FREE WOMEN
FREE MEN

FREE WOMEN
FREE MEN

SEX · GENDER · FEMINISM

CAMILLE PAGLIA

PANTHEON BOOKS, NEW YORK

Information on previous publication and illustration credits
appears on pages 311–317.

Library of Congress Cataloging-in-Publication Data
Name: Paglia, Camille, [date] author.
Title: Free women, free men : sex, gender, feminism / Camille Paglia.
Description: First Edition. New York : Pantheon, 2017. Includes index.
Identifiers: LCCN 2016034574 (print). LCCN 2016047713 (ebook).
ISBN 9780375424779 (hardcover). ISBN 9781101871812 (ebook).
Subjects: LCSH: Feminism. Sex role. BISAC: SOCIAL SCIENCE /
Women's Studies. SOCIAL SCIENCE / Feminism & Feminist Theory.
SOCIAL SCIENCE / Essays.
Classification: LCC HQ1155 .P34 2017 (print). LCC HQ1155 (ebook).
DDC 305.42—dc23.
LC record available at lccn.loc.gov/2016034574

www.pantheonbooks.com

Jacket design by Janet Hansen

Printed in the United States of America
First Edition
2 4 6 8 9 7 5 3 1

CONTENTS

INTRODUCTION

History moves in cycles. The plague of political correctness and assaults on free speech that erupted in the 1980s and were beaten back in the 1990s have returned with a vengeance. In the United States, the universities as well as the mainstream media are currently patrolled by well-meaning but ruthless thought police, as dogmatic in their views as agents of the Spanish Inquisition. We are plunged once again into an ethical chaos where intolerance masquerades as tolerance and where individual liberty is crushed by the tyranny of the group.

The premier principles of this book are free thought and free speech—open, mobile, and unconstrained by either liberal or conservative ideology. The liberal versus conservative dichotomy, dating from the split between left and right following the French Revolution, is hopelessly outmoded for our far more complex era of expansive technology and global politics. A bitter polarization of liberal and conservative has become so extreme and strident in both the Americas and Europe that it sometimes resembles mental illness, severed from the common sense realities of everyday life.

Our understanding of sexuality, a paradigmatic theme and indeed obsession of modern culture, has been clouded by its current politicization. Sex and gender have been redefined by ill-informed academic theorists as superficial, fictive phenomena produced by oppressive social forces, disconnected from biology. This hallucination has sowed confusion among young people and seriously damaged feminism. A gender theory without reference to biology is absurd on its face. But as a proponent of dynamic free will, I certainly do not subscribe to a wholesale biological determinism. As I wrote on the very first page of *Sexual Personae*, "Sexuality and eroticism are the intricate intersection of nature and culture." Furthermore, my key idea is that art itself is a line drawn against nature.

My dissident brand of feminism is grounded in my own childhood experience as a fractious rebel against the suffocating conformism of the 1950s, when Americans, exhausted by two decades of economic instability and war, reverted to a Victorian cult of domesticity that limited young girls' aspirations and confined them (in my jaundiced view) to a simpering, saccharine femininity. I have written elsewhere about my eccentric symbols of gender protest via transvestite Halloween costumes: Robin Hood at age five; the toreador from *Carmen* at six; a Roman soldier at seven; Napoleon at eight; Hamlet at nine. I took inspiration from wherever I could find it—from Classics Illustrated comic books and Courvoisier ads for Napoleon Cognac to the local church's Stations of the Cross and my parents' worn copy of *Stories from the Great Metropolitan Operas*.

But never in my passionate identification with heroic male figures was I encouraged by concerned but misguided adults to believe that I actually was a boy and that medical interventions could bring that hidden truth to life. On the contrary, by being forced to learn coping strategies for surviving in society, I was freed to develop my talents in other ways that have proved invaluable over time. When recently asked how I "identify" or describe myself, I replied, "Non-gendered entity." However, except in very rare conditions of true hermaphroditism (a congenital disorder), the DNA of every cell of the human body is inflexibly coded as male or female from birth to death. While respect and legal protection are owed to anyone who for whatever reason seeks to shift positions along the intricate spectrum of sexual personae (the Latin word for theater masks), changing sex is scientifically impossible.

Social pressures on girls in the late 1950s and early 1960s were heavy and relentless. The cultural dictators were chirpy, all-American blondes like Doris Day and Debbie Reynolds, with their compulsive cheerfulness. At Girl Scout camp, I melted into the woods to escape the happy mass singing of Doris's mega-hit, "Que Sera, Sera," around the campfire. At school, teachers appreciated my academic efforts but were routinely exasperated by my blundering inability to fit into the sedate, deferential girl slot. After my role in some pushing and shoving in line, my fifth-grade teacher made me stay after school to look up the word "aggressive" in the dictionary—as if it were a heinous mortal sin for girls. My eighth-grade teacher irately pulled me out of class to demand that I sit at my desk without moving or shaking any part of my body—a then baffling shaming incident that has made me enduringly sympathetic to the plight of physically active boys imprisoned in a public school system dominated by female teachers.

My only escapes from the repressive homogeneity of that period were through pop culture (wide-screen Hollywood epics and rock 'n' roll) and archaeology: I adored the monumentality and megalomania of Egyptian sculpture and architecture. When my parents could finally afford their first TV set (I was twelve), late-night movies became my gateway to the past. I discovered Katharine Hepburn, who electrified me. Her early films of the 1930s and '40s, where she often played hard-charging career women or lordly socialites, were a revelation. I had never seen a woman so sharply definitive and assertive, so fearlessly abrasive. What I did not realize at the time, given the scarcity of information about pop culture (still dismissed as evanescent trash), was that I was channeling through Hepburn the epochal defiant spirit of first-wave feminism: her mother and aunt had been nationally prominent activists for suffrage and birth control, and Hepburn herself had campaigned as a small child at suffrage events. I drew up a detailed chart of Hepburn films and studiously checked off each time I was lucky enough to see one, with broadcast date.

In high school, I went wild over Amelia Earhart, about whose mysterious 1937 disappearance over the Pacific I read in a 1961 article in *The Syracuse Herald-Journal*. For three years, to the puzzlement of my schoolmates, I feverishly pursued a research project about Earhart—systematically plowing through old newspapers and magazines in the sooty basement of the downtown Syracuse library, writing hundreds of letters of inquiry, and visiting spots associated with Earhart on side detours from family car trips. I was given access to Earhart's archives at Purdue University and had a private appointment at the National Air Museum in Washington, D.C., where a curator opened a vault to show me Earhart's medals and awards. I visited the house where Earhart was born in Atchison, Kansas, and the Opa Locka airfield in Florida where she left American soil on her last flight. I even briefly met her younger sister Muriel in a restaurant in Medford, Massachusetts.

Through Earhart, about whom I wrote a 77-page tenth-grade history project that I hoped to turn into a book, I learned first-hand about what would become my favorite period of feminism, the two decades just after American women won the right to vote in 1920. There were so many bold personalities and high achievers like Katharine Hepburn in every field—Dorothy Parker, Edna St. Vincent Millay, Dorothy Thompson, Lillian Hellman, Clare Boothe Luce, Pearl S. Buck, Anne Morrow Lindbergh, Mary McCarthy, Babe Didrikson, Margaret Bourke-White. What was distinctive in those emancipated women—and here loom my later problems with second-wave feminism—was that they never indulged in reflex male-bashing: they accepted and admired the enormity of what men had accomplished and were simply demanding a fair chance to prove that women could match or surpass it. Their inspirational record of unapologetic ambition and plucky, resourceful self-reliance was the foundation for my later philosophy of equal opportunity feminism.

My Earhart project gradually receded after the thunderclap of Simone de Beauvoir's *The Second Sex* (1949), the English translation of which was given to me for my sixteenth birthday in 1963 by a Belgian woman colleague of my father. I was stunned by de Beauvoir's imperious, authoritative tone and ambitious sweep through space and time. I began to dream of a book on the grand scale, a magnum opus that would incorporate all of my intense fixations, from archaeology to pop culture. That book, *Sexual Personae*, would take shape in the early 1970s as a study of androgyny for my doctoral dissertation at the Yale Graduate School. Revised and expanded, it was finally published in 1990 as a 700-page illustrated volume by Yale University Press, after rejections of the manuscript by seven publishers and five agents.

The vicious attacks on *Sexual Personae* by academic and establishment feminists (who in most cases had plainly not bothered to read it) will stand, I submit, as an indictment of the sorry process by which important political movements can undermine themselves through the blind insularity of their ruling coteries. Blow-by-blow chronicles of my public clashes with leading feminists and their acolytes, including documentation of their outlandish libels against me and my work, can be found in my two essay collections, *Sex, Art, and American Culture* (1992) and *Vamps & Tramps* (1994). Gloria Steinem in particular surely stained her legacy by her baseless remarks.

Compiled in this new collection is a selection of my most representative articles, excerpts, lectures, and interviews on sex, gender, and feminism since the release of *Sexual Personae* over a quarter century ago. I believe that my heterodox ideas and conclusions continue to have manifest resonance for many readers because they are based not on a priori theory and received opinion but on wide-ranging scholarly research and close observation of actual social behavior in our time. What is demonstrated here is the consistency and continuity of my libertarian feminist positions, which predate the publication of Betty Friedan's *The Feminine Mystique* in 1963 and her co-founding of the National Organization for Women in 1966, universally considered the birth of second-wave feminism. In its July 8, 1963 issue, *Newsweek* magazine published as its lead letter to the editor my protest about the exclusion of women from the American space program:

> Valentina Tereshkova has won the distinction of becoming the first woman to be launched into space 35 years to the day after Amelia Earhart was the first woman to fly across the Atlantic. Miss Earhart's lifelong fight for equal opportunity for American women apparently still remains to be won.
>
> CAMILLE A. PAGLIA
> Syracuse, N.Y.

The letter was headlined "Cosmonautka and Aviatrix" and accompanied by a dramatic photo of Earhart in her leather flying jacket, captioned, "After Earhart, orbit." I was 16, two years into my Earhart project and newly energized by Simone de Beauvoir, who was the ultimate and too rarely acknowledged source of Friedan's principal ideas.

Cultural histories of the mid-twentieth century have vastly overstated the role of the second-wave women's movement in the transformation and liberation of modern women. That tremendous change had already been in motion for other reasons from the early 1960s on. In the United States, my baby-boom generation was awakened and propelled forward by a great surge of optimism and idealism with the election in 1960 of the youthful, charismatic John F. Kennedy (for whom I had campaigned in Syracuse). Popular culture was an even more powerful force: the brash, body-based rhythms of rock 'n' roll, with its dual roots in African-American blues and working-class country music, were our percussive anthem, breaking into general cultural consciousness when Bill Haley's "Rock Around the Clock" was blasted at high volume over the credits of *The Blackboard Jungle* in movie theaters in 1955.

It was young women who were most jolted by Beatlemania. I have a reel-to-reel audio tape of a girls' party at my house on the night the Beatles appeared on *The Ed Sullivan Show* in February 1964. The noise level of our ecstatic response overwhelmed the microphone. That was the moment, nationwide, when American girls slew forever the decorous conventions of the 1950s. At their Shea Stadium concert the following year, the Beatles could not hear each other onstage and security guards covered their ears, so massive was the nonstop shrieking of girls exhilarated by their collective new freedom.

Barbra Streisand has never received due credit for her pioneering role in shattering female convention and laying the groundwork for second-wave feminism. Emerging from bohemian nightclubs where her campy patter and vintage costumes were shaped by gay male sensibility, Streisand embodied a scrappy non-conformism and confrontational toughness that strikingly contrasted with the emotional depth and elegant beauty of her singing. Her uncompromising ethnicity was career-risking: she refused to bob her prominent Jewish nose or moderate her harsh Brooklyn accent. A frequent guest on TV shows of the early 1960s, she was catapulted to fame by the Broadway musical, *Funny Girl*, which landed her on the covers of *Time* and *Life* in 1964.

As a huge Streisand devotee (I saw her onstage shortly before *Funny Girl* closed), I hailed her as a radical new woman who was smashing the genteel feminine code of the uber-WASP Doris Day–Debbie Reynolds regime. Entering Harpur College (the State University of New York at Binghamton) in the fall of 1964, I was amazed by the verve and audacity of the huge cadre of Jewish-American women students from metropolitan New York. They were politically progressive, mordantly funny, brutally blunt, and sexually free. Their unsparing realism often came from the harrowing experience of their grandparents' generation during the Holocaust. Streisand's rise from obscurity to stardom was a bellwether for a revolution stirring among American women well before the founding of NOW.

Young British women were also riding the zeitgeist in Swinging Sixties London, as England recovered from its postwar economic slump. Throughout my college years, I viewed the scintillating London of music, movies, and fashion as my distant spiritual home. In Binghamton, I somehow dug up gender-bending knockoffs of Carnaby Street–Portobello Road style gear—flowing Tom Jones or paisley shirts; men's chevron ties; flared, pin-striped hip-huggers; a sailor's maroon pea coat with gold military buttons; zipped Beatles boots with Cuban heels. Harpur's laid-back hippies, who affected a tattered, thrift-shop look, didn't like it one bit but prudently kept their distance. When I got to graduate school in 1968, I foolishly kept it all going—even adding a purple suede vest and a psychedelic orange-and-green stained-glass pendant on a leather thong from Greenwich Village. Needless to say, the tweedy Yale professors weren't thrilled.

The vivacious young women of London were photographed by John D. Green for a 1967 large-format book, *Birds of Britain*. In his introduction, Anthony Haden-Guest called "the new British girl" a "shock genetic mutation" produced by "the London Scene" and crossing social classes, from salesgirl to debutante. She was the mercurial, coltish Julie Christie in *Darling* (1965) and the volatile, enigmatic Vanessa Redgrave in *Blow-Up* (1966). Among the 55 sparklingly kinetic British girls in Green's book: Susannah York, Charlotte Rampling, Hayley Mills, Mary Quant, Jane Asher, Sarah Miles, Pattie Boyd, Cilla Black, Lulu, Dusty Springfield, and Marianne Faithfull.

The British youthquake, with its flamboyant "unisex" trend in clothing and hair styles for both men and women, proves that second-wave feminism was only one strand in the ongoing gender transformations of the 1960s. The formidable Diana Rigg was already in her black leather cat suit and throwing karate chops as Emma Peel in the hit British TV series, *The Avengers*, in 1966. The first and most influential militant female persona of the period was probably Ursula Andress as the fierce conch-hunter Honey Ryder in the first James Bond film, *Dr. No* (1962), where she steps from the sea in a dazzling white bikini and with a knife strapped to her hip. (I borrowed her heraldic knife for the Amazonian cover photo of *Vamps & Tramps*.) That bewitching scene, with its mythic evocation of an armed goddess born from the waves, would inspire the enduringly iconic poster for a 1966 British film, *One Million Years B.C.*, for which Raquel Welch as a cave woman in a ragged hide bikini spontaneously struck a combative, athletic pose. But the early hostility of second-wave feminism to the great sex symbols of film—indeed to all blatant eroticism in the entertainment industry—prevented those spectacular images from being incorporated into the history of women's modern advance.

Among my many quarrels with second-wave feminists was

my enthusiastic admiration for the sexy "Bond girls" and Dallas Cowboy Cheerleaders, as well as for Francesco Scavullo's glossy, glamorous, plunging-bodice covers for Helen Gurley Brown's *Cosmopolitan* magazine. (Feminist protestors, led by Kate Millett, staged a sit-in at Brown's offices in 1970.) Similarly, the hugely popular *Charlie's Angels* TV series (1976–81) was contemptuously dismissed as "jiggle" or "tits and ass" TV by feminist puritans. Hence my delight at the return of *Charlie's Angels* after the triumph of pro-sex feminism in the 1990s: thanks to producer-actress Drew Barrymore, there have been two successful *Charlie's Angels* films (2000 and 2003) and a TV series (2011).

Betty Friedan, a tireless, outspoken advocate for women's rights, was incontrovertibly the primary figure in the historic revival of organized feminist activism. But Betty Friedan did not create the formidable Germaine Greer in Australia, and she did not create me in the snow belt of upstate New York. I have repeatedly called Greer one of the emblematic women of the twentieth century. She remains the living person whom I most admire. Feminism would not have gone so wrong so fast had Greer retained the exuberant, slashingly satirical, all-conquering, and openly libidinous persona of her international debut after the publication of her first book, *The Female Eunuch*, in 1970. I have written and commented extensively about Greer, but there is room here for only one piece—my review of her 1995 study of women poets, *Slip-Shod Sibyls*.

The present book opens with half of the highly controversial first chapter of *Sexual Personae*, "Sex and Violence, or Nature and Art." Most feminists who fumed about it were usually reacting to out-of-context quotation of my signature one-liners (inspired by Oscar Wilde and innumerable Jewish comedians, including Joan Rivers). This chapter, with its dark overview of biology, is a protest against the omnipotence of nature and the outrage of gender. It is written from a trans-gender or should I say supragender point of view, like that of Tiresias, the invisible observer of sexual mores in T. S. Eliot's *The Waste Land.* Chapter One is merely an overture, inspired by Wagner. The rest of the book is quite different in tone, with chapters inspired in whole or in part by Bach, Chopin, Brahms, Rimsky-Korsakov, Debussy, Puccini, Satie, and Delius, in addition to movie music by Max Steiner, Miklós Rózsa, and Bernard Herrmann. Real readers, as opposed to lockstep ideologues, appreciated the sudden emotional shift (as in Hollywood soundtracks) into Chapter Two, "The Birth of the Western Eye," where art rescues humanity from the abyss of nature. Two excerpts are reprinted here: my diptych of a Stone Age statuette, the Venus of Willendorf, contrasted with the Egyptian bust of Queen Nefertiti. These passages are odes in the prose-poem style of the Oxford aesthete, Walter Pater, one of Wilde's principal mentors.

Sexual Personae was reasonably well-received by most reviewers. It was my piece on Madonna in *The New York Times* later in 1990 that made me instantly notorious. Background details of the circuitous genesis of this and my other articles in that inflammatory period can be found in "A Media History" in *Sex, Art, and American Culture.* In 2010, *The New York Times* featured this piece as one of its most significant and influential op-eds in the 40 years since it had invented that now standard form. What caused a storm was first, my open attack on the normally protected feminist establishment and second, my closing sally, "Madonna is the future of feminism," which was widely ridiculed as preposterous. But that prophecy would come true in the rise and resounding victory of long-silenced pro-sex feminism in the 1990s. Furthermore, my cheeky use of slang, which was debated by the editorial board, broke long-standing rules of decorum at *The New York Times* and opened the way for later writers like Maureen Dowd. Finally, the piece started a stampede for op-eds among humanities professors, who had previously considered writing for newspapers beneath their dignity. It was mainly historians, economists, and political scientists who had been doing op-eds before.

Six weeks later, New York *Newsday* published my op-ed on date rape, which remains the most controversial thing I have ever written. Syndicated in regional newspapers from coast to coast in haphazard truncated form, it caused a huge backlash. There was a coordinated campaign, evidently emanating from feminist groups in the Midwest, to harass the president of my university with demands for my firing. That article, often reprinted in freshman-composition course packs at state universities, caused me endless trouble throughout the 1990s. It led to picketing and protests at my outside campus lectures and to my own walk-offs (to avoid fisticuffs) from Austrian and British TV talk shows and even from the stage of Queen Elizabeth Hall in London. My lecture for the latter 1995 event, "The Modern Battle of the Sexes," was commissioned by the BBC and is reprinted here.

I still stand by every word of my date-rape manifesto. Women infantilize themselves when they cede responsibility for sexual encounters to men or to after-the-fact grievance committees, parental proxies unworthy of true feminists. My baby-boom generation demanded and won an end to the *in loco parentis* parietal rules, and it is tragic indeed how so many of today's young women seem to long for a return of those hovering paternalistic safeguards. As a career college teacher, I want our coddling, authoritarian universities to end all involvement with or surveillance of students' social lives and personal interactions, verbal or otherwise. If a real crime is committed, it should be reported to the police. Otherwise, college administrations should mind their own business and focus on facilitating and funding education in the classroom.

Many pieces in this book critique and lampoon prominent feminists, on campus and off. (My first scholarly publication, written in grad school, was "Lord Hervey and Pope," which appeared in *Eighteenth Century Studies* in 1973: Alexander Pope's scathing mock-epics, especially *The Dunciad*, remain a heavy influence.) My long 1991 review-essay for *Arion*, "Junk Bonds and Corporate Raiders," was primarily a hostile dissection of post-structuralism, which has in my view distorted gender studies and effectively destroyed the humanities. That was still my theme more than 20 years later in "Scholars in Bondage," my in-depth 2013 review for *The Chronicle of Higher Education* of three flawed new books by women academics on bondage and domination. Notable is my use of "corporate" in the *Arion* title: I was one of the few voices at the time denouncing the escalating corporatization of American universities, which was being exploited by careerist academics masquerading as leftists while obscenely driving up their own star salaries on the competitive national market. Similarly, in my 1992 essay, "The Nursery School Campus," for *The Times Literary Supplement,* I fired a prophetic warning shot about the takeover of American universities by an expanding class of intrusive administrators, leading to today's disastrous loss of faculty power.

Articles here where I took a contrarian position against the feminist establishment include my denial that Anita Hill was a feminist heroine; my attack on Catharine MacKinnon and Andrea Dworkin as Stalinist fanatics; and my defense of unconstrained reproductive rights while also acknowledging the ethical superiority of the pro-life argument in the abortion debate. Although I voted twice for Bill Clinton, I appear to be the only feminist who publicly condemned him for his abusive treatment of Monica Lewinsky and who protested the casuistry of feminist leaders like Gloria Steinem in hypocritically refusing for partisan reasons to apply basic sexual harassment rules to this deplorable case.

A recurrent theme in these pieces, as in my dissection of gender propaganda in the United Nations documents for its 1996 Conference on Women in Beijing, is the privileged bourgeois assumptions, self-preoccupied and status-conscious, in too much feminist thinking. (Attention to this long-standing problem has finally come to the fore as "intersectionality.") In the 1990s, when most other feminists were focused on policy matters, I was virtually alone in pressing the issue of the first woman president, for whom I insisted that military history rather than gender studies was the proper college training. I steadily protested the anti-male bias of second-wave feminism and took up the cudgels to defend men's wrestling and football (as in my sports credo, "Gridiron Feminism").

Female body image in art and popular culture is addressed in my lecture, "The Cruel Mirror," as well as in pieces on plastic surgery and the stiletto high heel. My celebration of Bravo TV's *Real Housewives* series is predictably oppositional: Gloria Steinem repeatedly criticized and dismissed the show. My 2014 University of Mississippi lecture on Southern women, published here for the first time, examines three female stereotypes: the old mountain woman, the mammy, and the Southern belle. In op-eds written for *Time,* I call for fertility issues to be addressed in school sex education; for an end to young women's frightening naïveté about sex crime; and for a repeal of the unjust Age-21 law regulating alcohol sales, which I connect to the sudden date-rape crisis of the 1980s, when riotous fraternity keg parties filled the social gap. My interviews with Deborah Coughlin for *Feminist Times* and Ella Whelan for *Spiked Review* highlight the ongoing common concerns of British and American feminism.

Ending the book is my essay on Robert Mapplethorpe's brilliant, half-transvestite portrait of Patti Smith for the album cover of *Horses* (1975), which I hung like a sacred icon on my wall at my first teaching job at Bennington College. Mutual friends who frequented CBGB's music club on New York's Bowery had recognized the cultural parallels between Smith and me and tried to bring us together. (We were briefly introduced in passing one afternoon when I was at the deserted CBGB's for a later performance by the proto-punk band Television, but it would have made no impression on her, given that I was unpublished and unknown.) I deeply admire Smith's respect for great male artists as well as her rejection of feminist rancor toward men. In a 2007 interview with *Bust* magazine, Smith said, "I never was really concerned with the idea of feminism. As a humanistic person, I'm interested in the human condition. I'm interested in men's rights just as much as women's rights. . . . I've never limited myself as an artist or as a human being to a genderized position."

The Mapplethorpe photo was a major inspiration for my 1991 *New York* magazine cover photo (reproduced here), taken in the armor room of the Philadelphia Museum of Art for Francesca Stanfill's very discerning profile: I am doing my glowering best to imitate my idol, Keith Richards, the original model for Smith's raffish 1970s rock-star hair cut. Also reproduced here, along with the covers of two gay magazines, are several examples of the theatrical scenarios I devised for routine photo shoots requested by magazines and newspapers to illustrate interviews or profiles. I sometimes brought props (whip, chains, sword, switchblade knife) to visually transmit my philosophy of street-smart Amazon feminism directly to the public, bypassing whatever untruths might be planted in the articles themselves by biased journalists or editors.

Like Mapplethorpe and unlike most feminists, I viewed fashion photography as a major modern art form. My longtime favorite photographers were Richard Avedon, David Bailey, and Helmut Newton, each of whom had a unique flair for capturing the essence of personality via moments of random choreography. Another inspiration for my outré photo shoots was David Bowie's stunning sexual personae during his Ziggy Stardust period of the early 1970s. (I regret there is no space to reprint my catalog essay, "Theater of Gender: David Bowie at the Climax of the Sexual Revolution," commissioned by the Victoria & Albert Museum for its 2013 exhibit of Bowie costumes in London.) It must be stressed that my flamboyant media presence lasted scarcely four years and was boosted by the official book tours for three bestsellers in a row (1991–94). After that, like the Roman general Cincinnatus returning to his plow, I simply resumed my cherished seclusion as a teacher and writer. As I often say, I'm just a schoolmarm!

The title of this book exalts freedom as an indispensable condition for the incubation and flourishing of individualism. My libertarian feminism, which takes the best from both liberalism and conservatism but is decidedly neither, places freedom of thought and speech above all ideology. I am an intellectual first and a feminist second—an ethical commitment to truth-seeking that I urge aspiring young writers and artists to adopt. The Free Speech Movement, led by a fiery Italian-American, Mario Savio, erupted at the University of California at Berkeley in 1964, the year I entered college. It was a cardinal moment for my generation. The anti-establishment stance of the Free Speech Movement represented the authentic populist revolution of the 1960s, which resisted encroachments of authority by a repressive elite. How is it possible that today's academic left has supported rather than protested campus speech codes as well as the grotesque surveillance and over-regulation of student life? American colleges have abandoned their educational mission and become government colonies, ruled by officious bureaucrats enforcing federal dictates. This despotic imperialism has no place in a modern democracy.

Erosion of liberals' fidelity to free speech can be partly traced to the Civil Rights Act of 1968 (following the landmark 1964 act), which imposed federal penalties for crimes committed because of "race, color, religion or national origin." The demarcation of certain groups for special protection, later extended to gender and sexual orientation, split them from the general populace by defining them as permanent victims, burdened by an inescapable past. I strongly oppose the categories of "hate speech" and "hate crimes" that arose from that law and others throughout North America and Europe. The laudable attempt to make reparation for past injustice unfortunately created segregated zones of new privilege and drew government into curbing the exercise of free speech. As I argued in *Vamps & Tramps*, government has no right to intrude into or speculate about the thinking or motivation of any citizen, except during the sentencing phase after criminal conviction.

The freedom to hate must be as protected as the freedom to love. It is only when hate crosses over into action that the law may properly intervene. Without complete freedom to explore the piercing extremes of human emotion, we will never have great art again. Even comedy, a genre descending from the bawdy fertility cults of antiquity, has always been predicated on the violation of taboos. The free speech idealism of the 1960s was galvanized by the daring, sardonic culture-hero, Lenny Bruce, who transformed stand-up comedy into biting and often profane social commentary, leading to his repeated arrest for obscenity. On today's campuses, students' rowdy natural instincts for mischievous transgression are being policed by dour, neo-Victorian agents of coercive compassion. Comedy has become yet another victim of political correctness.

Freedom in the gender realm means the freedom of each sex to define its history and destiny without blame or harassment. If women seek freedom, they must let men too be free. Men who demean or subjugate women are not free, because they are signaling their secret fear of female power, which remains near total in the still murky and anxiety-ridden realm of procreation. But men have every right to claim credit for their vast achievements in conceiving and constructing the entire framework of civilization, from the great irrigation projects of ancient Mesopotamia to today's global electronic grid. Impugned and silenced by feminism, men stoically go on doing the dirtiest, most dangerous and thankless work in modern society.

Feminism must end its sex war, which is stunting the maturation of both girls and boys. Upper-middle-class career women in the Americas and Europe blame men for their unhappiness. But the real cause is systemic. In the shift from the agrarian to industrial and now technological era, women have lost the daylong companionship and solidarity they once enjoyed with other women when they ruled the private sphere. In a new world where men and women share the same ambitions and workplace, perhaps a mutual incompatibility or creative tension between the sexes may have to be tolerated. But what is indisputable is that women do not gain by weakening men. An enlightened feminism, animated by a courageous code of personal responsibility, can only be built upon a wary alliance of strong women and strong men.

FREE WOMEN
FREE MEN

1

SEX AND VIOLENCE, OR NATURE AND ART

In the beginning was nature. The background from which and against which our ideas of God were formed, nature remains the supreme moral problem. We cannot hope to understand sex and gender until we clarify our attitude toward nature. Sex is a subset to nature. Sex is the natural in man.

Society is an artificial construction, a defense against nature's power. Without society, we would be storm-tossed on the barbarous sea that is nature. Society is a system of inherited forms reducing our humiliating passivity to nature. We may alter these forms, slowly or suddenly, but no change in society will change nature. Human beings are not nature's favorites. We are merely one of a multitude of species upon which nature indiscriminately exerts its force. Nature has a master agenda we can only dimly know.

Human life began in flight and fear. Religion rose from rituals of propitiation, spells to lull the punishing elements. To this day, communities are few in regions scorched by heat or shackled by ice. Civilized man conceals from himself the extent of his subordination to nature. The grandeur of culture, the consolation of religion absorb his attention and win his faith. But let nature shrug, and all is in ruin. Fire, flood, light-

[*Sexual Personae: Art and Decadence from Nefertiti to Emily Dickinson*, 1990, Chapter 1, excerpt]

ning, tornado, hurricane, volcano, earthquake—anywhere at any time. Disaster falls upon the good and bad. Civilized life requires a state of illusion. The idea of the ultimate benevolence of nature and God is the most potent of man's survival mechanisms. Without it, culture would revert to fear and despair.

Sexuality and eroticism are the intricate intersection of nature and culture. Feminists grossly oversimplify the problem of sex when they reduce it to a matter of social convention: readjust society, eliminate sexual inequality, purify sex roles, and happiness and harmony will reign. Here feminism, like all liberal movements of the past two hundred years, is heir to Rousseau. *The Social Contract* (1762) begins: "Man is born free, and everywhere he is in chains." Pitting benign Romantic nature against corrupt society, Rousseau produced the progressivist strain in nineteenth-century culture, for which social reform was the means to achieve paradise on earth. The bubble of these hopes was burst by the catastrophes of two world wars. But Rousseauism was reborn in the post-war generation of the Sixties, from which contemporary feminism developed.

Rousseau rejects original sin, Christianity's pessimistic view of man born unclean, with a propensity for evil. Rousseau's idea, derived from Locke, of man's innate goodness led to social environmentalism, now the dominant ethic of American human services, penal codes, and behaviorist therapies. It assumes that aggression, violence, and crime come from social deprivation—a poor neighborhood, a bad home. Thus feminism blames rape on pornography and, by a smug circularity of reasoning, interprets outbreaks of sadism as a backlash to itself. But rape and sadism have been evident throughout history and, at some moment, in all cultures.

This book takes the point of view of Sade, the most unread

major writer in Western literature. Sade's work is a comprehensive satiric critique of Rousseau, written in the decade after the first failed Rousseauist experiment, the French Revolution, which ended not in political paradise but in the hell of the Reign of Terror. Sade follows Hobbes rather than Locke. Aggression comes from nature; it is what Nietzsche is to call the will-to-power. For Sade, getting back to nature (the Romantic imperative that still permeates our culture from sex counseling to cereal commercials) would be to give free rein to violence and lust. I agree. Society is not the criminal but the force which keeps crime in check. When social controls weaken, man's innate cruelty bursts forth. The rapist is created not by bad social influences but by a failure of social conditioning. Feminists, seeking to drive power relations out of sex, have set themselves against nature. Sex *is* power. Identity is power. In Western culture, there are no nonexploitative relationships. Everyone has killed in order to live. Nature's universal law of creation from destruction operates in mind as in matter. As Freud, Nietzsche's heir, asserts, identity is conflict. Each generation drives its plow over the bones of the dead.

Modern liberalism suffers unresolved contradictions. It exalts individualism and freedom and, on its radical wing, condemns social orders as oppressive. On the other hand, it expects government to provide materially for all, a feat manageable only by an expansion of authority and a swollen bureaucracy. In other words, liberalism defines government as tyrant father but demands it behave as nurturant mother. Feminism has inherited these contradictions. It sees every hierarchy as repressive, a social fiction; every negative about woman is a male lie designed to keep her in her place. Feminism has exceeded its proper mission of seeking political equality for women and has ended by rejecting contingency, that is, human limitation by nature or fate.

Sexual freedom, sexual liberation. A modern delusion. We are hierarchical animals. Sweep one hierarchy away, and another will take its place, perhaps less palatable than the first. There are hierarchies in nature and alternate hierarchies in society. In nature, brute force is often the law. In society, there are protections for the weak. Society is our frail barrier against nature. When the prestige of state and religion is low, men are free, but they find freedom intolerable and seek new ways to enslave themselves, through drugs or depression. My theory is that whenever sexual freedom is sought or achieved, sadomasochism will not be far behind. Romanticism always turns into decadence. Nature is a hard taskmaster. It is the hammer and the anvil, crushing individuality. Perfect freedom would be to die by earth, air, water, and fire.

Sex is a far darker power than feminism has admitted. Behaviorist sex therapies believe guiltless, no-fault sex is possible. But sex has always been girt round with taboo, irrespective of culture. Sex is the point of contact between man and nature, where morality and good intentions fall to primitive urges. I called it an intersection. This intersection is the uncanny crossroads of Hecate, where all things return in the night. Eroticism is a realm stalked by ghosts. It is the place beyond the pale, both cursed and enchanted.

This book shows how much in culture goes against our best wishes. Integration of man's body and mind is a profound problem that is not about to be solved by recreational sex or an expansion of women's civil rights. Incarnation, the limitation of mind by matter, is an outrage to imagination. Equally outrageous is gender, which we have not chosen but which nature has imposed upon us. Our physicality is torment, our body the tree of nature on which Blake sees us crucified.

Sex is daemonic. This term, current in Romantic studies of the past twenty-five years, derives from the Greek *daimon*, meaning a spirit of lower divinity than the Olympian gods (hence my pronunciation "daimonic"). The outcast Oedipus becomes a daemon at Colonus. The word came to mean a man's guardian shadow. Christianity turned the daemonic into the demonic. The Greek daemons were not evil—or rather they were both good and evil, like nature itself, in which they dwelled. Freud's unconscious is a daemonic realm. In the day we are social creatures, but at night we descend to the dream world where nature reigns, where there is no law but sex, cruelty, and metamorphosis. Day itself is invaded by daemonic night. Moment by moment, night flickers in the imagination, in eroticism, subverting our strivings for virtue and order, giving an uncanny aura to objects and persons, revealed to us through the eyes of the artist.

The ghost-ridden character of sex is implicit in Freud's brilliant theory of "family romance." We each have an incestuous constellation of sexual personae that we carry from childhood to the grave and that determines whom and how we love or hate. Every encounter with friend or foe, every clash with or submission to authority bears the perverse traces of family romance. Love is a crowded theater, for as Harold Bloom remarks, "We can never embrace (sexually or otherwise) a single person, but embrace the whole of her or his family romance."[1] We still know next to nothing of the mystery of cathexis, the investment of libido in certain people or things. The element of free will in sex and emotion is slight. As poets know, falling in love is irrational.

Like art, sex is fraught with symbols. Family romance means that adult sex is always representation, ritualistic acting out of vanished realities. A perfectly humane eroticism may be impossible. Somewhere in every family romance is hostility and aggression, the homicidal wishes of the unconscious. Children are monsters of unbridled egotism and will, for they spring directly from nature, hostile intimations of immorality. We carry that daemonic will within us forever. Most people conceal it with acquired ethical precepts and meet it only in their dreams, which they hastily forget upon waking. The will-to-power is innate, but the sexual scripts of family romance are learned. Human beings are the only creatures in whom consciousness is so entangled with animal instinct. In Western culture, there can never be a purely physical or anxiety-free sexual encounter. Every attraction, every pattern of touch, every orgasm is shaped by psychic shadows.

The search for freedom through sex is doomed to failure. In sex, compulsion and ancient Necessity rule. The sexual personae of family romance are obliterated by the tidal force of regression, the backwards movement toward primeval dissolution, which Ferenczi identifies with ocean. An orgasm is a domination, a surrender, or a breaking through. Nature is no respecter of human identity. This is why so many men turn away or flee after sex, for they have sensed the annihilation of the daemonic. Western love is a displacement of cosmic realities. It is a defense mechanism rationalizing forces ungoverned and ungovernable. Like early religion, it is a device enabling us to control our primal fear.

Sex cannot be understood because nature cannot be understood. Science is a method of logical analysis of nature's operations. It has lessened human anxiety about the cosmos by demonstrating the materiality of nature's forces, and their frequent predictability. But science is always playing catch-up ball. Nature breaks its own rules whenever it wants. Science cannot avert a single thunderbolt. Western science is a product of the Apollonian mind: its hope is that by naming and classification, by the cold light of intellect, archaic night can be pushed back and defeated.

Name and person are part of the West's quest for form. The

West insists on the discrete identity of objects. To name is to know; to know is to control. I will demonstrate that the West's greatness arises from this delusional certitude. Far Eastern culture has never striven against nature in this way. Compliance, not confrontation is its rule. Buddhist meditation seeks the unity and harmony of reality. Twentieth-century physics, going full circle back to Heracleitus, postulates that all matter is in motion. In other words, there is no thing, only energy. But this perception has not been imaginatively absorbed, for it cancels the West's intellectual and moral assumptions.

The Westerner knows by seeing. Perceptual relations are at the heart of our culture, and they have produced our titanic contributions to art. Walking in nature, we see, identify, name, *recognize*. This recognition is our apotropaion, that is, our warding off of fear. Recognition is ritual cognition, a repetition-compulsion. We say that nature is beautiful. But this aesthetic judgment, which not all peoples have shared, is another defense formation, woefully inadequate for encompassing nature's totality. What is pretty in nature is confined to the thin skin of the globe upon which we huddle. Scratch that skin, and nature's daemonic ugliness will erupt.

Our focus on the pretty is an Apollonian strategy. The leaves and flowers, the birds, the hills are a patchwork pattern by which we map the known. What the West represses in its view of nature is the chthonian, which means "of the earth"—but earth's bowels, not its surface. Jane Harrison uses the term for pre-Olympian Greek religion, and I adopt it as a substitute for Dionysian, which has become contaminated with vulgar pleasantries. The Dionysian is no picnic. It is the chthonian realities which Apollo evades, the blind grinding of subterranean force, the long slow suck, the murk and ooze. It is the dehumanizing brutality of biology and geology, the Darwinian waste and bloodshed, the squalor and rot we must block from consciousness to retain our Apollonian integrity as persons. Western science and aesthetics are attempts to revise this horror into imaginatively palatable form.

The daemonism of chthonian nature is the West's dirty secret. Modern humanists made the "tragic sense of life" the touchstone of mature understanding. They defined man's mortality and the transience of time as literature's supreme subjects. In this I again see evasion and even sentimentality. The tragic sense of life is a partial response to experience. It is a reflex of the West's resistance to and misapprehension of nature, compounded by the errors of liberalism, which in its Romantic nature-philosophy has followed the Rousseauist Wordsworth rather than the daemonic Coleridge.

Tragedy is the most Western literary genre. It did not appear in Japan until the late nineteenth century. The Western will, setting itself up against nature, dramatized its own inevitable fall as a human universal, which it is not. An irony of literary history is the birth of tragedy in the cult of Dionysus. The protagonist's destruction recalls the slaughter of animals and, even earlier, of real human beings in archaic ritual. It is no accident that tragedy as we know it dates from the Apollonian fifth century of Athens's greatness, whose cardinal work is Aeschylus's *Oresteia*, a celebration of the defeat of chthonian power. Drama, a Dionysian mode, turned against Dionysus in making the passage from ritual to mimesis, that is, from action to representation. Aristotle's "pity and fear" is a broken promise, a plea for vision without horror.

Few Greek tragedies fully conform to the humanist commentary on them. Their barbaric residue will not come unglued. Even in the fifth century, as we shall see, a satiric response to Apollonianized theater came in Euripides's decadent plays. Problems in accurate assessment of Greek tragedy include not only the loss of three-quarters of the original body of work but the lack of survival of any complete satyr-play. This was the finale to the classic trilogy, an obscene comic burlesque. In Greek tragedy, comedy always had the last word. Modern criticism has projected a Victorian and, I feel, Protestant high seriousness upon pagan culture that still blankets teaching of the humanities. Paradoxically, assent to savage chthonian realities leads not to gloom but to humor. Hence Sade's strange laughter, his wit amid the most fantastic cruelties. For life is not a tragedy but a comedy. Comedy is born of the clash between Apollo and Dionysus. Nature is always pulling the rug out from under our pompous ideals.

Female tragic protagonists are rare. Tragedy is a male paradigm of rise and fall, a graph in which dramatic and sexual climax are in shadowy analogy. Climax is another Western invention. Traditional Far Eastern stories are picaresque, horizontal chains of incident. There is little suspense or sense of an ending. The sharp vertical peaking of Western narrative, as later of orchestral music, is exemplified by Sophocles's *Oedipus Rex*, whose moment of maximum intensity Aristotle calls *peripeteia*, reversal. Western dramatic climax was produced by the agon of male will. Through action to identity. Action is the route of escape from nature, but all action circles back to origins, the womb-tomb of nature. Oedipus, trying to escape his mother, runs straight into her arms. Western narrative is a mystery story, a process of detection. But since what is detected is unbearable, every revelation leads to another repression.

The major women of tragedy—Euripides's Medea and Phaedra, Shakespeare's Cleopatra and Lady Macbeth, Racine's Phèdre—skew the genre by their disruptive relation to male action. Tragic woman is less moral than man. Her will-to-power is naked. Her actions are under a chthonian cloud. They are a conduit of the irrational, opening the genre to intrusions of the barbaric force that drama shut out at its birth. Tragedy is a Western vehicle for testing and purification of the male will. The difficulty in grafting female protagonists onto it is a result not of male prejudice but of instinctive sexual strategics. Woman introduces untransformed cruelty into tragedy because she is the problem that the genre is trying to correct.

Tragedy plays a male game, a game it invented to snatch victory from the jaws of defeat. It is not flawed choice, flawed action, or even death itself which is the ultimate human dilemma. The gravest challenge to our hopes and dreams is the messy biological business-as-usual that is going on within us and without us at every hour of every day. Consciousness is a pitiful hostage of its flesh-envelope, whose surges, circuits, and secret murmurings it cannot stay or speed. This is the chthonian drama that has no climax but only an endless round, cycle upon cycle. Microcosm mirrors macrocosm. Free will is stillborn in the red cells of our body, for there is no free will in nature. Our choices come to us prepackaged and special delivery, molded by hands not our own.

Tragedy's inhospitality to woman springs from nature's inhospitality to man. The identification of woman with nature was universal in prehistory. In hunting or agrarian societies dependent upon nature, femaleness was honored as an immanent principle of fertility. As culture progressed, crafts and commerce supplied a concentration of resources freeing men from the caprices of weather or the handicap of geography. With nature at one remove, femaleness receded in importance.

Buddhist cultures retained the ancient meanings of femaleness long after the West renounced them. Male and female, the Chinese yang and yin, are balanced and interpenetrating powers in man and nature, to which society is subordinate. This code of passive acceptance has its roots in India, a land of sudden extremes where a monsoon can wipe out 50,000 people overnight. The femaleness of fertility religions is always double-edged. The Indian nature-goddess Kali is creator *and* destroyer, granting boons with one set of arms while cutting throats with the other. She is the lady ringed with skulls. The moral ambivalence of the great mother goddesses has been conveniently forgotten by those American feminists who have resurrected them. We cannot grasp nature's bare blade without shedding our own blood.

Western culture from the start has swerved from femaleness. The last major Western society to worship female powers was Minoan Crete. And significantly, that fell and did not rise again. The immediate cause of its collapse—quake, plague, or invasion—is beside the point. The lesson is that cultic femaleness is no guarantee of cultural strength or viability. What did survive, what did vanquish circumstance and stamp its mind-set on Europe was Mycenaean warrior culture, descending to us through Homer. The male will-to-power: Mycenaeans from the south and Dorians from the north would fuse to form Apollonian Athens, from which came the Greco-Roman line of Western history.

Both the Apollonian and Judeo-Christian traditions are transcendental. That is, they seek to surmount or transcend nature. Despite Greek culture's contrary Dionysian element, which I will discuss, high classicism was an Apollonian achievement. Judaism, Christianity's parent sect, is the most powerful of protests against nature. The Old Testament asserts that a father god made nature and that differentiation into objects and gender was after the fact of his maleness. Judeo-Christianity, like Greek worship of the Olympian gods, is a sky-cult. It is an advanced stage in the history of religion, which everywhere began as earth-cult, veneration of fruitful nature.

The evolution from earth-cult to sky-cult shifts woman

into the nether realm. Her mysterious procreative powers and the resemblance of her rounded breasts, belly, and hips to earth's contours put her at the center of early symbolism. She was the model for the Great Mother figures who crowded the birth of religion worldwide. But the mother cults did not mean social freedom for women. On the contrary, as can be seen in Hollywood history, cult objects are prisoners of their own symbolic inflation. Every totem lives in taboo.

Woman was an idol of belly-magic. She seemed to swell and give birth by her own law. From the beginning of time, woman has seemed an uncanny being. Man honored but feared her. She was the black maw that had spat him forth and would devour him anew. Men, bonding together, invented culture as a defense against female nature. Sky-cult was the most sophisticated step in this process, for its switch of the creative locus from earth to sky is a shift from belly-magic to head-magic. And from this defensive head-magic has come the spectacular glory of male civilization, which has lifted woman with it. The very language and logic modern woman uses to assail patriarchal culture were the invention of men.

Hence the sexes are caught in a comedy of historical indebtedness. Man, repelled by his debt to a physical mother, created an alternate reality, a heterocosm to give him the illusion of freedom. Woman, at first content to accept man's protections but now inflamed with desire for her own illusory freedom, invades man's systems and suppresses her indebtedness to him as she steals them. By head-magic she will deny there ever was a problem of sex and nature. She has inherited the anxiety of influence.

The identification of woman with nature is the most troubled and troubling term in this historical argument. Was it ever true? Can it still be true? Most feminist readers will disagree, but I think this identification not myth but reality.

All the genres of philosophy, science, high art, athletics, and politics were invented by men. But by the Promethean law of conflict and capture, woman has a right to seize what she will and to vie with man on his own terms. Yet there is a limit to what she can alter in herself and in man's relation to her. Every human being must wrestle with nature. But nature's burden falls more heavily on one sex. With luck, this will not limit woman's achievement, that is, her action in male-created social space. But it must limit eroticism, that is, our imaginative lives in sexual space, which may overlap social space but is not identical with it.

Nature's cycles are woman's cycles. Biologic femaleness is a sequence of circular returns, beginning and ending at the same point. Woman's centrality gives her a stability of identity. She does not have to become but only to be. Her centrality is a great obstacle to man, whose quest for identity she blocks. He must transform himself into an independent being, that is, a being free of her. If he does not, he will simply fall back into her. Reunion with the mother is a siren call haunting our imagination. Once there was bliss, and now there is struggle. Dim memories of life before the traumatic separation of birth may be the source of Arcadian fantasies of a lost golden age. The Western idea of history as a propulsive movement into the future, a progressive or Providential design climaxing in the revelation of a Second Coming, is a male formulation. No woman, I submit, could have coined such an idea, since it is a strategy of evasion of woman's own cyclic nature, in which man dreads being caught. Evolutionary or apocalyptic history is a male wish list with a happy ending, a phallic peak.

Woman does not dream of transcendental or historical escape from natural cycle, since she *is* that cycle. Her sexual maturity means marriage to the moon, waxing and waning in lunar phases. Moon, month, menses: same word, same world.

The ancients knew that woman is bound to nature's calendar, an appointment she cannot refuse. The Greek pattern of free will to hybris to tragedy is a male drama, since woman has never been deluded (until recently) by the mirage of free will. She knows there is no free will, since she is not free. She has no choice but acceptance. Whether she desires motherhood or not, nature yokes her into the brute inflexible rhythm of procreative law. Menstrual cycle is an alarming clock that cannot be stopped until nature wills it.

Woman's reproductive apparatus is vastly more complicated than man's, and still ill-understood. All kinds of things can go wrong or cause distress in going right. Western woman is in an agonistic relation to her own body: for her, biologic normalcy is suffering, and health an illness. Dysmenorrhea, it is argued, is a disease of civilization, since women in tribal cultures have few menstrual complaints. But in tribal life, woman has an extended or collective identity; tribal religion honors nature and subordinates itself to it. It is precisely in advanced Western society, which attempts to improve or surpass nature and which holds up individualism and self-realization as a model, that the stark facts of woman's condition emerge with painful clarity. The more woman aims for personal identity and autonomy, the more she develops her imagination, the fiercer will be her struggle with nature—that is, with the intractable physical laws of her own body. And the more nature will punish her: do not dare to be free! for your body does not belong to you.

The female body is a chthonian machine, indifferent to the spirit who inhabits it. Organically, it has one mission, pregnancy, which we may spend a lifetime staving off. Nature cares only for species, never individuals: the humiliating dimensions of this biologic fact are most directly experienced by women, who probably have a greater realism and wisdom than men because of it. Woman's body is a sea acted upon by the month's lunar wave-motion. Sluggish and dormant, her fatty tissues are gorged with water, then suddenly cleansed at hormonal high tide. Edema is our mammalian relapse into the vegetable. Pregnancy demonstrates the deterministic character of woman's sexuality. Every pregnant woman has body and self taken over by a chthonian force beyond her control. In the welcome pregnancy, this is a happy sacrifice. But in the unwanted one, initiated by rape or misadventure, it is a horror. Such unfortunate women look directly into nature's heart of darkness. For a fetus is a benign tumor, a vampire who steals in order to live. The so-called miracle of birth is nature getting her own way.

Every month for women is a new defeat of the will. Menstruation was once called "the curse," a reference to the expulsion from the Garden, when woman was condemned to labor pains because of Eve's sin. Most early cultures hemmed in menstruating women by ritual taboos. Orthodox Jewish women still purify themselves from menstrual uncleanness in the *mikveh*, a ritual bath. Women have borne the symbolic burden of man's imperfections, his grounding in nature. Menstrual blood is the stain, the birthmark of original sin, the filth that transcendental religion must wash from man. Is this identification merely phobic, merely misogynistic? Or is it possible there *is* something uncanny about menstrual blood, justifying its attachment to taboo? I will argue that it is not menstrual blood per se which disturbs the imagination—unstanchable as that red flood may be—but rather the albumen in the blood, the uterine shreds, placental jellyfish of the female sea. This is the chthonian matrix from which we rose. We have an evolutionary revulsion from slime, our site of biologic origins. Every month, it is woman's fate to face the abyss of time and being, the abyss which is herself.

The Bible has come under fire for making woman the fall guy in man's cosmic drama. But in casting a male conspirator, the serpent, as God's enemy, Genesis hedges and does not take its misogyny far enough. The Bible defensively swerves from God's true opponent, chthonian nature. The serpent is not outside Eve but in her. She is the garden *and* the serpent. Anthony Storr says of witches, "At a very primitive level, all mothers are phallic."[2] The Devil is a woman. Modern emancipation movements, discarding stereotypes impeding woman's social advance, refuse to acknowledge procreation's daemonism. Nature is serpentine, a bed of tangled vines, creepers and crawlers, probing dumb fingers of fetid organic life which Wordsworth taught us to call pretty. Biologists speak of man's reptilian brain, the oldest part of our upper nervous system, killer survivor of the archaic era. I contend that the premenstrual woman incited to snappishness or rage is hearing signals from the reptilian brain. In her, man's latent perversity is manifest. All hell breaks loose, the hell of chthonian nature that modern humanism denies and represses. In every premenstrual woman struggling to govern her temper, sky-cult wars again with earth-cult.

Mythology's identification of woman with nature is correct. The male contribution to procreation is momentary and transient. Conception is a pinpoint of time, another of our phallic peaks of action, from which the male slides back uselessly. The pregnant woman is daemonically, devilishly complete. As an ontological entity, she needs nothing and no one. I shall maintain that the pregnant woman, brooding for nine months upon her own creation, is the pattern of all solipsism, that the historical attribution of narcissism to women is another true myth. Male bonding and patriarchy were the recourse to which man was forced by his terrible sense of woman's power, her imperviousness, her archetypal confederacy with chthonian nature. Woman's body is a labyrinth in which man is lost.

It is a walled garden, the medieval *hortus conclusus*, in which nature works its daemonic sorcery. Woman is the primeval fabricator, the real First Mover. She turns a gob of refuse into a spreading web of sentient being, floating on the snaky umbilical by which she leashes every man.

Feminism has been simplistic in arguing that female archetypes were politically motivated falsehoods by men. The historical repugnance to woman has a rational basis: disgust is reason's proper response to the grossness of procreative nature. Reason and logic are the anxiety-inspired domain of Apollo, premier god of sky-cult. The Apollonian is harsh and phobic, coldly cutting itself off from nature by its superhuman purity. I shall argue that Western personality and Western achievement are, for better or worse, largely Apollonian. Apollo's great opponent Dionysus is ruler of the chthonian whose law is procreative femaleness. As we shall see, the Dionysian is liquid nature, a miasmic swamp whose prototype is the still pond of the womb.

We must ask whether the equivalence of male and female in Far Eastern symbolism was as culturally efficacious as the hierarchization of male over female has been in the West. Which system has ultimately benefited women more? Western science and industry have freed women from drudgery and danger. Machines do housework. The pill neutralizes fertility. Giving birth is no longer fatal. And the Apollonian line of Western rationality has produced the modern aggressive woman who can think like a man and write obnoxious books. The tension and antagonism in Western metaphysics developed human higher cortical powers to great heights. Most of Western culture is a distortion of reality. But reality *should* be distorted; that is, imaginatively amended. The Buddhist acquiescence to nature is neither accurate about nature nor just to human potential. The Apollonian has taken us to the stars.

Daemonic archetypes of woman, filling world mythology,

represent the uncontrollable nearness of nature. Their tradition passes nearly unbroken from prehistoric idols through literature and art to modern movies. The primary image is the femme fatale, the woman fatal to man. The more nature is beaten back in the West, the more the femme fatale reappears, as a return of the repressed. She is the spectre of the West's bad conscience about nature. She is the moral ambiguity of nature, a malevolent moon that keeps breaking through our fog of hopeful sentiment.

Feminism dismisses the femme fatale as a cartoon and libel. If she ever existed, she was simply a victim of society, resorting to destructive womanly wiles because of her lack of access to political power. The femme fatale was a career woman manqué, her energies neurotically diverted into the boudoir. By such techniques of demystification, feminism has painted itself into a corner. Sexuality is a murky realm of contradiction and ambivalence. It cannot always be understood by social models, which feminism, as an heir of nineteenth-century utilitarianism, insists on imposing on it. Mystification will always remain the disorderly companion of love and art. Eroticism *is* mystique; that is, the aura of emotion and imagination around sex. It cannot be "fixed" by codes of social or moral convenience, whether from the political left or right. For nature's fascism is greater than that of any society. There is a daemonic instability in sexual relations that we may have to accept.

The femme fatale is one of the most mesmerizing of sexual personae. She is not a fiction but an extrapolation of biologic realities in women that remain constant. The North American Indian myth of the toothed vagina (*vagina dentata*) is a gruesomely direct transcription of female power and male fear. Metaphorically, every vagina has secret teeth, for the male exits as less than when he entered. The basic mechanics of conception require action in the male but nothing more than passive receptivity in the female. Sex as a natural rather than social transaction, therefore, really is a kind of drain of male energy by female fullness. Physical and spiritual castration is the danger every man runs in intercourse with a woman. Love is the spell by which he puts his sexual fear to sleep. Woman's latent vampirism is not a social aberration but a development of her maternal function, for which nature has equipped her with tiresome thoroughness. For the male, every act of intercourse is a return to the mother and a capitulation to her. For men, sex is a struggle for identity. In sex, the male is consumed and released again by the toothed power that bore him, the female dragon of nature.

The femme fatale was produced by the mystique of connection between mother and child. A modern assumption is that sex and procreation are medically, scientifically, intellectually "manageable." If we keep tinkering with the social mechanism long enough, every difficulty will disappear. Meanwhile, the divorce rate soars. Conventional marriage, despite its inequities, kept the chaos of libido in check. When the prestige of marriage is low, all the nasty daemonism of sexual instinct pops out. Individualism, the self unconstrained by society, leads to the coarser servitude of constraint by nature. Every road from Rousseau leads to Sade. The mystique of our birth from human mothers is one of the daemonic clouds we cannot dispel by tiny declarations of independence. Apollo can swerve from nature, but he cannot obliterate it. As emotional and sexual beings we go full circle. Old age is a second childhood in which earliest memories revive. Chillingly, comatose patients of any age automatically drift toward the fetal position, from which they have to be pried by nurses. We are tied to our birth by unshakable apparitions of sense-memory.

Rousseauist psychologies like feminism assert the ultimate benevolence of human emotion. In such a system, the femme fatale logically has no place. I follow Freud, Nietzsche, and Sade in my view of the amorality of the instinctual life. At some level, all love is combat, a wrestling with ghosts. We are only *for* something by being *against* something else. People who believe they are having pleasant, casual, uncomplex sexual encounters, whether with friend, spouse, or stranger, are blocking from consciousness the tangle of psychodynamics at work, just as they block the hostile clashings of their dream life. Family romance operates at all times. The femme fatale is one of the refinements of female narcissism, of the ambivalent self-directedness that is completed by the birth of a child or by the conversion of spouse or lover into child.

Mothers can be fatal to their sons. It is against the mother that men have erected their towering edifice of politics and sky-cult. She is Medusa, in whom Freud sees the castrating and castrated female pubes. But Medusa's snaky hair is also the writhing vegetable growth of nature. Her hideous grimace is men's fear of the laughter of women. She that gives life also blocks the way to freedom. Therefore I agree with Sade that we have the right to thwart nature's procreative compulsions, through sodomy or abortion. Male homosexuality may be the most valorous of attempts to evade the femme fatale and to defeat nature. By turning away from the Medusan mother, whether in honor or detestation of her, the male homosexual is one of the great forgers of absolutist Western identity. But of course nature has won, as she always does, by making disease the price of promiscuous sex.

The permanence of the femme fatale as a sexual persona is part of the weary weight of eroticism, beneath which both ethics and religion founder. Eroticism is society's soft point, through which it is invaded by chthonian nature. The femme fatale can appear as Medusan mother or as frigid nymph, masquing in the brilliant luminosity of Apollonian high glamour. Her cool unreachability beckons, fascinates, and destroys. She is not a neurotic but, if anything, a psychopath. That is, she has an amoral affectlessness, a serene indifference to the suffering of others, which she invites and dispassionately observes as tests of her power. The mystique of the femme fatale cannot be perfectly translated into male terms. I will speak at length of the beautiful boy, one of the West's most stunning sexual personae. However, the danger of the *homme fatal*, as embodied in today's boyish male hustler, is that he will leave, disappearing to other loves, other lands. He is a rambler, a cowboy and sailor. But the danger of the femme fatale is that *she will stay*, still, placid, and paralyzing. Her remaining is a daemonic burden, the ubiquity of Walter Pater's *Mona Lisa*, who smothers history. She is a thorny symbol of the perversity of sex. She will stick.

We are moving in this chapter toward a theory of beauty. I believe that the aesthetic sense, like everything else thus far, is a swerve from the chthonian. It is a displacement from one area of reality to another, analogous to the shift from earth-cult to sky-cult. Ferenczi speaks of the replacement of animal nose by human eye, because of our upright stance. The eye is peremptory in its judgments. It decides what to see and why. Each of our glances is as much exclusion as inclusion. We select, editorialize, and enhance. Our idea of the pretty is a limited notion that cannot possibly apply to earth's metamorphic underworld, a cataclysmic realm of chthonian violence. We choose not to see this violence on our daily strolls. Every time we say nature is beautiful, we are saying a prayer, fingering our worry beads.

The cool beauty of the femme fatale is another transformation of chthonian ugliness. Female animals are usually less beautiful than males. The mother bird's dull feathers are camouflage, protecting the nest from predators. Male birds are creatures of spectacular display, of both plumage and parade, partly to impress females and conquer rivals and partly to divert enemies from the nest. Among humans, male ritual display is just as extreme, but for the first time the female becomes a lavishly beautiful object. Why? The female is adorned not simply to increase her property value, as Marxism would demystifyingly have it, but to assure her desirability. Consciousness has made cowards of us all. Animals do not feel sexual fear, because they are not rational beings. They operate under a pure biologic imperative. Mind, which has enabled humanity to adapt and flourish as a species, has also infinitely complicated our functioning as physical beings. We see too much, and so have to stringently limit our seeing. Desire is besieged on all sides by anxiety and doubt. Beauty, an ecstasy of the eye, drugs us and allows us to act. Beauty is our Apollonian revision of the chthonian.

Nature is a Darwinian spectacle of the eaters and the eaten. All phases of procreation are ruled by appetite: sexual intercourse, from kissing to penetration, consists of movements of barely controlled cruelty and consumption. The long pregnancy of the human female and the protracted childhood of her infant, who is not self-sustaining for seven years or more, have produced the agon of psychological dependency that burdens the male for a lifetime. Man justifiably fears being devoured by woman, who is nature's proxy.

Repression is an evolutionary adaptation permitting us to function under the burden of our expanded consciousness. For what we are conscious of could drive us mad. Crude male slang speaks of female genitalia as "slash" or "gash." Freud notes that Medusa turns men to stone because, at first sight, a boy thinks female genitals a wound, from which the penis has been cut. They are indeed a wound, but it is the infant who has been cut away, by violence: the umbilical is a hawser sawed through by a social rescue party. Sexual necessity drives man back to that bloody scene, but he cannot approach it without tremors of apprehension. These he conceals by euphemisms of love and beauty. However, the less well-bred he is—that is, the less socialized—the sharper his sense of the animality of sex and the grosser his language. The foulmouthed roughneck is produced not by society's sexism but by society's absence. For nature is the most foulmouthed of us all.

Woman's current advance in society is not a voyage from myth to truth but from myth to new myth. The rise of rational, technological woman may demand the repression of unpleasant archetypal realities. Ferenczi remarks, "The periodic pulsations in feminine sexuality (puberty, the menses, pregnancies and parturitions, the climacterium) require a much more powerful repression on the woman's part than is necessary for the man."[3] In its argument with male society, feminism must suppress the monthly evidence of woman's domination by chthonian nature. Menstruation and childbirth are an affront to beauty and form. In aesthetic terms, they are spectacles of frightful squalor. Modern life, with its hospitals and paper products, has distanced and sanitized these primitive mysteries, just as it has done with death, which used to be a grueling at-home affair. An awful lot is being swept under the rug: the awe and terror that are our lot.

The wound-like rawness of female genitals is a symbol of the unredeemability of chthonian nature. In aesthetic terms, female genitals are lurid in color, vagrant in contour, and architecturally incoherent. Male genitals, on the other hand, though they risk ludicrousness by their rubbery indecisiveness (a Sylvia Plath heroine memorably thinks of "turkey neck and turkey gizzards"), have a rational mathematical design, a syntax. This is no absolute virtue, however, since it may tend to confirm the male in his abundant misperceptions of reality. Aesthetics stop where sex begins. G. Wilson Knight declares, "All physical love is, in its way, a victory over physical secrecies and physical repulsions."[4] Sex is sloppy and untidy, a return to what Freud calls the infant's polymorphous perversity, a zestful rolling around in every body fluid. St. Augustine says, "We are born between feces and urine." This misogynistic view of the infant's sin-stained emergence from the birth canal is close to the chthonian truth. But excretion, through which nature for once acts upon the sexes equally, can be saved by comedy, as we see in Aristophanes, Rabelais, Pope, and Joyce. Excretion has found a place in high culture. Menstruation and childbirth are too barbaric for comedy. Their ugliness has produced the giant displacement of women's historical status as sex object, whose beauty is endlessly discussed and modified. Woman's beauty is a compromise with her dangerous archetypal allure. It gives the eye the comforting illusion of intellectual control over nature.

My explanation for the male domination of art, science, and politics, an indisputable fact of history, is based on an analogy between sexual physiology and aesthetics. I will argue that all cultural achievement is a projection, a swerve into Apollonian transcendence, and that men are anatomically destined to be projectors. But as with Oedipus, destiny may be a curse.

How we know the world and how it knows us are underlain by shadow patterns of sexual biography and sexual geography. What breaks into consciousness is shaped in advance by the daemonism of the senses. Mind is a captive of the body. Perfect objectivity does not exist. Every thought bears some emotional burden. Had we time or energy to pursue it, each random choice, from the color of a toothbrush to a decision over a menu, could be made to yield its secret meaning in the inner drama of our lives. But in exhaustion, we shut out this psychic supersaturation. The realm of number, the crystalline mathematic of Apollonian purity, was invented early on by Western man as a refuge from the soggy emotionalism and bristling disorder of woman and nature. Women who excel in mathematics do so in a system devised by men for the mastery of nature. Number is the most imposing and least creaturely of pacifiers, man's yearning hope for objectivity. It is to number that he—and now she—withdraws to escape from the chthonian mire of love, hate, and family romance.

Even now, it is usually men rather than women who claim logic's superiority to emotion. This they comically tend to do at moments of maximum emotional chaos, which they may have incited and are helpless to stem. Male artists and actors have a cultural function in keeping the line of emotion open from the female to male realms. Every man harbors an inner female territory ruled by his mother, from whom he can never entirely break free. Since Romanticism, art and the study of art have become vehicles for exploring the West's repressed emotional life, though one would never know it from half the deadening scholarship that has sprung up around them. Poetry is the connecting link between body and mind. Every idea in poetry is grounded in emotion. Every word is a palpation of the body. The multiplicity of interpretation surrounding a poem mirrors the stormy uncontrollability of emotion, where nature works her will. Emotion *is* chaos. Every benign emotion has a flip side of negativity. Thus the flight from emotion to number is another crucial strategy of the Apollonian West in its long struggle with Dionysus.

Emotion is passion, a continuum of eroticism and aggression. Love and hate are not opposites: there is only more passion and less passion, a difference of quantity and not of kind. To live in love and peace is one of the outstanding contradictions that Christianity has imposed on its followers, an ideal impossible and unnatural. Since Romanticism, artists and intellectuals have complained about the church's sex rules, but these are just one small part of the Christian war with pagan nature. Only a saint could sustain the Christian code of love. And saints are ruthless in their exclusions: they must shut out an enormous amount of reality, the reality of sexual personae and the reality of nature. Love for all means coldness to something or someone. Even Jesus, let us recall, was unnecessarily rude to his mother at Cana.

The chthonian superflux of emotion is a male problem. A man must do battle with that enormity, which resides in woman and nature. He can attain selfhood only by beating back the daemonic cloud that would swallow him up: mother-love, which we may just as well call mother-hate. Mother-love, mother-hate, for her or from her, one huge conglomerate of natural power. Political equality for women will make very little difference in this emotional turmoil that is going on above and below politics, outside the scheme of social life. Not until all babies are born from glass jars will the combat cease between mother and son. But in a totalitarian future that has removed procreation from woman's hands, there will also be no affect and no art. Men will be machines, without pain but also without pleasure. Imagination has a price, which we are paying every day. There is no escape from the biologic chains that bind us.

What has nature given man to defend himself against woman? Here we come to the source of man's cultural achievements, which follow so directly from his singular anatomy. Our lives as physical beings give rise to basic metaphors of apprehension, which vary greatly between the sexes. Here there can be no equality. Man is sexually compartmentalized. Genitally, he is condemned to a perpetual pattern of linearity, focus, aim, directedness. He must learn to aim. Without

aim, urination and ejaculation end in infantile soiling of self
or surroundings. Woman's eroticism is diffused throughout
her body. Her desire for foreplay remains a notorious area
of miscommunication between the sexes. Man's genital concentration is a reduction but also an intensification. He is a
victim of unruly ups and downs. Male sexuality is inherently
manic-depressive. Estrogen tranquilizes, but androgen agi-
tates. Men are in a constant state of sexual anxiety, living on
the pins and needles of their hormones. In sex as in life they
are driven *beyond*—beyond the self, beyond the body. Even in
the womb this rule applies. Every fetus becomes female unless
it is steeped in male hormone, produced by a signal from the
testes. Before birth, therefore, a male is already beyond the
female. But to be beyond is to be exiled from the center of life.
Men know they are sexual exiles. They wander the earth seeking satisfaction, craving and despising, never content. There is
nothing in that anguished motion for women to envy.

The male genital metaphor is concentration and projection. Nature gives concentration to man to help him overcome
his fear. Man approaches woman in bursts of spasmodic concentration. This gives him the delusion of temporary control
of the archetypal mysteries that brought him forth. It gives
him the courage to return. Sex is metaphysical for men, as it is
not for women. Women have no problem to solve by sex. Physically and psychologically, they are serenely self-contained.
They may choose to achieve, but they do not need it. They
are not thrust into the beyond by their own fractious bodies.
But men are out of balance. They must quest, pursue, court,
or seize. Pigeons on the grass, alas: in such parkside rituals
we may savor the comic pathos of sex. How often one spots
a male pigeon making desperate, self-inflating sallies toward
the female, as again and again she turns her back on him
and nonchalantly marches away. But by concentration and

insistence he may carry the day. Nature has blessed him with obliviousness to his own absurdity. His purposiveness is both a gift and a burden. In human beings, sexual concentration is the male's instrument for gathering together and forcibly fixing the dangerous chthonian superflux of emotion and energy that I identify with woman and nature. In sex, man is driven into the very abyss which he flees. He makes a voyage to nonbeing and back.

Through concentration to projection into the beyond. The male projection of erection and ejaculation is the paradigm for all cultural projection and conceptualization—from art and philosophy to fantasy, hallucination, and obsession. Women have conceptualized less in history not because men have kept them from doing so but because women do not need to conceptualize in order to exist. I leave open the question of brain differences. Conceptualization and sexual mania may issue from the same part of the male brain. Fetishism, for instance, a practice which like most of the sex perversions is confined to men, is clearly a conceptualizing or symbol-making activity. Man's vastly greater commercial patronage of pornography is analogous.

An erection is *a thought* and the orgasm an act of imagination. The male has to will his sexual authority before the woman who is a shadow of his mother and of all women. Failure and humiliation constantly wait in the wings. No woman has to prove herself a woman in the grim way a man has to prove himself a man. He must perform, or the show does not go on. Social convention is irrelevant. A flop is a flop. Ironically, sexual success always ends in sagging fortunes anyhow. Every male projection is transient and must be anxiously, endlessly renewed. Men enter in triumph but withdraw in decrepitude. The sex act cruelly mimics history's decline and fall. Male bonding is a self-preservation society, collegial reaffirmation through larger, fabricated frames of reference. Culture is man's iron reinforcement of his ever-imperiled private projections.

Concentration and projection are remarkably demonstrated by urination, one of male anatomy's most efficient compartmentalizations. Freud thinks primitive man preened himself on his ability to put out a fire with a stream of urine. A strange thing to be proud of but certainly beyond the scope of woman, who would scorch her hams in the process. Male urination really *is* a kind of accomplishment, an arc of transcendence. A woman merely waters the ground she stands on. Male urination is a form of commentary. It can be friendly when shared but is often aggressive, as in the defacement of public monuments by Sixties rock stars. To piss on is to criticize. John Wayne urinated on the shoes of a grouchy director in full view of cast and crew. This is one genre of self-expression women will never master. A male dog marking every bush on the block is a graffiti artist, leaving his rude signature with each lift of the leg. Women, like female dogs, are earthbound squatters. There is no projection beyond the boundaries of the self. Space is claimed by being sat on, squatter's rights.

The cumbersome, solipsistic character of female physiology is tediously evident at sports events and rock concerts, where fifty women wait in line for admission to the sequestered cells of the toilet. Meanwhile, their male friends zip in and out (in every sense) and stand around looking at their watches and rolling their eyes. Freud's notion of penis envy proves too true when the pub-crawling male cheerily relieves himself in midnight alleyways, to the vexation of his bursting female companions. This compartmentalization or isolation of male genitality has its dark side, however. It can lead to a dissociation of sex and emotion, to temptation, promiscuity, and disease. The modern gay man, for example, has sought ecstasy in the squalor of public toilets, for women perhaps the least erotic place on earth.

Man's metaphors of concentration and projection are echoes of both body and mind. Without them, he would be helpless before woman's power. Without them, woman would long ago have absorbed all of creation into herself. There would be no culture, no system, no pyramiding of one hierarchy upon another. Earth-cult must lose to sky-cult, if mind is ever to break free from matter. Ironically, the more modern woman thinks with Apollonian clarity, the more she participates in the historical negation of her sex. Political equality for women, desirable and necessary as it is, is not going to remedy the radical disjunction between the sexes that begins and ends in the body. The sexes will always be jolted by violent shocks of attraction and repulsion.

Androgyny, which some feminists promote as a pacifist blueprint for sexual utopia, belongs to the contemplative rather than active life. It is the ancient prerogative of priests, shamans, and artists. Feminists have politicized it as a weapon against the masculine principle. Redefined, it now means men must be like women and women can be whatever they like. Androgyny is a cancellation of male concentration and projection. Prescriptions for the future by bourgeois academics and writers carry their own bias. The reform of a college English department cuts no ice down at the corner garage. Male concentration and projection are visible everywhere in the aggressive energy of the streets. Fortunately, gay men of every social class have preserved the cult of the masculine, which will therefore never lose its aesthetic legitimacy. Major peaks of Western culture have been accompanied by a high incidence of male homosexuality—in classical Athens and Renaissance Florence and London. Male concentration and projection are self-enhancing, leading to supreme achievements of Apollonian conceptualization.

If sexual physiology provides the pattern for our experience of the world, what is woman's basic metaphor? It is mystery, *the hidden*. Karen Horney speaks of a girl's inability to see her genitals and a boy's ability to see his as the source of "the greater subjectivity of women as compared with the greater objectivity of men."[5] To rephrase this with my different emphasis: men's delusional certitude that objectivity is possible is based on the visibility of their genitals. Second, this certitude is a defensive swerve from the anxiety-inducing invisibility of the womb. Women tend to be more realistic and less obsessional because of their toleration for ambiguity, which they learn from their inability to learn about their own bodies. Women accept limited knowledge as their natural condition, a great human truth that a man may take a lifetime to reach.

The female body's unbearable hiddenness applies to all aspects of men's dealings with women. What does it look like in there? Did she have an orgasm? Is it really my child? Who was my real father? Mystery shrouds woman's sexuality. This mystery is the main reason for the imprisonment man has imposed on women. Only by confining his wife in a locked harem guarded by eunuchs could he be certain that her son was also his. Man's genital visibility is a source of his scientific desire for external testing, validation, proof. By this method he hopes to solve the ultimate mystery story, his chthonian birth. Woman is veiled. Violent tearing of this veil may be a motive in gang rapes and rape-murders, particularly ritualistic disembowelings of the Jack the Ripper kind. The Ripper's public nailing up of his victim's uterus is exactly paralleled in tribal ritual of South African Bushmen. Sex crimes are always male, never female, because such crimes are conceptualizing assaults on the unreachable omnipotence of woman and nature. Every woman's body contains a cell of archaic night, where all knowing must stop. This is the profound meaning behind striptease, a sacred dance of pagan origins which, like prostitution, Christianity has never been able to stamp out. Erotic dancing by males cannot be comparable, for a nude woman carries off the stage a final concealment, that chthonian darkness from which we come.

Woman's body is a secret, sacred space. It is a temenos, or ritual precinct, a Greek word I adopt for the discussion of art. In the marked-off space of woman's body, nature operates at its darkest and most mechanical. Every woman is a priestess guarding the temenos of daemonic mysteries. Virginity is categorically different for the sexes. A boy becoming a man quests for experience. The penis is like eye or hand, an extension of self reaching outward. But a girl is a sealed vessel that must be broken into by force. The female body is the prototype of all sacred spaces from cave shrine to temple and church. The womb is the veiled Holy of Holies, a great problem, as we shall see, for sexual polemicists like William Blake who seek to abolish guilt and covertness in sex. The taboo on woman's body is the taboo that always hovers over the place of magic. Woman is literally the occult, which means "the hidden." These uncanny meanings cannot be changed, only suppressed, until they break into cultural consciousness again. Political equality will succeed only in political terms. It is helpless against the archetypal. Kill the imagination, lobotomize the brain, castrate and operate: then the sexes will be the same. Until then, we must live and dream in the daemonic turbulence of nature.

Everything sacred and inviolable provokes profanation and violation. Every crime that *can* be committed *will* be. Rape is a mode of natural aggression that can be controlled only by the social contract. Modern feminism's most naive formulation is its assertion that rape is a crime of violence but not of sex, that it is merely power masquerading as sex. But sex *is* power, and all power is inherently aggressive. Rape is male power fighting female power. It is no more to be excused than is murder or any other assault on another's civil rights. Society is woman's protection against rape, not, as some feminists absurdly maintain, the cause of rape. Rape is the sexual expression of the will-to-power, which nature plants in all of us and which civilization rose to contain. Therefore the rapist is a man with too little socialization rather than too much. Worldwide evidence is overwhelming that whenever social controls are weakened, as in war or mob rule, even civilized men behave in uncivilized ways, among which is the barbarity of rape.

The latent metaphors of the body guarantee the survival of rape, which is a development in degree of intensity alone of the basic movements of sex. A girl's loss of virginity is always in some sense a violation of sanctity, an invasion of her integrity and identity. Defloration *is* destruction. But nature creates by violence and destruction. The commonest violence in the world is childbirth, with its appalling pain and gore. Nature gives males infusions of hormones for dominance in order to hurl them against the paralyzing mystery of woman, from whom they would otherwise shrink. Her power as mistress of birth is already too extreme. Lust and aggression are fused in male hormones. Anyone who doubts this has probably never spent much time around horses. Stallions are so dangerous they must be caged in barred stalls; once gelded, they are docile enough to serve as children's mounts. The hormonal disparity in humans is not so gross, but it is grosser than Rousseauists like to think. The more testosterone, the more elevated the libido. The more dominant the male, the more frequent his contributions to the genetic pool. Even on the microscopic level, male fertility is a function not only of number of sperm but of their motility, that is, their restless movement, which increases the chance of conception. Sperm are miniature assault troops, and the ovum is a solitary citadel that must be breached. Weak or passive sperm just sit there like dead ducks. Nature rewards energy and aggression.

Profanation and violation are part of the perversity of sex, which never will conform to liberal theories of benevolence. Every model of morally or politically correct sexual behavior *will be subverted*, by nature's daemonic law. Every hour of every day, some horror is being committed somewhere. Feminism, arguing from the milder woman's view, completely misses the blood-lust in rape, the joy of violation and destruction. An aesthetics and erotics of profanation—evil for the sake of evil, the sharpening of the senses by cruelty and torture—have been documented in Sade, Baudelaire, and Huysmans. Women may be less prone to such fantasies because they physically lack the equipment for sexual violence. They do not know the temptation of forcibly invading the sanctuary of another body.

Our knowledge of these fantasies is expanded by pornography, which is why pornography should be tolerated, though its public display may reasonably be restricted. The imagination cannot and must not be policed. Pornography shows us nature's daemonic heart, those eternal forces at work beneath and beyond social convention. Pornography cannot be separated from art; the two interpenetrate each other, far more than humanistic criticism has admitted. Geoffrey Hartman rightly says, "Great art is always flanked by its dark sisters, blasphemy and pornography."[6] *Hamlet* itself, the cardinal Western work, is full of lewdness. Criminals through history, from Nero and Caligula to Gilles de Rais and the Nazi commandants, have never needed pornography to stimulate their exquisite, gruesome inventiveness. The diabolic human mind is quite enough.

1. *The Anxiety of Influence: A Theory of Poetry* (New York, 1973), 94.

2. *Sexual Deviation* (Harmondsworth, Middlesex, 1964), 63.

3. "The Analytic Conception of the Psycho-Neuroses" (1908), in *Further Contributions to the Theory and Technique of Psycho-analysis*,

ed. John Rickman, trans. Jane Isabel Suttie et al. (New York, 1926), 25.

4. *Lord Byron's Marriage* (London, 1957), 261.

5. "On the Genesis of the Castration Complex in Women," *International Journal of Psychoanalysis* 5 (1924): 53.

6. *Beyond Formalism: Literary Essays 1958–1970* (New Haven, 1970), 23.

2

THE VENUS OF WILLENDORF

Our first exhibit from Western art is the so-called Venus of Willendorf, a tiny statuette (height 4³/₈") from the Old Stone Age found in Austria. In it we see all the strange laws of primitive earth-cult. Woman is idol and object, goddess and prisoner. She is buried in the bulging mass of her own fecund body.

The Venus of Willendorf is comically named, for she is unbeautiful by every standard. But beauty has not yet emerged as a criterion for art. In the Old Stone Age, art is magic, a ritual re-creation of what-is-desired. Cave paintings were not meant to be seen. Their beauty for us is incidental. Bison and reindeer crowd the walls, following rock ridges and grooves. Art was invocation, a summoning: mother nature, let herds return that man might eat. Caves were the bowels of the goddess, and art was a sexual scribbling, an impregnation. It had rhythm and vitality but no visual status. The Venus of Willendorf, a cult-image half-molded from a rough stone, is unbeautiful because art has not yet found its relation to the eye. Her fat is a symbol of abundance in an age of famine. She is the too-muchness of nature, which man longs to direct to his salvation.

Venus of Willendorf carries her cave with her. She is blind,

[*Sexual Personae*, 1990, Chapter 2, "The Birth of the Western Eye"]

Venus of Willendorf, ca. 30,000 B.C.
(Bridgeman-Giraudon/Art Resource, N.Y.)

masked. Her ropes of corn-row hair look forward to the invention of agriculture. She has a furrowed brow. Her facelessness
is the impersonality of primitive sex and religion. There is
no psychology or identity yet, because there is no society, no
cohesion. Men cower and scatter at the blast of the elements.
Venus of Willendorf is eyeless because nature can be seen but
not known. She is remote even as she kills and creates. The
statuette, so overflowing and protuberant, is ritually invisible.
She stifles the eye. She is the cloud of archaic night.

Bulging, bulbous, bubbling. Venus of Willendorf, bent
over her own belly, tends the hot pot of nature. She is eternally pregnant. She broods, in all senses. She is hen, nest, egg.

The Latin *mater* and *materia*, mother and matter, are etymo-logically connected. Venus of Willendorf is the nature-mother as primeval muck, oozing into infant forms. She is female but not feminine. She is turgid with primal force, swollen with great expectations. She has no feet. Placed on end, she would topple over. Woman is immobile, weighed down by her inflated mounds of breast, belly, and buttock. Like Venus de Milo, Venus of Willendorf has no arms. They are flat flippers scratched on the stone, unevolved, useless. She has no thumbs and therefore no tools. Unlike man, she can neither roam nor build. She is a mountain that can be climbed but can never move.

Venus is a solipsist, navel-gazing. Femaleness is self-referential and self-replicating. Delphi was called the ompha-los or navel of the world, marked by a shapeless holy stone. A black meteorite, a primitive image of Cybele, was brought to Rome from Phrygia to save the city in the last Punic War. The Palladium, a Zeus-sent image of Athena upon which Troy's fate depended, was probably such a meteorite. Today, the Kaaba, the inner sanctuary of the Great Mosque of Mecca, enshrines a meteorite, the Black Stone, as the holiest relic of Islam. The Venus of Willendorf is a kind of meteorite, a quirky found object, lumpish and mystic. The Delphic omphalos-stone was cone, womb, and beehive. The braided cap of Venus of Wil-lendorf is hive-like—prefiguring the provocative beehives of French court wigs and shellacked swinging-Sixties towers. Venus buzzes to herself, queen for all days, woman for all seasons. She sleeps. She is hibernation and harvest, the turn-ing wheel of the year. The egg-shaped Venus thinks in circles. Mind under matter.

Sex, I said, is a descent to the nether realms, a daily sink-ing from sky-cult to earth-cult. It is abdominal, abominable, daemonic. Venus of Willendorf is going down, disappearing into her own labyrinth. She is a tuber, rooted from a pocket of earth. Kenneth Clark divides female nudes into the Vegetable and the Crystalline Aphrodite. Inert and self-communing, Venus of Willendorf represents the obstacle of sex and vegetable nature. It is at her shrine that we worship in oral sex. In the bowels of the earth mother, we feel but do not think or see. Venus dwindles to a double pubic delta, knees clamped and cramped in the sharp pelvic angle of the wide-hipped child-bearing woman, which prevents her from running with ease. Female jiggle is the duck-like waddle of our wallowing Willendorf, who swims in the underground river of liquid nature. Sex is probings, plumbing, secretions, gushings. Venus is drowsing and dowsing, hearkening to the stirring in her sac of waters.

Is the Venus of Willendorf just to female experience? Yes. Woman is trapped in her wavy, watery body. She must listen and learn from something beyond and yet within her. The Venus of Willendorf, blind, tongueless, brainless, armless, knock-kneed, seems a depressing model of gender. Yet woman is depressed, pressed down, by earth's gravitation, calling us back to her bosom. We will see that malign magnetism at work in Michelangelo, one of his great themes and obsessions. In the West, art is a hacking away at nature's excess. The Western mind makes definitions. That is, it draws lines. This is the heart of Apollonianism. There are no lines in the Venus of Willendorf, only curves and circles. She is the formlessness of nature. She is mired in the miasmic swamp I identify with Dionysus. Life always begins and ends in squalor. The Venus of Willendorf, slumping, slovenly, sluttish, is in a rut, the womb-tomb of mother nature. Never send to know for whom the belle tolls. She tolls for thee.

3

NEFERTITI

Our second exhibit from Western art is the bust of Nefertiti. How familiar it is, and yet how strange. Nefertiti is the opposite of the Venus of Willendorf. She is the triumph of Apollonian image over the humpiness and horror of mother earth. Everything fat, slack, and sleepy is gone. The Western eye is open and alert. It has forced objects into their frozen frame. But the liberation of the eye has its price. Taut, still, and truncated, Nefertiti is Western ego under glass. The radiant glamour of this supreme sexual persona comes to us from a palace-prison, the overdeveloped brain. Western culture, moving up toward Apollonian sunlight, discards one burden only to stagger under another.

The bust, found by a German expedition at Amarna in 1912, dates from the reign of Akhenaten (1353–36 B.C.). Queen Nefertiti, wife of the pharaoh, wears a wig-crown peculiar to the eighteenth dynasty and seen elsewhere only on Akhenaten's formidable mother, Queen Tiy. The bust is painted limestone with plaster additions; the eye is inset rock crystal. The ears and uraeus, the royal serpent on the brow, are broken. Scholars have debated whether the piece is a studio model for court artists.

[From *Sexual Personae*, 1990, Chapter 2, "The Birth of the Western Eye"]

Nefertiti (copy)
(Foto Marburg/Art Resource, N.Y.)

The Nefertiti bust is one of the most popular artworks in the world. It is printed on scarves and molded in necklace pendants and coffee-table miniatures. But never in my experience is the bust exactly reproduced. The copyist softens it, feminizes and humanizes it. The actual bust is intolerably severe. It is too uncanny an object for domestic display. Even art books lie. The bust is usually posed in profile or at an angle, so that the missing left pupil is hidden or shadowed. What happened to the eye? Perhaps it was unnecessary in a model and never inserted. But the eye was often chiseled out of statues and paintings of the dead. It was a way of making a hated rival a nonperson and extinguishing his or her survival in the afterlife. Akhenaten's reign was divisive. His creation

Nefertiti, ca. 1350 B.C.
(Foto Marburg/Art Resource, N.Y.)

of a new capital and efforts to crush the powerful priesthood, his establishment of monotheism and innovations in artistic style were nullified under his son or son-in-law, Tutankhamen, the short-lived boy-king. Nefertiti may have lost her eye in the wreck of the eighteenth dynasty.

As we have it, the bust of Nefertiti is artistically and ritualistically complete, exalted, harsh, and alien. It fuses the naturalism of the Amarna period with the hieratic formalism of Egyptian tradition. But Amarna expressiveness ends in the grotesque. This is the least consoling of great artworks. Its popularity is based on misunderstanding and suppression of its unique features. The proper response to the Nefertiti bust is fear. The queen is an android, a manufactured being. She is a new gorgoneion, a "bodiless head of fright." She is paralyzed and paralyzing. Like the enthroned pharaoh Chephren, Nefertiti is suave, urbane. She gazes toward the far distance, seeing what is best for her people. But her eyes, with their catlike rim of kohl, are cold. She is self-divinized authority. Art shows Akhenaten half-feminine, his limbs shrunken and belly bulging, possibly from birth defect or disease. This portrait shows his queen half-masculine, a vampire of political will. Her seductive force both lures in and warns away. She is Western personality barricaded behind its aching, icy line of Apollonian identity.

Nefertiti's head is so massive it threatens to snap the neck like a stalk. She is like a papyrus blossom swaying on its river reed. The head is swollen to the point of deformity. She seems futuristic, with the enlarged cerebrum foreseen as the destiny of our species. The crown is filled like a funnel with a rain of hierarchic energy, flooding the fragile brain-pan and violently pushing the face forward like the prow of a ship. Nefertiti is like the Winged Victory of Samothrace, garments plastered back by the wind of history. As cargo, Nefertiti carries her own excess of thought. She is weighed down by Apollonian wakefulness, a sun that never sets. Egypt invented the pillar, which Greece would refine. With her slim aristocratic neck, Nefertiti is a pillar, a caryatid. She bears the burden of state upon her head, rafters of the temple of the sun. The golden brow-band is a ritual bridle, squeezing, constricting, limiting. Nefertiti presides from the temenos of power, a sacred precinct she can never leave.

Venus of Willendorf is all body, Nefertiti all head. Her shoulders have been cut away by radical surgery. Early in its history, Egypt invented the bust, a portrait style still in use. It may have been a robust double, the *ka* that enters and exits through false doors. The shoulders of the Nefertiti bust have shriveled to become their own pedestal. No physical force remains. The queen's body is bound and invisible, like a mummy. Her face gleams with the newness of rebirth. Tense with self-creation, she is a goddess as mother-father. The pregnancy of Venus of Willendorf is displaced upward and redefined. Willendorf is chthonian belly-magic, Nefertiti Apollonian head-magic. Thinking makes it so. Nefertiti is a royal highness, propelling herself like a jet into sky-cult. Forward thrust. Nefertiti leads with her chin. She has "great bones." She is Egyptian stone architecture, just as Venus of Willendorf is earthen ovals, woman as quivering poached egg. Nefertiti is femaleness made mathematical, femaleness sublimized by becoming harder and more concrete.

I said Egypt invented elegance, which is reduction, simplification, condensation. Mother nature is addition and multiplication, but Nefertiti is subtraction. Visually, she has been reduced to her essence. Her sleek contoured face is one step from the wizened. She is abbreviation, a symbol or pictogram, a pure idea of pagan pictorialism. One can never be too rich or too thin, decreed the Duchess of Windsor. I said the idea of beauty is based on enormous exclusions. So much is excluded from the Nefertiti bust that we can feel its silhouette straining against the charged atmosphere, a combat of Apollonian line. The name Nefertiti means "The Beautiful One Cometh." Her haughty face is carved out of the chaos of nature. Beauty is a state of war, a frigid blank zone under siege.

Nefertiti is ritualized Western personality, a streamlined *thing*. She is forbiddingly clean. Her eyebrows are shaved and redrawn with male width and frown. She is as depilated as a priest. She has the face of a mannequin, static, posed, self-proffering. Her *knowingness* is both fashionable and hieratic. The modern mannequin of window or runway is an androgyne, because she is femaleness impersonalized by masculine abstraction. If a studio model, the Nefertiti bust is as much a mannequin as the royal dummy of a London tailor shop. As queen and mannequin, Nefertiti is both exposed and enclosed, a face and a mask. She is naked yet armored, experienced yet ritually pure. She is sexually unapproachable because bodiless: her torso is gone; her full lips invite but remain firmly pressed together. Her perfection is for display, not for use. Akhenaten and his queen would greet their court from a balcony, the "window of appearance." All art is a window of appearance. Nefertiti's face is the sun of consciousness rising over a new horizon, the frame or mathematical grid of man's victory over nature. The idolatrous *thingness* of Western art is a theft of authority from mother nature. Nefertiti's mismatched eyes, deliberate or accidental, are a symbol of Egyptian duality. Like the cat, she sees in and sees out. She is frozen Apollonian poseur and Gorgonesque daemonic seer. The Greek Graiai, three old divine sisters, had one eye that they passed from hand to hand. Fontenrose connects this to the double pupil of a Lydian queen: "What she had, it seems to me, was a removable eye of wondrous power. It was an eye that could penetrate the invisible."[1] Nefertiti, the half-blind mannequin, sees more by being less. Mutilation is mystic expansion. Modern copyists suppress the missing eye because it is fatal to popular canons of beauty. Maimed eyes seem mad or spectral, as in the veiled vulture's eye of Poe's "The Tell-Tale Heart." Nefertiti is a mutant and visionary materialist, a thing that sees. In Egypt, matter is made numinous by the first electricity of mind. In the Egyptian cult of seeing, Nefertiti is thought in flight from its origins.

From Venus of Willendorf to Nefertiti: from body to face, touch to sight, love to judgment, nature to society. Nefertiti is like Athena born from the brow of Zeus, a head-heavy armored goddess. She is beautiful but desexed. She is hieratic decorum and reserve, her head literally a reservoir of containment and curtailment, like her stunted torso. Her ponderous, ostentatious crown is the cold breeding ground of Greek categorical thought. Her tight brow-band is stringency, rigor, channeled ideas. The miasmic cloud of mother nature has lifted. Nefertiti's imperious jutting face is the cutting edge of Western conceptualization and projection. In her profile, all roads lead to the eye. From the side, diagonals converge in peaking vectors of force. From the front, she rears up like a cobra head, woman as royal intimidator. She is the eye-intense West, the over-enlargement and grandiosity of head-culture. The bust of Nefertiti is eye-pleasing but oppressive. It looks forward to Bellini's androgynous *Doge Loredan*, to Neapolitan silver reliquary busts, to 1950s fantasy drawings of smiling armless women in chic evening gowns. Authority, good will, aloofness, asceticism. Epiphany as a totem of vibrating passivity. With her welcoming but uncanny smile, Nefertiti is Western personality in its ritual bonds. Exquisite and artificial, she is mind-made image forever caught in radiant Apollonian freeze-frame.

1. Joseph Fontenrose, *Python: A Study of Delphic Myth and Its Origins* (Berkeley, 1959) 285–86.

4

MADONNA: ANIMALITY AND ARTIFICE

Madonna, don't preach.

Defending her controversial new video, "Justify My Love," on *Nightline* last week, Madonna stumbled, rambled, and ended up seeming far less intelligent than she really is.

Madonna, 'fess up.

The video is pornographic. It's decadent. And it's fabulous. MTV was right to ban it, a corporate resolve long overdue. Parents cannot possibly control television, with its titanic omnipresence.

Prodded by correspondent Forrest Sawyer for evidence of her responsibility as an artist, Madonna hotly proclaimed her love of children, her social activism, and her condom endorsements. Wrong answer. As Baudelaire and Oscar Wilde knew, neither art nor the artist has a moral responsibility to liberal social causes.

"Justify My Love" is truly avant-garde, at a time when that word has lost its meaning in the flabby art world. It represents a sophisticated European sexuality of a kind we have not seen since the great foreign films of the 1950s and 1960s. But it does not belong on a mainstream music channel watched around the clock by children.

[*The New York Times*, December 14, 1990]

On *Nightline*, Madonna bizarrely called the video a "cele-bration of sex." She imagined happy educational scenes where curious children would ask their parents about the video. Oh, sure! Picture it: "Mommy, please tell me about the tired, tied-up man in the leather harness and the mean, bare-chested lady in the Nazi cap." Okay, dear, right after the milk and cookies.

Sawyer asked for Madonna's reaction to feminist charges that, in the neck manacle and floor-crawling of an earlier video, "Express Yourself," she condoned the "degradation" and "humiliation" of women. Madonna waffled: "But I chained myself! I'm in charge." Well, no. Madonna the producer may have chosen the chain, but Madonna the sexual persona in the video is alternately a cross-dressing dominatrix and a slave of male desire.

But who cares what the feminists say anyhow? They have been outrageously negative about Madonna from the start. In 1985, *Ms.* magazine pointedly feted quirky, cuddly singer Cyndi Lauper as its woman of the year. Great judgment: gim-micky Lauper went nowhere, while Madonna grew, flour-ished, metamorphosed, and became an international star of staggering dimensions. She is also a shrewd business tycoon, a modern new woman of all-around talent.

Madonna is the true feminist. She exposes the puritan-ism and suffocating ideology of American feminism, which is stuck in an adolescent whining mode. Madonna has taught young women to be fully female and sexual while still exercis-ing control over their lives. She shows girls how to be attrac-tive, sensual, energetic, ambitious, aggressive, and funny—all at the same time.

American feminism has a man problem. The beaming Betty Crockers, hangdog dowdies, and parochial prudes who call themselves feminists want men to be like women. They fear and despise the masculine. The academic feminists think their nerdy bookworm husbands are the ideal model of human manhood.

But Madonna loves real men. She sees the beauty of masculinity, in all its rough vigor and sweaty athletic perfection. She also admires the men who are actually like women: transsexuals and flamboyant drag queens, the heroes of the 1969 Stonewall rebellion, which started the gay liberation movement.

"Justify My Love" is an eerie, sultry tableau of jaded androgynous creatures, trapped in a decadent sexual underground. Its hypnotic images are drawn from such sadomasochistic films as Liliana Cavani's *The Night Porter* and Luchino Visconti's *The Damned*. It's the perverse and knowing world of the photographers Helmut Newton and Robert Mapplethorpe.

Contemporary American feminism, which began by rejecting Freud because of his alleged sexism, has shut itself off from his ideas of ambiguity, contradiction, conflict, ambivalence. Its simplistic psychology is illustrated by the new cliché of the date-rape furor: " 'No' always means 'no.' " Will we ever graduate from the Girl Scouts? "No" has always been, and always will be, part of the dangerous, alluring courtship ritual of sex and seduction, observable even in the animal kingdom.

Madonna has a far profounder vision of sex than do the feminists. She sees both the animality and the artifice. Changing her costume style and hair color virtually every month, Madonna embodies the eternal values of beauty and pleasure. Feminism says, "No more masks." Madonna says we are nothing but masks.

Through her enormous impact on young women around the world, Madonna is the future of feminism.

5

RAPE AND MODERN SEX WAR

Rape is an outrage that cannot be tolerated in civilized society. Yet feminism, which has waged a crusade for rape to be taken more seriously, has put young women in danger by hiding the truth about sex from them.

In dramatizing the pervasiveness of rape, feminists have told young women that before they have sex with a man, they must give consent as explicit as a legal contract's. In this way, young women have been convinced that they have been the victims of rape. On elite campuses in the Northeast and on the West Coast, they have held consciousness-raising sessions, petitioned administrations, demanded inquests. At Brown University, outraged, panicky "victims" have scrawled the names of alleged attackers on the walls of women's restrooms. What marital rape was to the Seventies, "date rape" is to the Nineties.

The incidence and seriousness of rape do not require this kind of exaggeration. Real acquaintance rape is nothing new. It has been a horrible problem for women for all of recorded history. Once fathers and brothers protected women from rape. Once the penalty for rape was death. I come from a fierce Italian tradition where, not so long ago in the motherland, a rapist would end up knifed, castrated, and hung out to dry.

[New York *Newsday*, January 27, 1991]

But the old clans and small rural communities have broken down. In our cities, on our campuses far from home, young women are vulnerable and defenseless. Feminism has not prepared them for this. Feminism keeps saying the sexes are the same. It keeps telling women they can do anything, go anywhere, say anything, wear anything. No, they can't. Women will always be in sexual danger.

One of my male students recently slept overnight with a friend in a passageway of the Great Pyramid in Egypt. He described the moon and sand, the ancient silence and eerie echoes. I will never experience that. I am a woman. I am not stupid enough to believe I could ever be safe there. There is a world of solitary adventure I will never have. Women have always known these somber truths. But feminism, with its pie-in-the-sky fantasies about the perfect world, keeps young women from seeing life as it is.

We must remedy social injustice whenever we can. But there are some things we cannot change. There are sexual differences that are based in biology. Academic feminism is lost in a fog of social constructionism. It believes we are totally the product of our environment. This idea was invented by Rousseau. He was wrong. Emboldened by dumb French language theory, academic feminists repeat the same hollow slogans over and over to each other. Their view of sex is naive and prudish. Leaving sex to the feminists is like letting your dog vacation at the taxidermist's.

The sexes are at war. Men must struggle for identity against the overwhelming power of their mothers. Women have menstruation to tell them they are women. Men must do or risk something to be men. Men become masculine only when other men say they are. Having sex with a woman is one way a boy becomes a man.

College men are at their hormonal peak. They have just left their mothers and are questing for their male identity. In groups, they are dangerous. A woman going to a fraternity party is walking into Testosterone Flats, full of prickly cacti and blazing guns. If she goes, she should be armed with resolute alertness. She should arrive with girlfriends and leave with them. A girl who lets herself get dead drunk at a fraternity party is a fool. A girl who goes upstairs alone with a brother at a fraternity party is an idiot. Feminists call this "blaming the victim." I call it common sense.

For a decade, feminists have drilled their disciples to say, "Rape is a crime of violence but not of sex." This sugar-coated Shirley Temple nonsense has exposed young women to disaster. Misled by feminism, they do not expect rape from the nice boys from good homes who sit next to them in class.

Aggression and eroticism are deeply intertwined. Hunt, pursuit, and capture are biologically programmed into male sexuality. Generation after generation, men must be educated, refined, and ethically persuaded away from their tendency toward anarchy and brutishness. Society is not the enemy, as feminism ignorantly claims. Society is woman's protection against rape. Feminism, with its solemn Carry Nation repressiveness, does not see what is for men the eroticism or fun element in rape, especially the wild, infectious delirium of gang rape. Women who do not understand rape cannot defend themselves against it.

The date-rape controversy shows feminism hitting the wall of its own broken promises. The women of my Sixties generation were the first respectable girls in history to swear like sailors, get drunk, stay out all night—in short, to act like men. We sought total sexual freedom and equality. But as time passed, we woke up to cold reality. The old double standard protected women. When anything goes, it's women who lose.

Today's young women don't know what they want. They see that feminism has not brought sexual happiness. The theatrics of public rage over date rape are their way of restoring the old sexual rules that were shattered by my generation. Because nothing about the sexes has really changed. The comic film *Where the Boys Are* (1960), the ultimate expression of Fifties man-chasing, still speaks directly to our time. It shows smart, lively women skillfully anticipating and fending off the dozens of strategies with which horny men try to get them into bed. The agonizing date-rape subplot and climax are brilliantly done. The victim, Yvette Mimieux, makes mistake after mistake, obvious to the other girls. She allows herself to be lured away from her girlfriends and into isolation with boys whose character and intentions she misreads. *Where the Boys Are* tells the truth. It shows courtship as a dangerous game in which the signals are not verbal but subliminal.

Neither militant feminism, which is obsessed with politically correct language, nor academic feminism, which believes that knowledge and experience are "constituted by" language, can understand preverbal or nonverbal communication. Feminism, focusing on sexual politics, cannot see that sex exists in and through the body. Sexual desire and arousal cannot be fully translated into verbal terms. This is why men and women misunderstand each other.

Trying to remake the future, feminism cut itself off from sexual history. It discarded and suppressed the sexual myths of literature, art, and religion. Those myths show us the turbulence, the mysteries and passions of sex. In mythology we see men's sexual anxiety, their fear of woman's dominance. Much sexual violence is rooted in men's sense of psychological weakness toward women. It takes many men to deal with one woman. Woman's voracity is a persistent motif. Clara Bow, it was rumored, took on the USC football team on weekends. Marilyn Monroe, singing "Diamonds Are a Girl's Best Friend," rules a conga line of men in tuxes. Half-clad Cher, in the video for "If I Could Turn Back Time," deranges a battleship of screaming sailors and straddles a pink-lit cannon. Feminism, coveting social power, is blind to woman's cosmic sexual power.

To understand rape, you must study the past. There never was and never will be sexual harmony. Every woman must take personal responsibility for her sexuality, which is nature's red flame. She must be prudent and cautious about where she goes and with whom. When she makes a mistake, she must accept the consequences and, through self-criticism, resolve never to make that mistake again. Running to Mommy and Daddy on the campus grievance committee is unworthy of strong women. Posting lists of guilty men in the toilet is cowardly, infantile stuff.

The Italian philosophy of life espouses high-energy confrontation. A male student makes a vulgar remark about your breasts? Don't slink off to whimper and simper with the campus shrinking violets. Deal with it. On the spot. Say, "Shut up, you jerk! And crawl back to the barnyard where you belong!" In general, women who project this take-charge attitude toward life get harassed less often. I see too many dopey, immature, self-pitying women walking around like melting sticks of butter. It's the Yvette Mimieux syndrome: make me happy. And listen to me weep when I'm not.

The date-rape debate is already smothering in propaganda churned out by the expensive Northeastern colleges and universities, with their overconcentration of boring, uptight academic feminists and spoiled, affluent students. Beware of the deep manipulativeness of rich students who were neglected by their parents. They love to turn the campus into hysterical psychodramas of sexual transgression, followed by assertions of parental authority and concern. And don't look for sexual enlightenment from academe, which spews out mountains of books but never looks at life directly.

As a fan of football and rock music, I see in the simple, swaggering masculinity of the jock and in the noisy posturing of the heavy-metal guitarist certain fundamental, unchanging truths about sex. Masculinity is aggressive, unstable, combustible. It is also the most creative cultural force in history. Women must reorient themselves toward the elemental powers of sex, which can strengthen or destroy.

The only solution to date rape is female self-awareness and self-control. A woman's number one line of defense is herself. When a real rape occurs, she should report it to the police. Complaining to college committees because the courts "take too long" is ridiculous. College administrations are not a branch of the judiciary. They are not equipped or trained for legal inquiry. Colleges must alert incoming students to the problems and dangers of adulthood. Then colleges must stand back and get out of the sex game.

6

JUNK BONDS AND CORPORATE RAIDERS: ACADEME IN THE HOUR OF THE WOLF

Women's studies is institutionalized sexism. It too must go. Gender studies is no alternative: "gender" is now a biased, prudish code word for social constructionism. Sexology is an old and distinguished field. As sex studies, frankly admitting it is sex we are tirelessly interested in, it would take in the hundred-year history of international commentary on sex; it would make science its keystone; and it would allow both men and women as well as heterosexuals and homosexuals to work together in the fruitful dialogue of dislike, disagreement, and debate, the tension, confrontation, and dialectic that lead to truth. Women's studies is a comfy, chummy morass of unchallenged groupthink. It is, with rare exception, totally unscholarly. Academic feminists have silenced men and dissenting women. Sunk in a cocoon of smug complacency, they are blind to their own clichéd Rousseauist ideology. Feminists are always boasting of their "diversity" and pluralism. This is like white Protestants, in the nineteenth and pre-Sixties twentieth centuries when they controlled American politics, finance, and academe, claiming diversity on the basis of their

[*Arion*, Spring 1991, excerpt]

dozens of denominations. But blacks, Jews, and Italian Catholics, standing on the outside, could clearly see the monolithic homogeneity that the WASP insiders were blissfully, arrogantly unaware of. If any field ever deserved a punishing Foucauldian analysis, it's women's studies, which is a prisoner of its own futile, grinding, self-created discourse. Women's studies needed a syllabus and so invented a canon overnight. It puffed up clunky, mundane contemporary women authors into Oz-like, skywriting dirigibles. Our best women students are being force-fed an appalling diet of cant, drivel, and malarkey. Pioneering work in sex studies will come only from men and women conservatively trained in high-level intellectual history.

American feminism's nosedive began when Kate Millett, that imploding beanbag of poisonous self-pity, declared Freud a sexist. Trying to build a sex theory without studying Freud, women have made nothing but mud pies. In Great Britain and France, feminists did not make this silly mistake, but unfortunately their understanding of Freud has been tainted by the swindling Lacan. Now the missing but indispensable Freud is being smuggled back into America by the Lacan feminists, with their paralyzing puritanism. It's all ass-backwards. Just read Freud, for pity's sake, and forget Lacan. It's outrageous that women undergraduates are being made to read Lacan who haven't read Freud and therefore have no idea what Lacan is doing. Freud is one of the major thinkers in world history. One reads him not for his conclusions, which were always tentative and in process, but for the bold play of his speculative intelligence. He shows you how to conceptualize, how to frame long, overarching arguments, how to verbalize ambiguous, nonverbal psychic phenomena. Reading him, you feel new tracks being cut in your brain. Cheap gibes about Freud, epidemic in women's studies, are a symptom of emotional juvenility. American feminists, sniveling about Freud without reading him, have sentenced themselves and their work to mediocrity and irrelevance.

Simone de Beauvoir's brilliant, imperious *The Second Sex*, now 40 years old, is the only thing undergraduate sex studies needs. Add Freud to de Beauvoir, and you have intellectual training at its best. The later French women choking the current syllabus don't come up to Simone de Beauvoir's anklebones: that damp sob sister, Hélène Cixous, with her diarrhea prose, or Luce Irigaray, the pompous lapdog of Parisian café despots doing her grim, sledgehammer elephant walk through small points. American feminism is awash with soupy Campbellism: schlockmeisters like Marija Gimbutas, the Pollyanna of poppycock, with her Mommy goddess tales conveniently exalting her Lithuanian ancestors into world-class saintly pacifists. The chirpy warblers Gilbert-Gubar, those unlearned, unreadable bores, with their garbled, rumbling, hollow, rolling-trashcan style. Carolyn Heilbrun, Mrs. Fifties Tea Table, who spent her academic time, while my generation was breaking its head against social and sexual convention, spinning daydreams about a WASP persona, Amanda Cross, and who spoke out only when it was safe to do so. Heilbrun's late self-packaging as a feminist is a triumph of American commerce. The gauzy, ethnicity-evading style of her dazzlingly research-free books is the height of wishful, reactionary gentility. Women's studies is a jumble of vulgarians, bunglers, whiners, French faddicts, apparatchiks, doughface party-liners, pie-in-the-sky utopianists, and bullying, sanctimonious sermonizers. Reasonable, moderate feminists hang back and, like good Germans, keep silent in the face of fascism. For fifteen years, the established women academics irresponsibly let women's studies spread uncritiqued and unchecked (I call this period "While Vendler Slept"). Great women scholars like Jane Harrison and Gisela

Richter were produced by the intellectual discipline of the masculine classical tradition, not by the wishy-washy sentimentalism of clingy, all-forgiving sisterhood, from which no first-rate book has yet emerged. Every year, feminists provide more and more evidence for the old charge that women can neither think nor write.

7

THE MIT LECTURE:
CRISIS IN THE AMERICAN UNIVERSITIES

Thank you, Professor Manning, for that most gracious introduction. And may I say what a pleasure it is to be here, a mere
stone's throw from Harvard.

I address you tonight after several sex changes and a great
deal of ambiguity over sexual orientation over twenty-five
years. I am the Sixties come back to haunt the present.

Now, speaking here at MIT confronted me with a dilemma.
I asked myself, should I try to act like a lady? I can do it. It's
hard, it takes a lot out of me, I can do it for a few hours. But
then I thought, *Naw.* These people, both my friends and my
enemies who are here, aren't coming to see me act like a lady.
So I thought I'd just be myself—which is, you know, abrasive,
strident, and obnoxious. So then you all can go outside and
say, "What a bitch!"

Now, the reason I'm getting so much attention: I think
it's pretty obvious that we're in a time where there's a kind
of impasse in contemporary thinking. And what I represent

[Excerpt from transcript of lecture at the Massachusetts Institute of
Technology, Cambridge, September 19, 1991. Introduction by
Kenneth Manning, Professor of the History of Science]

is independent thought. What I represent is the essence of the Sixties, which is free thought and free speech. And a lot of people don't like it. A lot of people who are well-meaning on both sides of the political spectrum want to shut down free speech. And my mission is to be absolutely as painful as possible in every situation.

So I've been attacking what I regard as the ideology of date rape. At the same time as I consider rape an outrage, I consider the propaganda and hysteria about date rape *equally* outrageous from the Sixties point of view, utterly reactionary from a Sixties point of view. And I will continue to attack it. And I will continue to attack the well-meaning people who think they're protecting women and in fact are infantilizing them. . . .

One of the main reasons that I am so angry is that last year at the University of Pennsylvania I went to a lecture—and I'm going to start identifying her. I haven't for a year, but I just spilled the beans to a Cornell magazine, so I might as well keep doing it. It was Diana Fuss of Princeton, a very prominent feminist theorist. She seems to be a very nice woman. This is the *pity* of it! She was such a nice woman. I had never heard of her, I didn't know her. I went to this lecture and I thought, "This is *awful*, what is happening here!" A lecture hall filled with young women from the University of Pennsylvania, okay, and this Diana Fuss, this really nice, very American kind of a woman—we're not talking, like, cosmopolitan here, and I mean cosmopolitan with a small *c!*—what she did was show a series of slides that she had made of contemporary ads and pictorials from *Harper's Bazaar* and so on.

Let me tell the full story of what happened that night. Now, normally if you're in a boring lecture, you can, like, tune out. You know, you can plan your meals, do your laundry in your head, and things like that, okay? In this case, it was *torture* to me, because she was showing these *gorgeous* pictures up on the screen, beautiful pictures that were stimulating the mind, stimulating the imagination, you understand? And at the same time she was *trashing* these pictures with this horrible Lacan, labyrinthine thing. So I was just out of my—I was out of control. People turned around and said "*Shh!*" to me. I was *writhing* in my seat [*imitates electrocution-like spasms*]. It was *awful*. Let me give you an example. There was a Revlon ad of a woman in a blue pool of water, and she was beautifully made up, and there was obviously a reflector being used to shine the sunlight especially intensely on her face. This was a beautiful ad. And Diana Fuss was going, "Decapitation—mutilation."

Then there was a beautiful picture from *Harper's Bazaar*, I think, of a black woman wearing a crimson turtleneck. But instead of the collar turned over, you know, it was up like this, around the chin. It was very beautiful. It was like a flower. And she was wearing aviator glasses that I recognized, from the 1930s! Now Diana Fuss said, "She's blinded." *I* would have said, "She has mystic vision." Anyway, with the turtleneck, what do you think? "Strangulation, bondage!" It went on like this, picture after picture after picture. I thought, "This is *psychotic*." Such radical misinterpretation of reality is psychotic. But it's a whole system. Psychosis is a system. People within that system feel it's very rational.

Now, what I hated about this was you had two hundred young women, who didn't understand a *word* of what she was saying—it was all that Lacan gibberish—and they're all going, "Ohhh, *wow*! The woman from Princeton—a big woman from Princeton. She's so brilliant!" And I thought, "This is *evil*." Diana Fuss is not evil. She's a nice woman. But if what you're *doing* is evil, I'm sorry, it has to *stop*. This is perverted. It really is perverted. When you destroy young people's ability to take pleasure in beauty, you are a pervert! So I stood up, I was very agitated—and she was such a good sport. I mean, here was this maniac she never heard of, my book had just come out, and I was waving my arms around. I said I didn't mean to condemn her, because I understood that what she was doing was the result of ten years of feminists doing this. But nevertheless, I asked, why is it, why is it that feminists have so much trouble dealing with beauty and pleasure, I said, to which gay men have made such *outstanding* cultural contributions? *Why*—if gay men can respond? This is why I get along so well with gay men, and I don't get along with lesbian feminists. This is why my sexuality is a complete neuter! I don't fit in anywhere! I'm like this wandering being, the Ancient Mariner—it's just awful.

So anyway, afterwards I went down to speak to Diana Fuss because I wanted to find out how much she knows about art, because she's a product of English departments. And I spoke to her a little bit, and I could see she knew nothing about art. And I also could tell she knew nothing about popular culture. Now you see the problem here. You cannot just suddenly open a magazine and look at a picture of a nude woman and then free associate, using Lacan. You cannot do that! Because fashion magazines are part of the history of art. These are great photographers, great stylists—and gay men have made enormous contributions to fashion photography. Anyway, I made a huge statement that night—the whole audience gasped. I went, "The history of fashion photography from 1950 to 1990 is one of the great moments in the history of art!" And everyone went, "*How* can you *say* that?" Because obviously fashion is an oppression of women.

And beauty, according to, um, Miss, um, Naomi Wolf, is a heterosexist conspiracy by men in a room to keep feminism back—and all that *crap* that's going on. I call her, by the way, "Little Miss Pravda." She and I are head-to-head on MTV this week, in case you want to know! But I won't appear with her. *Oprah's* tried to get me on with her: I won't go on with her. A talk show in Italy wanted to fly me over to appear with her. *No.* I always say, "Would Caruso appear with Tiny Tim?" If you want to see what's wrong with Ivy League education, look at *The Beauty Myth,* that book by Naomi Wolf. This is a woman who graduated from Yale magna cum laude, is a Rhodes scholar, and cannot write a coherent paragraph. This is a woman who cannot do historical analysis, and she is a Rhodes scholar? If you want to see the damage done to intelligent women today in the Ivy League, look at that book. It's a *scandal.* Naomi Wolf is an intelligent woman. She has been ill-served by her education. But if you read Lacan, this is the result. Your brain turns to pudding! She has a case to make. She cannot make it. She's full of paranoid fantasies about the world. Her education was completely removed from reality.

Now, I want to totally reform education, so that we get really first-rate, top-level intellectual work by women. We're not going to get it. There's a lost generation of women coming out of these women's studies programs—a lost generation. If you spend your whole time reading Gilbert-Gubar, Hélène Cixous, and all the rest of that French *rot*—thank God, I didn't have that. Thank God, I had only men and Simone de Beauvoir—and Jane Harrison and Gisela Richter. There were great women writers as well as great women scholars. I held myself to *the highest standards.* I didn't say, we're going to make new standards, women's standards, and give us women's awards, the women's sweepstakes, and all that stuff. No one takes women's work seriously right now. Do you think that men take it seriously? Do you think anyone reads Gilbert-Gubar? I mean, who reads Gilbert-Gubar? or Carolyn Heilbrun, that mediocre, genteel crap, coming from a woman who's Jewish and who is still writing in a genteel style. This is feminism? *This* is feminism?

This is third-rate, tenth-rate stuff. It's appalling that our young women are being assigned to read things like Lacan when they're sophomores and haven't read Freud. What good does it do to read Lacan if you haven't read Freud? All of Lacan is just a commentary on Freud. This is *ridiculous.* It's a *horrible* situation. We need massive reform, at every level.

Now back to my little survey here. So by the time the women's movement broke forth in the late 1960s, it was practically impossible for me to be reconciled with my "sisters." And there were, like, screaming fights. The big one was about the Rolling Stones. Boy, I was bounced *fast*, right out of the movement. And I had this huge argument. Because I said you cannot apply a political agenda to art. When it comes to art, we have to make other distinctions. We had this huge fight about the song "Under My Thumb." I said it was a great song, not only a great song but I said it was a work of art. And these feminists of the New Haven Women's Liberation Rock Band went into a rage, surrounded me, practically spat in my face, literally my back was to the wall. They're screaming in my face: "Art? Art? Nothing that demeans women can be art!" There it is. *There it is!* Right from the start. The fascism of the contemporary women's movement.

Feminism is 200 years old. Ever since Mary Wollstonecraft wrote that manifesto in 1792. It's 200 years old. It's had many phases. We can criticize the present phase without necessarily criticizing feminism. I want to save feminism from the feminists. What I identify with is the prewar feminism of Amelia Earhart, of Katharine Hepburn—who had an enormous impact on me—that period of women where you had independence, self-reliance, personal responsibility, and not blaming other people for your problems. I want to bring that back. And my life has been a good example of it. Because my career was a disaster, but I did not blame it on anyone. I took personal responsibility for my own work. If I could not be published in my own lifetime, I would leave it beyond the grave, as Emily Dickinson did, and torture people in the next life!

So in the late 1960s, I saw immediately—and still we have this problem, twenty years down the line from the birth of contemporary feminism—that there are two huge areas that feminism has excluded that need to be integrated within it. That's what I'm doing. That's my contribution. One of them that was excluded was aesthetics. Right from the start there was a problem with aesthetics, a difficulty with dealing with beauty and with art. If you think that's an old problem, it isn't. The present prominence of Naomi Wolf and her book indicates that what I'm criticizing is still a contemporary problem. The accolades on the back of that book from leading feminists, including Germaine Greer—who said, "This is the most important book—since my *own* book!"—show that that's still an issue.

So: aesthetics. Because one of my earliest faculties was my responsiveness to beauty. I think it may be something innate in Italians, I honestly think it may be. There's an art thing, an art gene that we've got. Early on, I was in love with beauty. I don't feel *less* because I'm in the presence of a beautiful person. I don't go [*imitates crying and dabbing tears*], "Oh, I'll *never* be that beautiful!" What a ridiculous attitude to take!—the Naomi Wolf attitude. When men look at sports, when they look at football, they don't go [*crying*], "Oh, I'll *never* be that fast, I'll *never* be that strong!" When people look at Michelangelo's *David*, do they commit suicide? No. See what I mean? When you see a strong person, a fast person, you go, "Wow! That is fabulous." When you see a beautiful person: "How beautiful." That's what I'm bringing back to feminism. You go, "What a beautiful person, what a beautiful man, what a beautiful woman, what beautiful hair, what beautiful boobs!" Okay, now I'll be charged with sexual harassment, probably. I won't even be able to get out of the room!

We should not have to apologize for reveling in beauty. Beauty is an eternal human value. It was not a trick invented by nasty men in a room someplace on Madison Avenue. I say in *Sexual Personae* that it was invented in Egypt. For 3,000 years at the height of African civilization you had a culture based on beauty. We have two major cultures in the world today, France and Japan, organized around the idea of beauty. It is *so* provincial, feminism's problem with beauty. We have *got* to get over this. Obviously, any addiction—like if you're addicted to plastic surgery—that's a problem. Of course it's a problem. Addiction to anything is a problem. But this blaming anorexia on the media—this is Naomi's thing—oh *please!* Anorexia is coming out of these white families, these pushy, perfectionist white families, who all end up with their daughters at Yale. Naomi arrives in England, and "Gee, all the women Rhodes scholars have eating disorders. Gee, it must be . . . *the media!*" Maybe it's that *you* are a parent-pleasing, teacher-pleasing little kiss-ass! Maybe you're a *yuppie!* Maybe *you*, Miss Yuppie, have figured out *the system*. Isn't it interesting that Miss Naomi, the one who has succeeded in *the system*, the one who has been given the prizes by the system, she who is the princess of the system, *she's* the one who's bitchin' about it? *I'm* the one who's been poor and rejected—shouldn't *I* be the one bitching about it? *No*—because I'm a scholar, okay, and she's a twit!

The second area where feminism is deficient is in its psychology. Right from the start, Kate Millett banned Freud as a sexist. And so we have this horror that has arisen over the last twenty years of feminism trying to build a sex theory without Freud, one of the greatest masters, one of the great analysts of human personality in history. Now, you don't have to *assent* to Freud. I don't read Freud and go, "Oh, wow, he is the ultimate word on the human race"—that's not how I *read*! I follow him, and I go, "This is interesting. Now maybe he needs to be supplemented." So I'll supplement from wherever—a little bit from Jung, a little bit from Frazer, whom I very much admire, sometimes from astrology. I mean, I find all kinds of things everywhere. Soap opera—I love soap opera—Lana Turner—I'll take it from anywhere. I'm very syncretic. I'm very eclectic. But I mean Freud has to be the *basis* of any psychology. We should be reading him first, not these minor women, and build up from there. All this obsession with "Well, did you read Jeffrey Masson's thing on the seduction theory?" Oh, please, who *cares*? All this "Let's unmask Big Daddy"—this obsession with the weaknesses of big figures. This is infantile. It's infantile. You read major figures not because everything they say is the gospel truth but because they expand your imagination, they expand your IQ, okay, they open up brain cells you didn't even know you have.

So we have these two large areas: we have aesthetics missing from contemporary feminism and we have psychology. It's an incoherent psychology right now. Another thing, I feel, and others might not agree, is that its politics is also naive, a politics which blames all human problems on white male imperialists who have victimized women and people of color. This view of history is coming from people who know nothing about history. Because when you think of the word "imperialist," if you automatically just think "America," then you don't know anything. Because someone who's studied the history of ancient Egypt knows that imperialism was practically invented in Egypt and in the ancient Near East. If you want to talk about imperialism, let's talk about Japan or Persia or all kinds of things. It's not just a white male monopoly.

What we need, you see, is really systematic training in political science and history. It's obvious there's a need for this now. There was, following the Sixties, an appetite for history, but the people in academe were not willing to do the work necessary to master history and anthropology and so on. Instead, it was sort of like, "Hey, we need history! Let's see. Oh—there's Foucault!" It was sort of like that. It's sort of like ducks when they're born—the first thing they see, you know? So if they see a vacuum cleaner, they think it's their mother. They'll follow the vacuum cleaner. That's what happened. Foucault is the vacuum cleaner that everyone followed.

All I can say is thank God, by the time Lacan and Foucault appeared on the cultural landscape, I had already done all my preparations. I had been reading very deeply not only in college but especially during graduate school in the Yale library, so by the time they arrived I was intellectually prepared to see how specious they are. And therefore it never affected me. And now, of course, there are people who spent twenty years of their lives on these characters, and now, of course, they're a little irritated when someone says, "Oh, that was a waste." It's sort of like a period where people were told, because they had no taste of their own, that they should furnish their house in zebra Naugahyde furniture. So they went heavily into this, okay, their whole house is furnished in it. Then suddenly, twenty years down the road, someone like me appears and says, "Guess what—that's *out* now. Not only that, but it was in terrible taste to begin with." So you can see why they're mad at me. They're mad because they're stuck with that furniture! They have twenty years of furniture!

But time for something *new*. I think, you know, that there's something happening. I can really feel it. Like for twenty years, no one would listen to me. I just hit a wall. No one heard what I was saying, no one understood anything about what my book was doing, people just looked at me with blank faces. And suddenly people are listening. It's not me that's changed. The culture is changing. Something is happening. It's a twenty-year astrological cycle that's happening. I was very moved, a few months ago—Arsenio had on the Fifth Dimension, reunited!

The Fifth Dimension, which had quarreled, the catfights, all
that, they had reunited, and they were singing "Aquarius" on
Arsenio! I was very moved! I said, "Something is happening.
The Sixties are coming back." Some of the lines of that song I
really identify with: "The mind's true liberation." This is what
I stand for: "The mind's true liberation."

And unfortunately what's happening today, with this kind
of very sanctimonious and sermonizing talk about sex that's
coming out of the rape counselors and so on, people do not
realize, with all their good intentions, how oppressive this is to
sex, what a disaster this is to the mind, what a disaster this is to
the spirit, to allow the rape counselors to take over the cultural
stage. Now the work that they do is good, and it's wonderful
that they're there. But we cannot have this scenario being projected of male rapaciousness and brutality and female victimage. We have *got* to make women realize they are *responsible*,
that sexuality is something that belongs to them. They have
an enormous power in their sexuality. It's up to them to use it
correctly and to be wise about where they go and what they do.
And I'm accused of being "anti-woman" because of this attitude? Because I'm bringing common sense back to the rape
discourse?

Now when people say to me, "Oh, you're always talking
about feminists as if they're monolithic. We're not monolithic.
We're very pluralistic. We have so many different views."
No, excuse me: the date-rape issue shows that I am correct.
Because there is *one voice* speaking about date rape from coast
to coast, *one voice*, one stupid, shrewish, puritanical, sermonizing, hysterical voice. And where are all these sophisticated
feminists supposedly out there? Where *are* they? Totally impotent, locked in their little burrows wherever they are, whether
they're in the East Village or Harvard. Wherever they are,
they're impotent. There's not one voice raised to bring some

sense into this hysteria. Now, I am an experienced teacher. I sympathize with the problems of freshmen, and so I believe that date-rape awareness is an excellent thing to do when students arrive, not only for the men, to warn the men that breaches of civilized behavior will not be tolerated, but also to warn the women. . . .

The idea that feminism is the first group that ever denounced rape is a gross libel to men. Throughout history, rape has been condemned by honorable men. Honorable men do not murder; honorable men do not steal; honorable men do not rape. It goes all the way back through history. Tarquin's rape of Lucretia caused the fall of the tyrants and the beginning of the Roman Republic. This idea that somehow suddenly feminism miraculously found out that women were being exploited and raped through history is ridiculous. We have got to remove things like rape from the women's studies context and pull it back into ethics. It belongs in *ethics*. We have to ask how should *everyone*—not just men—how should everyone be trained as a child to behave in society. We must put it in a general philosophical context. This idea of focusing in, suddenly, at the freshman year of college—it's too late! Guess *what*—you're not going to convert anyone with a few films on date-rape education, a few demonstrations, and a few pamphlets being passed out. You're not going to change anyone's mind. Look—ethics has *always* condemned such abuses. You do not have this endless series of atrocities through history. Men have also protected women. Men have given women sustenance. Men have provided for women. Men have died to defend the country for women. We must look back and acknowledge what men have done *for women*.

Men's creation of the technological world of today has made *me* possible. I remember my paternal grandmother on the back porch in Endicott, scrubbing the clothes on a washboard. She had nine children. I remember that. I, her grand-daughter, could have the leisure to write this book, thanks to the technological world and modern capitalism, which has such a bad rep. Look around the world, okay, and see what the reality is. Oh, I thank God I was born an American, I thank God. When I got to Europe—I feel the smog of convention hanging everywhere in Europe, even in England, which is a very free-speaking and free-thinking country. In America, woman is at her freest. Never in history have women been freer than they are here. And this idea, this bitching, bitching, kvetching about capitalism and America and men, this whining—it's infantile, it's an adolescent condition, it's *bad* for women. It's very, very bad to convince young women that they have been victims and that their heritage is nothing but victimization. This is another perversion.

8

THE STRANGE CASE OF CLARENCE THOMAS AND ANITA HILL

Anita Hill is no feminist heroine. A week ago, in the tense climax of the Senate Judiciary Committee's hearings into the nomination of Clarence Thomas to the Supreme Court, the important issue of sexual harassment, one of the solid innovations of contemporary feminism, was used and abused for political purposes.

In an atrocious public spectacle worthy of the show trials of a totalitarian regime, uncorroborated allegations about verbal exchanges ten years old were paraded on the nation's television screens. The Judiciary Committee should have thoroughly investigated the charges but conducted the proceedings privately. It was an appalling injustice to both Anita Hill and Clarence Thomas to pit them and their supporters against each other. The Senate turned itself into the Roman Colosseum, with decadent, jaded patricians waving thumbs down over a blood-drenched arena.

Five years ago, because of the absence of a sexual harassment policy at my university, I initiated a workshop on the question in my women's studies class. I collected sexual

[*The Philadelphia Inquirer*, October 21, 1991]

harassment guidelines and documents from Philadelphia-area universities, distributed them to the class, and guided the formulation of proposals, which we presented to the dean. Such guidelines are crucial not only to warn potential offenders but to help women stand their ground in specific encounters. In our democratic society, however, we must also protect the rights of the accused. Frivolous claims of misconduct do occur.

I listened carefully to Anita Hill's testimony at the Senate hearings. I found her to be sincere and intelligent. But I reject her claim of sexual harassment. What exactly transpired between her and Clarence Thomas we can never know. That Hill was distressed by references to sex may indeed be the case. But since they were never threatening and never led to pressure for a date, I fail to see how they constitute sexual harassment. Many religious men, as well as women, find conversations about sex or pornography inappropriate and unacceptable. This is not a gender issue. It is our personal responsibility to define what we will and will not tolerate.

The sexual revolution of my Sixties generation broke the ancient codes of decorum that protected respectable ladies from profanation by foul language. We demanded an end to the double standard. What troubles me about the "hostile workplace" category of sexual harassment policy is that women are being returned to their old status of delicate flowers who must be protected from assault by male lechers. It is anti-feminist to ask for special treatment for women.

America is still burdened by its Puritan past, which erupts again and again in public scenarios of sexual inquisition, as in Hawthorne's *The Scarlet Letter*. If Anita Hill was thrown for a loop by sexual banter, that's her problem. If by the age of twenty-six, as a graduate of the Yale Law School, she could find no convincing way to signal her displeasure and disinterest, that's her deficiency. We cannot rely on rigid rules and regulations to structure everything in our lives. There is a blurry line between our professional and private selves. We are sexual beings, and as Freud demonstrated, eroticism pervades every aspect of our consciousness.

Hill woodenly related the content of conversations without any reference to their context or tone. The senators never asked about joking, smiles, facial expressions, hers as well as his. Every social encounter is a game being played by two parties. I suspect Hill's behavior was compliant and, to use her own word about a recent exchange with a Thomas friend, "passive." Judging by her subsequent cordial behavior toward Thomas, Hill chose to put her career interests above feminist principle. She went along to get along. Hence it is hypocritical of her, ten years later, to invoke feminist principle when she did not have the courage to stand on it before. For feminists to make a heroine out of Hill is to insult all those other women who have taken a bolder, more confrontational course and forfeited career advantage.

In this case, the sexual harassment issue was a smoke screen, cynically exploited to serve another issue, abortion rights. Although I am firmly pro-choice, I think there should be no single-issue litmus test for nominees to the Supreme Court. And the strategy backfired. Thomas, who had seemed bland and evasive for the prior hundred days of the hearings, emerged under fire with vastly increased stature. He was passionate, forceful, dignified.

Make no mistake: it was not a White House conspiracy that saved this nomination. It was Clarence Thomas himself. After eight hours of Hill's testimony, he was driven as low as any man could be. But step by step, with sober, measured phrases, he regained his position and turned the momentum against his accusers. It was one of the most powerful moments I have ever witnessed on television. Giving birth to himself, Thomas reenacted his own credo of the self-made man.

9

THE NURSERY SCHOOL CAMPUS: THE CORRUPTING OF THE HUMANITIES IN THE U.S.

Is there intellectual life in America? At present, the answer is no. Since the decline of the great era of literary journalism, when Edmund Wilson, the Algonquin wits, and the politically engaged *Partisan Review* writers were active, America has lacked a general literate culture hospitable to ideas. Mary McCarthy went off to Paris, and Susan Sontag, after half-a-dozen promising years, withdrew into French preciosity and irrelevance. When she was attacked for her laudable interest in pop culture, Sontag dropped it like a hot potato and has never since regained the status she enjoyed in the 1960s.

During that decade, a vital artistic and intellectual consciousness was taking shape. Passionate, prophetic voices, heirs to the visionary tradition of Emerson, Whitman, and Hart Crane, spoke in the central works of Allen Ginsberg, Norman O. Brown, and Leslie Fiedler, but they had few successors. The actual achievements of 1960s thinkers were few and limited, and the line of continuity was broken.

America's current intellectual crisis originates in the

[*The Times Literary Supplement* (London), May 22, 1992]

tragic loss of the boldest and most innovative members of the 1960s generation. Drugs may have expanded the mind, but they arrested its long-term productivity, whose promise was glimpsed in the so-called psychedelic phase of rock music.

The students most affected by the Sixties did not as a rule enter the professions, whose stultifying rules for advancement have remained unchanged for fifty years. Instead, they surrendered their places to less talented contemporaries, careerists in the dull, timid Fifties style.

Nowhere was this truer than in academia. The effect upon American universities of the student rebellions was fleeting. Genuine radicals did not go on to graduate school. If they did, they soon dropped out, or were later defeated by the faculty recruitment and promotion process, which rewards conformism and sycophancy. The universities were abandoned to the time-servers and mercenaries who now hold many of the senior positions there. Ideas had been relegated to the universities, but the universities belonged to the drudges.

There is a widespread notion that these people are dangerous leftists, "tenured radicals" in Roger Kimball's phrase, who have invaded the American establishment with subversive ideas. In fact, they are not radicals at all. Authentic leftism is nowhere to be seen in our major universities. The multiculturalists and the politically correct on the subjects of race, class, and gender actually represent a continuation of the genteel tradition of respectability and conformity. They have institutionalized American *niceness*, which seeks, above all, not to offend and must therefore pretend not to notice any differences or distinctions among people or cultures.

The politically correct professors, with their hostility to the "canon" of great European writers and artists, have done serious damage to the quality of undergraduate education at the best American colleges and universities. Yet they are people without deep beliefs. Real radicals stand for something and risk something; these academics are very pampered fat cats who have never stood on principle at any point in their careers. Nothing has happened to them in their lives. They never went to war; they were never out of work or broke. They have no experience or knowledge of anything outside the university, least of all working-class life. Their politics are a trendy tissue of sentimental fantasy and unsupported verbal categories. Guilt over their own privilege has frozen their political discourse into a simplistic world melodrama of privilege versus deprivation.

Intellectual debate in the humanities has also suffered because of the narrowness of training of those who emerged from the overdepartmentalized and overspecialized universities of the post-war period. The New Criticism, casting off the old historicism of German philology, produced a generation of academics trained to think of literature as largely detached from historical context. This was ideal breeding ground for French theory, a Saussurean paradigm dating from the 1940s and '50s that was already long passé when American academics got hold of it in the early 1970s. French theory, far from being a symbol of the 1960s, was on the contrary a useful defensive strategy for well-positioned, pedantic professors actively resisting the ethnic and cultural revolution of that subversive decade. Foucault, a glib game-player who took very little research a very long way, was especially attractive to literary academics in search of a shortcut to understanding world history, anthropology, and political economy.

The 1960s failed, I believe, partly because of unclear thinking about institutions, which it portrayed in dark, conspiratorial, Kafkaesque terms. The positive role of institutions in economically complex societies was neglected. The vast capitalist distribution network is so efficient in America that it is invisible to our affluent, middle-class humanists. Capitalism's contribution to the emergence of modern individualism, and therefore feminism, has been blindly suppressed. This snide ahistoricism is the norm these days in women's studies programs and chichi, Foucault-afflicted literature departments. Leftists have damaged their own cause, with whose basic principles I as a 1960s libertarian generally agree, by their indifference to fact, their carelessness and sloth, their unforgivable lack of professionalism as scholars. The Sixties world-view, which integrated both nature and culture, has degenerated into clamorous, competitive special-interest groups.

The universities led the way by creating a ghetto of black studies, which begat women's studies, which in turn begat gay studies. Not one of these makeshift, would-be disciplines has shown itself capable of re-creating the broad humane picture of Sixties thought. Each has simply made up its own rules and fostered its own selfish clientele, who have created a closed system in which scholarship is inseparable from politics. It is, indeed, questionable whether or not the best interests of blacks, women, and gays have been served by these political fiefdoms. The evidence about women's studies suggests the opposite: that these programs have hatched the new thought police of political correctness. No conservative presently in or out of government has the power of intimidation wielded by these ruthless forces. The silencing of minority opinion has been systematic in faculty recruitment and promotion. The winners of that rat race seem genuinely baffled by such charges, since, of course, their conventional, fashionable opinions have never been stifled.

While lecturing at major American universities this year, I have come into direct conflict with the politically correct establishment. At Harvard and elsewhere I was boycotted by the feminist faculty, and at several colleges leaflets were distributed, inaccurately denouncing me as a voice of the far right. Following my lecture at Brown, I was screamed at by soft, inexperienced, but seethingly neurotic middle-class white girls, whose feminist party-line views on rape I have rejected in my writings. Rational discourse is not possible in an atmosphere of such mob derangement.

Sociologically, the roots of the campus crisis can be found in the rapid expansion of the college-going population in America in the decades following the Second World War. After the "baby-boomers," the post-war demographic bulge, passed through, colleges were forced to retrench, and they turned to aggressive marketing strategies to maintain enrollment. As costs continued to rise, they were locked into a strictly commercial relationship with parents. Intellectual matters soon took a backseat to the main issue: providing a "nice time" for students with paying parents.

By the early 1970s, American universities had become top-heavy with full-time administrators who took to speaking of the campus as a "community," which, faculty soon discovered, was governed by invisible codes of acceptable speech, opinions, and behavior. In the past fifteen years, some of these administrators, especially Student Life deans and the freshmen orientation staff, have forged a disquieting alliance with women's studies programs, and are indoctrinating their charges with the latest politically correct attitudes on dating, sexual preference, and so on. Many of the students, neglected by their prosperous, professional parents, are pathetically grateful for these attentions. Such coddling has led, in my view, to the outrageous speech codes which are designed to shield students from the realities of life. The campus is now not an arena of ideas but a nursery school where adulthood can be indefinitely postponed. Faculty who are committed to the great principle of free speech are therefore at war with paternalistic administrators in league with misguided parents.

In the summer-camp mentality of American universities, the ferocity of genuine intellectual debate would just seem like spoiling everyone's fun. Ambitious humanities professors go about their business behind a brick wall of "theory," which they imagine is the *dernier cri* but which has long been out of fashion, even in Paris. Drab, uncultivated philistines, without broad knowledge of the arts, have seized the top jobs in the Ivy League, simply because they have the right opinions and know the right people. In the past twenty years, conferences became the infernal engine driving the academic profession. The conference crowd, an international party circuit of literary luminaries ever on the move, was put together by the new humanities centers. These programs had the initially laudable aim of fostering interdisciplinary exchanges outside the repressive framework of the conservative, static, and over-tenured university departments. But the epidemic of French theory was abroad in the world. The humanities centers quickly became careerist stockyards, where greedy speculation and insider trading were as much the rules of the game as on Wall Street.

Quieter, more traditional academics were outmaneuvered by the conference crowd, and scholarship was the victim. The humanities centers are now controlled by small, amoral cadres that are intricately intertwined with each other nationally by cronyism, favoritism, patronage and collusion. It is essential for American intellectual life that they be brought under scrutiny. And, indeed, that is beginning to happen: in April, a prominent woman scholar filed a lawsuit against the Massachusetts Institute of Technology for tolerating an internal *putsch* by a cabal of politically correct faculty members with close ties to the cultural studies center at Harvard University.

The solution to the present dilemma is for academic liberals to speak out against the rampant corruption of their profession. The reform of education is too often being left to the neoconservatives these days. My own proposals for reform include the abolition of all literary conferences and the replacement of women's studies with sex studies, based on the rigorous study of world history, anthropology, psychology, and science. Today, in politically correct America, questions of quality, learning, and intellectual distinction are out of style.

10

THE RETURN OF CARRY NATION: CATHARINE MACKINNON AND ANDREA DWORKIN

I am a pornographer. From earliest childhood, I saw sex suffusing the world. I felt the rhythms of nature and the aggressive energies of animal life. Art objects, in both museum and church, seemed to blaze with sensual beauty. The authority figures of church, school, and family denied or suppressed what I saw, but like Madonna, I kept to my pagan vision. I belong to the Sixties generation that tried and failed to shatter all sexual norms and taboos. In my book, *Sexual Personae*, I injected lewdness, voyeurism, homoeroticism and sadomasochism into the entire Western high-art tradition.

Because I am a pornographer, I am at war with Catharine MacKinnon and Andrea Dworkin. These obsessed, moralistic women, feminism's oddest odd couple, are Carry Nation reborn. They were co-authors of the Minneapolis and Indianapolis ordinances against pornography that were declared unconstitutional. They have produced, individually and in collaboration, an enormous amount of material ranging from tortured autobiographical confessions to legal case histories and academic Marxist critiques.

[*Playboy*, October 1992]

MacKinnon was among the first to argue for the establishment of sexual harassment as a legal category. But her positive
contributions to women's issues must be weighed against the
responsibility she bears for fomenting the crazed sexual hysteria that now grips American feminism. Date rape has swelled
into a catastrophic cosmic event, like an asteroid threatening
the earth in a Fifties science-fiction film. Anita Hill, a competent but priggish, self-interested yuppie, has been canonized as a virgin martyr ruined by the depraved emperor—who
never laid a hand on her.

MacKinnon is a totalitarian. She wants a risk-free, state-
controlled world. She believes rules and regulations will solve
every human ill and straighten out all those irksome problems
between the sexes that have been going on for five thousand
years. As a lawyer, MacKinnon is deft and pragmatic. But
as a political thinker, cultural historian, or commentator on
sex, she is incompetent. For a woman of her obvious intelligence, her frame of reference is shockingly small. She has
the dull instincts and tastes of a bureaucrat. It's all work and
no play in MacKinnon Land. Literature, art, music, film,
television—nothing intrudes on MacKinnon's consciousness
unless it has been filtered through feminism, which has taught
her, she likes to say, "everything I know." There's the rub. She
is someone who, because of her own private emotional turmoil, locked on to Seventies-era feminism and never let go.

MacKinnon has a cold, inflexible, and fundamentally
unscholarly mind. She is a propagandist and casuist, good at
constructing ad hoc arguments from expedience for specific
political aims. But her knowledge of intellectual or world history is limited, and as a researcher she has remarkably poor
judgment in evaluating sources. She wildly overpraises weak
feminist writers and has no feeling whatever for psychology,
a defect that makes her conclusions about sex ridiculous.

She is a Stalinist who believes that art must serve a political agenda and that all opposing voices are enemies of humanity who must be silenced. MacKinnon and Dworkin are fanatics, zealots, fundamentalists of the new feminist religion. Their alliance with the reactionary, anti-porn far right is no coincidence.

MacKinnon is a classic WASP who painstakingly builds huge, rigid structures of words in complete obliviousness to the organic, sensual, and visual. She is a twentieth-century puritan whose upbringing—a stern Minnesota judge as father, Episcopalian and conservative Republican—seems straight out of Hawthorne. MacKinnon's pinched, cramped, body-denying Protestant culture made her peculiarly susceptible to Andrea Dworkin, whose let-it-all-hang-out ethnicity was initially liberating. MacKinnon's stolid lack of psychology drew her to Dworkin's boiling emotionalism and self-analytic, self-lacerating Jewishness. In return, MacKinnon, the third-generation Smith College WASP insider, satisfied Dworkin's longings for establishment acceptance, a nagging theme in her writing.

Dworkin, like Kate Millett, has turned a garish history of mental instability into feminist grand opera. Dworkin publicly boasts of her bizarre multiple rapes, assaults, beatings, breakdowns and tacky traumas, as if her inability to cope with life were the patriarchy's fault rather than her own. She pretends to be a daring truth-teller but never mentions her most obvious problem: food. Hence she is a hypocrite. Dworkin's shrill, kvetching, solipsistic prose has a sloppy, squalling infantilism. This attracted MacKinnon, with her dour background of Protestant high seriousness, which treats children like miniature adults. MacKinnon's impersonal prose is dry, bleached, parched. Her hereditary north-country, anal-retentive style, stingy and nitpicking, was counterbalanced by Dworkin's raging undifferentiated orality, her buckets of chicken soup spiked with spite.

Dworkin, wallowing in misery, is a "type" that I recognize after twenty-two years of teaching. I call her The Girl with the Eternal Cold. This was the pudgy, clumsy, whiny child at summer camp who was always spilling her milk, dropping her lollipop in the dirt, getting a cramp on the hike, a stone in her shoe, a bee in her hair. In college, this type—pasty, bilious, and frumpy—is constantly sick from fall to spring. She coughs and sneezes on everyone, is never prepared with tissue and sits sniffling in class with a roll of toilet paper on her lap. She is the ultimate teacher's pest, the morose, unlovable child who never got her mama's approval and therefore demands attention at any price. Dworkin seized on feminism as a mask to conceal her bitterness at this tedious, banal family drama.

MacKinnon and Dworkin have become a pop duo, like Mutt and Jeff, Steve and Eydie, Ron and Nancy. MacKinnon, starved and weather-beaten, is a fierce gargoyle of American Gothic. With her witchy tumbleweed hair, she resembles the batty, gritty pioneer woman played by Agnes Moorehead on *The Twilight Zone*. Or she's Nurse Diesel, the preachy secret sadist in Mel Brooks's *High Anxiety*.

Dworkin is Pee-wee Herman's Large Marge, the demon trucker who keeps returning to the scene of her fatal accident. I see MacKinnon and Dworkin making a female buddy picture like *Thelma & Louise*. Their characters: Penny Wise and Pound Foolish, the puritan Gibson Girl and her fuming dybbuk, the glutton for punishment. Or they'd be perfect for the starring roles in a TV docudrama about prissy, repressed J. Edgar Hoover and his longtime companion, Clyde Tolson, bugging hotel rooms and sticking their noses into everyone's business.

MacKinnon and Dworkin detest pornography because it symbolizes everything they don't understand and can't control about their own bodies. Current feminism, with its anti-science and social constructionist bias, never thinks about nature. Hence it cannot deal with sex, which begins in the body and is energized by instinctual drives. MacKinnon and Dworkin's basic error is in identifying pornography with society, which they then simplistically define as patriarchal and oppressive. In fact, pornography, which erupts into the open in periods of personal freedom, shows the dark truth about nature, concealed by the artifices of civilization. Pornography is about lust, our animal reality that will never be fully tamed by love. Lust is elemental, aggressive, asocial. Pornography allows us to explore our deepest, most forbidden selves.

The MacKinnon-Dworkin party line on pornography is preposterous. "Pornography is sex discrimination," they declared in their Minneapolis ordinance. In a manifesto, they call pornography "hate literature." "Most women hate pornography; all pornography hates women." MacKinnon and Dworkin display an astounding ignorance of the ancient, sacred pornographic tradition of non-Western societies, as well as that of our own gay male culture. Dworkin's blanket condemnation of fellatio as disgusting and violent should make every man furious.

MacKinnon and Dworkin are victim-mongers, ambulance chasers, atrocity addicts. MacKinnon begins every argument from big, flawed premises such as "male supremacy" or "misogyny," while Dworkin spouts glib Auschwitz metaphors at the drop of a bra. Here's one of their typical maxims: "The pornographers rank with Nazis and Klansmen in promoting hatred and violence." Anyone who could write such a sentence knows nothing about pornography *or* Nazism. Pornography does not cause rape or violence, which predate pornography by thousands of years. Rape and violence occur not because of patriarchal conditioning but because of the opposite, a breakdown of social controls. MacKinnon and Dworkin, like most feminists today, lack a general knowledge of criminology or psychopathology and hence have no perspective on or insight into the bloody, lurid human record, with its disasters and triumphs.

In this mechanized technological world of steel and glass, the fires of sex have to be stoked. This is why pornography must continue to play a central role in our cultural life. Pornography is a pagan arena of beauty, vitality, and brutality, of the archaic vigor of nature. It should break every rule, offend all morality. Pornography represents absolute freedom of imagination, as envisioned by the Romantic poets. In arguing that a hypothetical physical safety on the streets should take precedence over the democratic principle of free speech, MacKinnon aligns herself with the authoritarian Soviet commissars. She would lobotomize the village in order to save it.

An enlightened feminism of the twenty-first century will embrace all sexuality and will turn away from the delusionalism, sanctimony, prudery, and male-bashing of the MacKinnon-Dworkin brigade. Women will never know who they are until they let men be men. Let's get rid of Infirmary Feminism, with its bedlam of bellyachers, anorexics, bulimics, depressives, rape victims, and incest survivors. Feminism has become a catch-all vegetable drawer where bunches of clingy sob sisters can store their moldy neuroses.

Pornography lets the body live in pagan glory, the lush, disorderly fullness of the flesh. When it defines man as the enemy, feminism is alienating women from their own bodies. MacKinnon never deals with woman as mother, lover, or whore. Snuff films are her puritan hallucinations of hellfire. She traffics in tales of terror, hysterical fantasies of death and dismemberment, which shows that she does not understand the great god Dionysus, with his terrible duality. The demons

are within us. MacKinnon and Dworkin, peddling their dis-
eased rhetoric, are in denial, and what they are blocking is life
itself, in all its grandeur and messiness. Let's send a message
to the Mad Hatter and her dumpy dormouse to stop trying to
run other people's tea parties.

11

A WHITE LIBERAL
WOMEN'S CONFERENCE

The United Nations conference on women will finally be under way next week in Beijing, with Hillary Rodham Clinton scheduled to attend. No matter how chaotic the proceedings or repressive China's officials, Mrs. Clinton's presence, along with that of tens of thousands of delegates, observers, and journalists, may already be giving courage to dissidents and could even hasten internal reform.

But what of the content of the conference itself? Is it driven by a radical feminist, "anti-family" agenda, as far-right critics have charged?

To judge by the official U.N. documents, the answer isn't a simple no. At times, Western feminist ideology does indeed ride roughshod over the concerns of delegates from the Third World.

The documents include a 149-page "Draft Platform for Action," the product of more than a year of intense negotiations by the U.N. Commission on the Status of Women, which faced fierce lobbying by conference delegates and special interest groups (like the Women's Environment and Develop-

[*The New York Times*, September 1, 1995]

ment Organization, headed by Bella Abzug). Many bracketed passages—dealing with contentious subjects like abortion and sexual orientation, which American delegates are trying to force into the platform—are still in dispute.

Then there is the glossy press kit, consisting of 60 pages of color-coded "fact sheets," distributed by the U.N. Department of Public Information. It's difficult to tell who actually wrote it, but the tone is strikingly doctrinaire and strident. Straightforward figures on worldwide illiteracy and life expectancy alternate with lurid headlines like "Male Power, Privilege and Control," "Prejudiced Before Birth," and "Occupational Segregation."

There are absurd statistics: one chart trumpets the long-discredited fabrication that in the United States "one in five adult women has been raped." Another chart proclaims that 92 million urban women have unsafe drinking water and 133 million lack proper sanitation—without a word about the men who presumably share these privations.

Other statistics show that 75 percent of refugees and "displaced persons" are women and children—again blotting out the men who, dead or imprisoned after fighting for their family and land, did not have the luxury of flight.

Nevertheless, the draft document, despite its mind-numbing, bureaucratic prose, has many admirable passages. Most welcome, after years of dilettantish Marxism among feminist theorists, is its frank endorsement of capitalism: commercial banking, financial management, and investment portfolios are cited as the best means to woman's economic independence. There are also stirring calls for basic health care, the right to choose one's spouse, and freedom from physical and sexual abuse and forced prostitution.

Yet the document is a maelstrom of clashing and perhaps irreconcilable ideologies. The delegates at Beijing come from societies at every stage of development. Thus there are surreal switches of perspective, as when harsh matters of survival—bare subsistence levels of food and water—are addressed on one page and computer access to the Internet celebrated on another.

A grotesque, paranoid picture is projected of the historical "domination over and discrimination against women by men" with their "gender-based violence."

Men are never depicted as devoted friends or loving spouses who sacrifice for women and children. The words "father," "husband," and "wife" rarely appear, unlike "mother," which is ubiquitous. Religion is scarcely mentioned; art exists only for approved social messages.

Human communication is reduced to "gender-stereotypes" and to "demeaning" and "degrading" female images in the media and pornography that are said to cause violence against women. Education curriculums, particularly in science, are "gender-biased," undermining "girls' self-esteem." The main problem is society's lack of "gender awareness." What is needed is "gender-sensitive" government intervention, programs for "gender-impact analysis," "affirmative action," "centers for women's studies," and oversight by international organizations.

A Guatemalan delegate sent an open letter to conference organizers on behalf of Central and South American delegates, protesting the document's heavy use of the word "gender" and demanding to know what it meant. The word is standard academic jargon for socially constructed sex roles, and the delegates were offended by its implicit denial of biological sex differences. The outcome? A 14-member committee was appointed to investigate the matter, but the language stayed.

The Beijing conference offers a superb opportunity for

feminism to get back on track and to make the progressive principle of equal rights under the law its paramount concern. Much of the turmoil over the platform reflected the healthy competition of ideas in any broad political movement.

But American feminists must go to Beijing to learn, not to preach and convert. They should leave their clichéd rhetoric and male-bashing propaganda at home. A genuine multiculturalism would recognize that delegates from the Third World have a right to define women's lives in their own terms.

12

LOOSE CANONS

WHY HAS THERE NEVER BEEN A FEMALE SHAKESPEARE? CAMILLE PAGLIA TESTS THE THEORY THAT WOMEN CAN'T WRITE POETRY

REVIEW OF GERMAINE GREER, *SLIP-SHOD SIBYLS*

On March 12, 1975 I made a pilgrimage to see the celebrated Germaine Greer, who was lecturing at the State University of New York at Albany, an hour's drive from where I was teaching in Vermont. Five years earlier, Greer's first book, *The Female Eunuch*, a scathing exposé of sexual images in popular culture, had electrified the nascent women's liberation movement, and she herself, with her flamboyant clothing and bold, bawdy manner, had made an enormous splash in the American media. Greer seemed to embody the brash, mercurial spirit of a whole new generation.

But the reserved, steely author who spoke to the packed hall in Albany was quite another person. All trace of humor or physicality was gone. Greer's tenacious subject was now the deplorable economic condition of women in Pakistan. Dur-

[*The Observer Review* (London), October 8, 1995]

ing the question period, I nervously raised my hand from the crowd and asked if Greer, a former English professor, would be writing on literary subjects again soon. Her reply was stern and swift: "There are *far* more important things in the world than literature!"

As a proponent of Wildean aestheticism who believed, and still believes, that art is the highest achievement of humanity, I was stunned by Greer's defection to the increasingly Stalinist ranks of feminist utilitarians. Since that moment twenty years ago, Greer has published many books—on women painters, human fertility, the menopause, and her vanished father. There have been a collection of essays and three editions of seventeenth-century women's poetry. Aside from her slim volume on Shakespeare released a decade ago, Greer's massive new book, *Slip-Shod Sibyls,* must be considered her first and long overdue major statement on general literary history and criticism.

Greer's argument here is directed toward those feminists and their sympathizers who want the educational curriculum proportionately adjusted to reflect the contributions of women (or ethnic minorities—a red-hot controversy the book avoids). The claim has constantly been made that history was written by heterosexual white men and that, given the systematic suppression of women, there are unacknowledged female geniuses waiting to be rediscovered and restored to the canon.

This premise of contemporary feminism has been a sentimental illusion from the start. Greer rightly turns her artillery against it, and from a startling new position: she maintains that, at least in English literature, women have never been ignored or stopped from publication. On the contrary, male patrons have been all too eager to get women's writing into print. In her view, it is coddling and condescending over-praise, not simple obstruction, that has done most damage to women poets. Treated as wondrous "freaks of nature," they drifted into melodramatic "exhibitionism," accepted too much intrusive advice from male mentors, and never fully developed their own voices beyond the saccharine.

Hence, Greer asserts, the absence of pre-modern female poets from the curriculum is not entirely due to sexism but rather to a lack of quality in the available material. "Women did this to themselves," she flatly remarks. It is foolish and counterproductive for feminists to promote mediocre work merely because it is of female provenance. Greer is implicitly acknowledging that a quarter century of feminist scholarship, while reviving a host of minor figures, has failed to find a single major woman writer or artist unknown to or unheralded by the prior critical establishment. Following the Second World War, male Anglo-American academics produced a massive corpus of superb, often reverential writing on Jane Austen, Charlotte and Emily Bronte, George Eliot, Emily Dickinson, Virginia Woolf, and others. Though feminists boasted they would rewrite cultural history, they have yet to make any significant revision of the 5000-year chronology and evolution of Western artistic styles, as traditionally taught.

Greer's new strategy of critique of feminist theory is most welcome, since for some time it has been apparent that feminism has more to fear from its own ideological excesses than from conservative political opposition. Feminist theory is a lucrative industry guaranteeing academic employment in America, where for every competent feminist book, there are twenty others shot through with inaccuracies, distortions, and propaganda. And this glut has produced no classics: only one modern feminist book—Simone de Beauvoir's *The Second Sex*, over forty years old—has earned distinction in intellectual history.

As a magnum opus sweeping from Greek antiquity to

the present, *Slip-Shod Sibyls*, in conception, tantalizingly approaches what one could imagine as a worthy sequel to de Beauvoir's great book. The problem is that Greer has not clarified, perhaps even to herself, who her audience is. Her powerful "Prologue" is addressed to the broadest possible readership and assumes no special insider's knowledge of feminist factionalism. If the entire book had been executed in this taut, sinewy, aggressive prose, it would have made an international sensation, and we would be toasting, in the desert of poststructuralism and postmodernism, the rebirth of serious literary criticism.

Take this magnificent sally from the book's first page:

> The fact of their sex certainly prevented middle-class women from acquiring the same kind of education as was available to men of the same class, but the usefulness of that education to the poet is far from obvious. No male poet becomes great by merely following the rules. If we ask ourselves why we have no female Blake, for example, we will have to probe deeper, beyond questions of literacy or privilege or patronage or support or even recognition. Homer and Milton were blind; can we claim that being female is a worse handicap than being blind?

In crisp passages like these, we see operating a learned, fastidious mind vastly superior to that of the pedestrian lot of women's studies professors—or to that of the woozy slatterns and twittering triflers who have provoked Greer lately in the London media.

But *Slip-Shod Sibyls* has too many shifting targets, which finally limit the probable reach of the book. At times, Greer seems to be skirmishing with a handful of British literary feminists, unnamed but clearly very middlebrow and very dull. As a consequence, she neglects to lay out, and mark her battle lines in, the larger field of contemporary cultural conflict. She shows little awareness of or interest in the life-and-death quarrels that have raged for twenty years about narrative, textuality, authorship, identity, commodification, and so on. Certainly, as a master of the cut direct, she is fully capable of skewering sterile academic fads with a tossed-off phrase, but she has not taken the time to do so.

The body of the book opens with a fascinating if somewhat chaotic meditation on the image of the Muse, which has relegated woman to the role of inspirer rather than creator. One wishes both Homer's Muse and Robert Graves's eerie White Goddess were more fairly dealt with, but Greer's jetting down the centuries to Sylvia Plath is exhilarating. In subsequent chapters, Greer surveys the emergence of the "poetess," nursery rhymes, hymn-writing, pederasty, fraternal incest, and death by henbane.

The strongest critical writing in the book is on Shakespeare's comedies (oddly off the main topic), a grisly war poem by the Duchess of Newcastle, and Christina Rossetti's "Goblin Market"—whose repressed infantile sensuality Greer intricately and vividly reveals. The chapter on Sappho (where I am politely criticized, though evidently because Greer has missed my discussions of ancient poetry in *The Princeton Encyclopedia of Poetry and Poetics* and elsewhere) repeatedly underestimates how much about classical literature can in fact be reasonably inferred from the enormous mass of contextual evidence, and then overestimates the credulity of modern scholars to romantic myths about Sappho.

In other chapters, Greer's instincts as an editor seem at cross-purposes with the needs of her present exposition. Several seventeenth-century writers—Katherine Philips, Aphra

Behn, and Anne Wharton—are treated in a plodding, bibliographic manner, but the low point of the book is an excruciating 100-page chapter on the mundane Letitia Landon that leaves one gasping for air. These chapters contain far too much lengthy quotation, plot summary, and minute textual variations that properly belong in an appendix.

The book's signal failure is its astonishing omission of Emily Dickinson, with whom Greer is so little familiar that she praises Charlotte Mew for lines that are a blatant Dickinson pastiche. The material is too cursory on contemporary woman poets, who, even when praised, are portrayed as hysterics pushed into suicidal self-dramatization by men. Greer's natural period is the seventeenth century, with its trumpet-like formal oratory; she seems uneasy with the lurid, sinuous, Whitman-influenced arias of the American Confessional school.

Ultimately, the author is the most interesting person in this book. When the history of modern women is written, Germaine Greer will be seen as one who, like Jane Austen, permanently redefined female intellect. Following her swift, swerving, sometimes reckless train of thought is like watching a champion slalom racer, jabbing the snow and hurtling past the trembling markers. As the world's premier woman of letters, she is a living legend. Her new book is a pivotal contribution to the now thriving reform movement within feminism.

13

MEN'S SPORTS VANISHING

A misguided interpretation of feminism is destroying men's sports on campuses across the nation. Colgate University dropped baseball, Notre Dame University ended wrestling, and San Francisco State University canceled football. UCLA even dropped the swimming and diving program that won 16 Olympic gold medals.

Title IX, a 1972 amendment to the 1964 Civil Rights Act, has been distorted by cowardly and self-serving university administrators who are scapegoating men's athletics instead of fighting for principle against intrusive Washington bureaucrats.

As originally conceived, Title IX was necessary to pressure slow-moving universities to expand athletic opportunities for female students. Men's sports were lavishly funded, while women had few varsity programs. Poor equipment, part-time coaches, and no locker rooms, weight training, or transportation budget—women's sports were separate and definitely unequal.

But just as happened with affirmative action, a nobly intentioned government mandate turned into a clumsy, brutal quota system. The Department of Education's Office of Civil Rights has threatened withdrawal of federal funds from insti-

[*USA Today*, April 9, 1996]

tutions that fail to demonstrate an ambiguously defined gender equity in athletics.

As the courts have interpreted it, notably in a successful 1991 lawsuit by female athletes against Brown University (which has appealed), allocations for sports must absurdly follow the exact proportion of males to females in the general undergraduate population, even though the number of men wanting to join teams far exceeds that of women.

Instead of publicly denouncing this tyrannical experiment in hurry-up social engineering, university administrations have taken the easy route of liquidating men's sports in order to achieve a fraudulent equity that exists only on paper. As a result, over a hundred men's wrestling programs have been terminated, and men's gymnastics has been virtually annihilated. Men's golf, fencing, and ice hockey also have been targeted.

In 1993, Princeton University abruptly ended its prestigious 90-year-old men's wrestling program, the core of the nation's oldest intercollegiate sports league. The administration's claim that it was motivated by economic pressures, rather than by fear of the feminist establishment, was quickly exposed as false when it refused to accept a $2.3 million gift raised to permanently endow the program by the Friends of Princeton Wrestling, an ad hoc group of concerned alumni.

After three years of fruitless appeals, not only has men's wrestling not recovered full varsity status at Princeton, but women's water polo—one of the most marginal, elitist, low spectator-interest sports imaginable—has been made a team and may be elevated to varsity instead. This is how many universities have complied with Title IX: to inflate the women's rosters, exclusive prep school sports like crew, lacrosse, and field hockey have been substituted for truly ethnically and racially diverse sports like wrestling, which cuts across social class lines.

When the Princeton alumni were stonewalled by their

intransigent administration, they turned to me for help—an ironic role reversal in which a female warrior rides to the rescue to slay the dragon. At a recent event sponsored by the Princeton Debate Panel, I attacked the corrupt master class of arrogant, overpaid administrators whose ranks have grotesquely swelled on U.S. campuses in the past 30 years and who have diverted the educational mission into a suffocating social-welfare ideology. My solution for freeing up money for college sports: fire a few deans and subdeans.

Wrestling, the oldest sport in the world and the sixth most popular sport in high school, is in fact highly economical. It requires virtually no equipment, and practice sessions can be easily accommodated to students' academic schedules—as is not the case with football and its all-consuming team drills. With its one-on-one encounters, wrestling is a great equalizer that embodies individualism and the democratic spirit. This ancient sport develops discipline, quickness, balance, and control. Wrestling is as much about mental preparation and strategy as physical development.

The destruction of men's wrestling at Princeton is an outrageous and blatant case of gender bias. Title IX was meant to eliminate sexual discrimination, not create it. Women's liberation cannot be achieved on the smoking ruins of men's traditions. This shameful scandal is harming feminism, not helping it. Title IX has become a license for vandalism. If it cannot be intelligently enforced, Title IX should be repealed.

AFTERWORD

The wrestling program was formally reinstated by Princeton University in 1997. It remained self-funded until 2004, when the Friends of Princeton Wrestling achieved its endowment goal of $3 million, restoring the program's eligibility for university funding.

14

CODDLING WON'T ELECT WOMEN, TOUGHENING WILL

WOMEN'S STUDIES PROGRAMS AND OBSESSION WITH SEXUAL-HARASSMENT RULES HAMPER DEVELOPMENT OF STRONG FEMALE LEADERS

With the reelection of Bill Clinton, the gender gap seems here to stay in American politics. Exit polls show that while men and women supported Bob Dole in equal numbers, more women than men voted for Clinton by at least a 16 percent margin.

Commentators are scrambling to explain this discrepancy, which is unconvincingly blamed on Republican opposition to abortion or on frantic, semimythical "soccer moms" who are less hostile than men to authority and look to government programs for relief. Conservatives lament that polls show women allegedly less concerned than men about the "character" of the president.

The pursuit of the women's vote, along with Democratic claims that Clinton owes his reelection to women, unfortu-

[*USA Today*, November 12, 1996]

nately has reinforced outmoded sexist stereotypes. Why is it assumed that women always vote their private interest?

Pollsters' clumsy questions didn't catch the real truth about the last two presidential elections: a majority of women realistically assessed the candidates and concluded that Bill Clinton has the greater imagination, flexibility, and mental and physical energy to lead America at this historical moment.

Discussion of the gender gap is too skewed in one direction. It's insulting to portray women as mysterious, distracted, half-enslaved beings whom male candidates must court and fawn over. We need more attention to what female candidates must do to appeal to men.

Women themselves must close the gender gap. Though they have advanced as governors and senators, there are still too few women in high elected office in America. Even worse, of the pool of prominent women, only a handful would make credible presidential candidates. Funding problems alone cannot explain this. The real gender gap is in the Oval Office.

Producing a female president must go to the top of the agenda. Then it will be clear how orthodox feminism, with its third-rate women's studies programs and its promotion of overzealous sexual-harassment regulations in schools and offices, is hampering the development of strong female leaders.

Outrageously, even before this election, the media already had anointed the contenders for the next presidential campaign, virtually all white males. My own Democratic Party, that bastion of political correctness, should be embarrassed that the only leading exceptions—Colin Powell and Governor Christine Todd Whitman—are both Republicans. Indeed, it is hard-nosed conservative women like Margaret Thatcher who first attained national leadership.

For all its lip service to feminism, American liberalism

has been too focused on "feel good" social welfare issues to produce world-class female leaders. The Democratic Party's anti-military bias in the post-Vietnam era has weakened the presidential chances of its own women. Until a female candidate can show she is prepared to be Commander-in-Chief and, if necessary, to wage war, she will not win the confidence of the electorate.

Current gender-gap propaganda calls for softening up male candidates so that they talk the talk—all cooing, clucking empathy—that women supposedly want. But it's more critical to toughen up our female candidates to set them on the track to the White House.

We must rethink young women's education. Future politicians of both sexes should be studying military history and tactics, which will always be needed in an unstable world. Warfare's offensive and defensive strategies also apply to the cutthroat world of politics, where attack ads work because they genuinely embody the competitive clash of ideas.

Women's studies courses, which encourage resentful, separatist thinking, are a dead end. Tomorrow's female leaders must have a broader, more universal perspective. Hence they should be studying men's history instead and emulating the best in the human record.

Young women also need decisive role models, who remain rare. Senator Dianne Feinstein, for example, has a deft, magisterial mind but seems to be tiring. Christie Whitman wonderfully combines personal warmth with military bearing but has been weakened by health problems. The shrill, bullying Senator Barbara Boxer represents feminist dogma at its most arrogant, while retiring Representative Patricia Schroeder, with her unctuous maternal mannerisms, represents feminist sentimentality at its most saccharine.

Of female politicians today, perhaps Geraldine Ferraro,

the only woman to share the national ticket of a major party, best exemplifies the ideal qualities of a leader. An ethnic New Yorker once thought too strident for middle America, she has been seasoned by international diplomacy and now projects a shrewd, cordial, yet tenaciously combative persona that should be a model for all young women with presidential dreams.

15

ACADEMIC FEMINISTS MUST BEGIN TO FULFILL THEIR NOBLE, ANIMATING IDEAL

What is the future of academic feminism? As women's studies evolves into gender studies, how should we reexamine and strengthen it?

Feminism is one of the great progressive social movements of the modern period begun by the French Revolution. Like the movements to abolish slavery and eradicate child labor, it is the fruit of the Western Enlightenment, which produced the concepts of individualism and civil liberties that have inspired insurgents against dictatorial regimes around the world.

Because of feminism's noble, animating ideal—equal treatment of the sexes before the law—one might expect the feminist movement to have the wholehearted support of every person of good will. That there is so much skepticism about feminism in the United States—and that, as polls show, so few young women identify themselves as feminist—can no longer be explained away with such facile formulas as "backlash" or "the war against women" (which are the titles of propaganda-filled books by Susan Faludi and Marilyn French). Instead, it's time for every American feminist to admit that

[*The Chronicle of Higher Education*, July 25, 1997]

both mainstream and academic feminism have been guilty of ideological excesses that require correction.

The reform wing of feminism to which I belong burst into public view in the early 1990s, but it actually has a long lineage. The most radically pro-sex of us began our struggles with the puritanism and groupthink of feminist leaders from the moment the women's movement revived in the late 1960s, after its dormancy following the winning of suffrage in 1920. The innovative, prankish dance critic Jill Johnston, for example, personified a feisty, libidinous, pugnaciously physical 1960s feminism that was erased from cultural memory. This process occurred both in the mainstream feminism of *Ms.* magazine and in the new bureaucratic-minded women's studies programs of the 1970s.

To establish itself as a discipline and quickly prove its own academic legitimacy in the '70s, campus feminism became addicted to theory, which took two principal forms. The first, derived from Kate Millett's *Sexual Politics* (1970), reduced complex artworks to their political content and attacked famous male artists and authors for their alleged sexism. That atrocious book, which appeared while I was a graduate student, drove every talented, young, intellectual woman I knew away from the women's movement. Millett, who is responsible for the current eclipse of D. H. Lawrence, Ernest Hemingway, and Henry Miller in the college curriculum, did enormous damage to American cultural life. She made vandalism chic.

The second major theoretical style adopted by campus feminism was a French import, derived from the highly abstruse and convoluted deconstruction and poststructuralism. These approaches invaded literature departments in the 1970s and later spread to other fields in the humanities. While the practitioners of French theory professed leftist and even Marxist values, they had little connection to actual poli-

tics and none whatever to ordinary people, who were conde-
scended to and excluded by theorists' elitist jargon. Why the
shifty, cynical, and verbose psychoanalyst Jacques Lacan—a
classic white, European male—became the idol of so many
credulous Anglo-American feminists remains a mystery.
Simple careerism may explain it: from the late 1970s through
the 1980s, attaching oneself to feminism or to French theory
guaranteed employment, promotion, and, at the top, huge
financial rewards. The academic marketplace reinforced cutthroat ambition and herd behavior, eventually seriously compromising the direct, sympathetic study of literature and art
that should be the humanities' proper mission.

In the 1980s, the feminist law professor Catharine MacKinnon's implacable opposition to pornography, as well as her
advocacy of stringent sexual-harassment regulations, became
a dominant strain in academic feminism. The increasingly powerful deans of "student life" and their proliferating
subdeans—spawned by expensive American colleges and
universities trying to attract tuition-paying parents—were
converts to MacKinnonism and its dated scenario of male
oppressors and frail female victims. By the end of the 1980s,
MacKinnon's feverish rhetoric and totalitarian politics had
helped produce an epidemic of date-rape hysteria, to which
colleges nervous about bad publicity responded with secret
kangaroo courts that suspended the civil rights of male students and faculty members.

Feminist theory of the 1970s and 1980s was, virtually
without exception, social constructionist, attributing gender
differences entirely to social conditioning. Hormones did not
exist. Even the psychologist Carol Gilligan's hazy, sentimental,
bourgeois notions of woman's innate moral superiority carefully avoided the taint of biology. Any reference to nature was
buried in kitschy, sanitized "Goddess" figures or automatically

dismissed as "essentialist"—a sloppy term used by amateurish academics innocent of philosophy.

Women's studies programs were thrown together in the 1970s and 1980s without the most basic consideration of science. Sweeping generalizations about gender were made by humanists with little or no knowledge of endocrinology, genetics, anthropology, or social psychology. The anti-science bias of poststructuralism worsened matters, producing the repressed doublespeak of Foucault followers (such as the derivative and unlearned "queer theorist" Judith Butler), who substituted turgid wordplay for scientific inquiry.

A massive sea change in the 1990s has begun to reduce the campus prestige and influence of the French and feminist theorists. Most undergraduate students are no longer paying attention to them—even though our ossified system of lifetime tenure will allow them to drain the treasuries of their institutions and distort graduate education and department hiring for at least the next fifteen years. What are the reasons for this recent cultural shift? The unmasking in the late 1980s of the deconstructionist pioneer Paul de Man as a Nazi sympathizer sent shock waves through the humanities and did much to discredit deconstruction. Sudden scrutiny by journalists sent star professors accustomed to conference high jinks scurrying underground. The present atmosphere in many humanities departments is cautious and demoralized. Still, some theorists continue to hurt themselves. For example, the recent brazen memoir by Jane Gallop, a leading Lacanian feminist—with its casuistical defense of her sexual affairs with her professors and graduate students—has cast a glaring light on the intrinsic amorality of French theory.

Academic feminism, as well as the mainstream feminist establishment, lost control of the discourse on gender when a series of controversial issues spilled into the media and became a focus of raging national debate on op-ed pages and radio and television talk shows. The first was date rape, featured in cover stories of news magazines in 1989 and 1990. The next was workplace sexual harassment, dramatized by Anita Hill's charges during Clarence Thomas's stormy Supreme Court confirmation hearings in 1991.

Such practical matters, for which campus theorists were ill-prepared, were discussed and developed with great speed as talk shows multiplied on CNN, CNBC, and PBS, amplified by the refreshingly unedited coverage of lectures and public events by C-SPAN. Scores of lively women across the political spectrum could now be heard, without the censorship of the New York–based network news shows, which had long been under the thumb of Gloria Steinem and the National Organization for Women, with their intimate ties to the Democratic Party. The free exchange of ideas on the expanding Internet was also crucial in ending the era of political correctness.

The election of the Southern centrist Bill Clinton in 1992 removed the Reagan-Bush administration officials whom many academics, in their smug sense of enlightened leftism, loved to deride, and it also began to break down the outmoded polarity of liberal versus conservative. Again, academic feminism (which was overinvested in liberal, social-welfare doctrine, sometimes approaching overt socialism) failed to keep pace with changes in the real world, here or in the former Soviet Union. It completely missed the rise of libertarianism (my own philosophy as a Clinton Democrat), which opposes government intrusion into private behavior and combines endorsement of a modified capitalism with adamant support of free speech (no minor matter in the early 1990s, when campus speech codes were spreading).

Because they were locked into the slower pace and the exclusivity of academic conferences and scholarly journals, campus feminists also have had little to say on most other controversial issues and public figures of the 1990s: Robert Mapplethorpe's photographs and the attack on the National Endowment for the Arts; gays in the military and gay marriage; Hillary Clinton; Paula Jones; partial-birth abortions; sexual harassment and adultery in the military.

Arcane French theory, based on linguistic paradigms predating World War Two, looks pretty foolish these days, when most people are concerned with bread-and-butter issues such as childcare, the divorce rate, drug use, and decaying public education. And by a delicious irony, hormones are back, as the baby-boom generation hits menopause. Germaine Greer, the most wonderful of the early feminists before she turned against sex, has devoted an entire book, *The Change*, to declining estrogen levels in aging women.

Furthermore, science has ceased to be the enemy for women seeking earlier warning and intervention for breast and ovarian cancers and for career women who postponed pregnancy and are experiencing fertility problems as their biological clocks run down. And for HIV-positive persons who are putting their faith in the new protease inhibitors and, beyond that, in a future AIDS vaccine. And for gays who (much too prematurely) claim that a handful of limited studies have confirmed the existence of a "gay gene," thus proving homosexuality inborn, natural, and not a moral issue. In view of these pressing developments, the absence of science in the gender studies curriculum seems all the more outrageous.

The arrival on the national scene in the early 1990s of a new generation of young feminists has also helped shift the center of gravity away from academic feminism toward real-life issues. The early books of writers such as Naomi Wolf and Susan Faludi, despite sometimes haphazard research and skewed reasoning, at least addressed the real society we live in, with its omnipresent media and conflicted sexual relationships. As Ivy League graduates, both women were heavily influenced by academic feminist ideology, from which Wolf began to move away in her later books. As girlish new personalities with strong opinions, Wolf and Faludi made the older, established American feminists seem tired and out of touch. Perhaps inadvertently, they also tolled the death knell for absurdly idolized French feminists such as Hélène Cixous and Luce Irigaray, whose tedious works had been forced down the throats of American women students in the 1980s.

A rich and dynamic popular culture also has overwhelmed the pallid, moralistic messages of academic feminism. For example, Madonna's embrace of pornographic scenarios and glamorous high fashion has subverted not "patriarchal hegemonic categories" (as tone-deaf humanities professors still like to say) but puritanical, MacKinnon-style feminism (which by this point is close to comatose). Since Madonna, younger women no longer feel that makeup and sexy outfits are incompatible with feminism. Progress has been especially striking in the gay world: the "lipstick lesbians" of the early 1990s, who first emerged on the West Coast, broke the stereotype of the dour, preachy, overall-clad, granola-eating lesbian feminist. The cover of *Hot, Throbbing Dykes to Watch Out For*, the latest book by Alison Bechdel, a lesbian syndicated cartoonist, says it all: the erotica shelves of a feminist bookstore are shown bulging with titles perused by eager shoppers, while the small section labeled "Feminist Theory" is nearly bare and filled with cobwebs.

We are left, then, with the duty to restructure gender studies to bring the field into line with recent cultural changes and the educational needs of the next century. It is an unhappy fact that women's studies programs sprang into existence without the most elementary intellectual or scholarly oversight. Furthermore, many of them have been conducted as autocratic fiefdoms, insulated from critique on their own campuses and connected to each other nationally by a network of self-interested operatives who control hiring, grants, and publications.

Reasonable, well-intentioned feminists do exist on campus, but they cannot pretend that they are typical or that, before I launched my attack in 1990 in my book *Sexual Personae* and in the media, they dared to speak publicly about their discontent. Those who believe academic feminists are tolerant and open to dissent have never challenged the thought police, as both the philosopher Christina Hoff Sommers and I have done, walking into hostile mob scenes that no sane person would think possible on an American campus. Sommers's 1994 book *Who Stole Feminism? How Women Have Betrayed Women* has been subjected to malicious and baseless attack by politically correct academics.

What should be the credentials for an instructor of women's studies? Faculty members and administrators have been utterly cowardly in their refusal to confront this question. Because women's studies as an academic entity was a product of the 1970s, its senior practitioners reflect the already hardened, male-bashing ideology of that period, with its disrespect for science as well as great art. Those whose feminism predates the 1970s have been out of sync with and often ostracized by academic feminism from the start. Critics who claim that I am anti-feminist, for example, ignore the fact that my own feminism goes back to my letter published by *Newsweek* in July 1963, demanding "equal opportunity for American women."

A foundation in basic science should be required of anyone teaching gender issues to undergraduates. Familiarity with traditional, rigorous research techniques in history, sociology, and anthropology is also necessary; the literary training of many of today's academic feminists is simply not enough. Postmodernism, a glitzy, game-playing style promulgated by incestuous humanities centers and that rubbish factory, Routledge, is a terrible preparation for gender studies, which requires patient, accurate observation of ordinary life.

A first step that colleges and universities can take to reduce cronyism and insure accountability is to insist that gender studies courses honestly represent all sides in the debate. If dissident feminists and conservative critics of feminism are not included in the readings, students are getting indoctrination, not education.

Second, gender studies must break out of the ghetto of academic publishing. Faculty members should consider assigning the kind of general-release books whose sales in the many millions indicate that they have struck a chord with the mass audience: Deborah Tannen's *You Just Don't Understand: Women and Men in Conversation*; John Gray's *Men Are from Mars, Women Are from Venus*; and even the comedian Tim Allen's *Don't Stand Too Close to a Naked Man*.

These popular books, with their quirky humor, draw upon the wisdom of actual experience to present a picture of sexual relations far more persuasive than anything current academic theorists have yet produced.

16

GRIDIRON FEMINISM

This week, after being written off for dead in a month-long flurry of grumpy magazine articles, the National Football League stormed back and retook center stage.

On Sunday, the Philadelphia Eagles left their execrable preseason and lackluster opener behind in a stunning upset of the reigning Super Bowl champions, the Green Bay Packers. Then on Monday night, the tenacious Kansas City Chiefs outmuscled the dangerous Oakland Raiders, the street fighters of the league.

These two scrappy, physical games—both decided in the final, thrilling seconds of play—demonstrate that football is still America's premier sport. While the game may never regain the mass popularity it enjoyed in the 1970s, neither baseball, basketball, soccer, nor ice hockey shows any sign of displacing football from the national psyche.

In recent years, there have been escalating attacks from bleeding-heart liberals and politically correct feminists, who condemn football for its inculcation of violence and misogyny, allegedly encouraging a climate of date rape and domestic violence. Football has also been targeted by campus special-interest groups who object to its devouring of the lion's share of athletic department budgets, to the detriment of women's sports (none of which consistently draw football's massive, ticket-buying crowds of both sexes).

I would argue instead not only that football is congruent with an enlightened feminism but that football is one of the best educational tools for showing women how to advance in the "hostile workplace"—which current sexual harassment regulations try to control through intrusive, after-the-fact legal remedies.

Football is a living encyclopedia of military strategy, the intricate patterns of offense and defense in the art of warfare first systematized in the Greco-Roman era. Ambitious young women who hope to rise in politics or business should be taking military-history courses rather than women's studies, which locks them in juvenile attitudes of self-pity and resentment of men.

Football, which I call the religion of my brand of Amazon feminism, contains abundant inspiration and instruction for daily life. Ideally, all sports teams should be sexually integrated and merit-based from grade school on, though few girls will have the brawn to succeed in football beyond the collegiate level.

Simply as a spectator sport, however, football is an American art form, a blend of practical, bone-crushing action with mental ingenuity and foxy foresight worthy of chess. Though domed stadiums and the abomination of synthetic AstroTurf (laid over injury-producing concrete) are used in many professional and some university venues, most football games are still played on grass in the open air, subject to the unpredictable elements.

Unlike baseball, with its sentimental pastoral fantasies, football does not wimp out at the first drop of rain. Like an army on the march, football forges ahead through downpours and snowstorms. It has a courageous, truthful view of savage pagan nature.

The raw material world is one of football's major themes. With its muscular masses, brute collisions, and soaring trajectories, football is a crash course in basic physics. Each play is a gamble with grave risks. Any punishing hit or pileup can permanently maim or cripple. Bloodshed is a constant.

Football is an imperialistic Western drama of the mapped grid and the tyrannical clock. It's all about masculine territory—winning it, losing it, shooting like lightning over it, or having your face shoved in the mud when you don't. Even at its best, football sadomasochistically rockets back and forth between humiliation and triumph: each gain of a yard means a defender's defeat.

Football's elaborate, expensive equipment is its Homeric armaments, and its jumble of combatants on the field resembles the chaotic clash of warriors described by the *Iliad* before the walls of Troy. Football grinds through supplies and resources, just as it eats up men. Its huge, specialized squads and staffs of trainers and coordinators are battalions necessary to cope with the inevitable attrition of players during practice sessions and actual engagement.

Poststructuralism, that stale teething biscuit of the nattering nerds of trendy academe, cannot rival the dazzling analytic complexity of football. The massive playbooks that each professional team annually constructs and masters are continually revised in action. While coaches scrutinize opponents from the sidelines or a skybox, quarterbacks and runners must "read" the defense and make instantaneous adjustments, with a score of grappling men in wild motion around them. Football demands a militant hard body and a poetically fluid mind.

Television is doing an increasingly bad job of packaging football. The halftime highlights of ABC's *Monday Night*

Football, for example, which used to be a gorgeous compendium of informative clips from the weekend's games, are now a stupid, jittery collage of MTV clichés. Only ex-coach John Madden among the play-by-play commentators still makes a serious effort to teach interested spectators the subtle mechanics of the game. The crucial role of the defense is particularly ignored these days.

I have learned an enormous amount from watching football since childhood and have usefully applied those lessons in my war against the feminist and academic establishment. I block and tackle with pleasure and love in particular to run "misdirection" plays on feminist leaders—who must be baseball fans, since they still haven't caught on.

If I could be reborn as a football player, I would choose the position of tight end—the big guy who catches the ball over his shoulder and tramples over defenders at the goal line. Or free safety—who roams at will in the open field, shrewdly hangs back as a play develops, then pounces out of nowhere to smash a fleet, franchise runner to the ground.

As the Pentagon has become infested with gender-equity propaganda, disastrously compromising military readiness, only football retains the old heroic values of excellence, fortitude, and valor. "Suck it up!" gleefully hoot the announcers from the broadcast booth. To toughen up our future female leaders, we need to turn them on to football.

Football will keep us strong!

17

THE MODERN BATTLE
OF THE SEXES

As the millennium approaches, we can look back on 200 years of women's advance in society after the industrial revolution. Women all over the world are moving, country by country, into positions of power in business and politics. That progress is inevitable and unstoppable. However, as we survey personal relationships, it is clear that the sexual weather is cloudy and stormy. There is an atmosphere of tension, of suspicion, of mutual recrimination between the sexes which feminism has not helped but in fact materially worsened. How did we get to this point? What prognosis is there for the future?

Modern feminism is one of the great progressive movements inspired by the American and French Revolutions. Analogous to the movement to abolish slavery as well as child labor, it is a goal that is still not accepted everywhere in the world but that has emerged from European concepts of natural rights and civil liberties.

Mary Wollstonecraft's 1792 polemical essay, *A Vindication*

[Third lecture in *Sounding the Century* (a six-part series), Queen Elizabeth Hall, London, December 1, 1997. Broadcast by BBC Radio 3, March 7, 1998] *of the Rights of Woman,* is rightly regarded as the first manifesto of the modern women's movement, though it had little discernible effect at the time. It was directly inspired by the radicalism of the French Revolution, which had promised sexual equality but failed to deliver it and whose excesses in turn disillusioned a whole generation of Romantic idealists. Today's organized women's movement has its roots in the nineteenth-century drive for woman suffrage, the right to vote and thus fully participate in the political process. This was a long struggle that was not fully supported even by all women, some of whom felt that women would lose their femininity or their position of moral superiority within the home if they were to enter the rough arena of masculine politics. In America, it was surprisingly the Western frontier states that were the first to give women the right to vote, in the closing decades of the nineteenth century. In a rural or pioneer environment, it was easier to see women as the pragmatic equals of men, due to the dawn-to-dusk physical labor required. Having lived as a child for an eventful year on a working farm, I witnessed with admiration the extraordinary energy and brute muscular power and boldness of country women in action. It was ironically in the more sophisticated, cosmopolitan Northeastern states, the crucible of American democracy, that there was most resistance to giving women the right to vote—because of the glaring differential between the sexual personae of the middle-class man and the middle-class woman, with her delicacy and refinement. In the United States, it took the 19th Amendment to the Constitution, ratified in 1920, to guarantee women the right to vote from coast to coast.

For me, that first moment after the winning of suffrage, in the 1920s and 1930s, is indeed the classic moment for women in the twentieth century. From Marlene Dietrich and Coco Chanel to Dorothy Parker and Eleanor Roosevelt, there was an enormous number of women who came into the public eye and who showed with class and style what it was to be a modern woman, free of the shackles of the past. The women of that generation accepted the achievements of the men of the past and simply wanted to show that women could perform at that level. There was resistance to everything that held women back but not the kind of wholesale male-bashing or derisive denigration of men that would later become so entrenched a feature of the second wave of feminism that continues at present.

A fundamental argument in early feminism is still causing acrimony today. I am an equity feminist—that is, I believe in equality of the sexes before the law and the removal of all obstacles to women's advance in society. However, I oppose special protections for women, which had been sought from the start by some leading feminists. What has been conveniently swept under the rug is that even the noblest of woman suffrage leaders, Susan B. Anthony, was also active in the temperance movement—that is, the crusade to ban alcohol sales in the United States. This was seen as a woman's issue, because working-class men were thought to waste their take-home pay on drink and because alcoholism was regarded as a major cause of wife battering and child abuse and therefore the decay of family life. This conservative, puritanical element is very strongly rooted in American culture, dating from the founding of New England by Puritan refugees and the Pilgrim forefathers who are still endlessly pictured and honored at our national holiday of Thanksgiving.

The temperance cause would indeed succeed with the ratification in 1919 of the 18th Amendment to the Constitution, which led to fourteen years of Prohibition in the United States. The banning of alcohol sales produced a flourishing underground economy—bootlegging and rum-running on a huge scale. It facilitated the creation of an international crime syndicate that would eventually shift over into the drug trade. We are still paying the price today for that foolish attempt by the American government to intrude into people's private lives. And cultural histories must begin to honestly acknowledge the lamentable role that organized feminism played in that misjudgment.

The temperance debate would be replayed again a century later in feminism by the school of thought represented by Catharine MacKinnon and Andrea Dworkin. The argument would no longer be about alcohol but pornography. Feminism has been split by this issue. From the mid-1970s to the late 1980s, the anti-pornography wing was at its most powerful. MacKinnon and Dworkin translated their opposition to pornography into successful enactment of local legislation in two American communities. These laws, which banned the sale of pornography, including mainstream men's magazines like *Playboy* and *Penthouse*, were later thrown out as unconstitutional by higher courts. MacKinnon and Dworkin believe that pornography is by definition "anti-woman" and that it leads directly to abuse, rape, and murder. But their claim of a cause and effect relationship between pornography and rape has never been substantiated, despite innumerable studies. There is no solid evidence, aside from scattered copycat incidents, often by adolescents, that atrocities in art, literature, and popular culture lead directly to crime. Nothing, in my view, legitimizes an infringement of the civil liberties of ordinary citizens who have the right to determine what they privately read or view.

I represent the pro-sex wing of feminism that has turned the tide and that is close to winning the culture wars of the past fifteen years. MacKinnon and Dworkin were still dominant early in this decade. Indeed, when I made my first book tours of Britain in 1992 and 1994, Dworkin was treated as a deity by many women journalists and writers. The reform wing to which I belong has since grown massively in size, and we have the momentum. And I think that a younger generation of women are no longer in sympathy with the censorious, anti-pleasure wing of feminism. They have been heavily influenced by popular culture. Madonna in particular played a pivotal role in showing that it is possible for young women to be ambitious, creative, talented, and assertive, and yet dress in a sexy, fashionable manner. The Spice Girls have certainly taken up Madonna's mission, now that she has flagged, and are carrying it again around the world. Indeed, I take particular pleasure in the fact that in the song "The Lady Is a Vamp," from their latest album, the Spice Girls are wonderfully illustrating the thesis of my book, Vamps & Tramps, where I argued that white middle-class women, stuck in the sterile, sanitized office world, need to recover the outlaw vamp in themselves.

Western culture of the twentieth century has probably seen the greatest changes in women in all of world history. The respectable lady of 1907 would be shocked indeed by the kind of aggressive, outspoken, and even raunchy women that are all around us in 1997. These changes have occurred with such speed that we are suffering a kind of sexual vertigo. We are trying to find our balance. Thirty years after the sexual revolution of my generation, there are signs that many people are looking back toward tradition again, seeking, particularly after they have children, firm compass points by which to live. To dismiss this as merely "conservative" would be quite wrong, for the epidemic of divorce as well as the spread of drugs among the young should tell us that all is not well with Western culture.

The transition away from 1960s values may well have been the arrival of Diana Spencer on the scene in 1981. There was an unexpectedly immense international response, particularly by young people, to the fairy-tale wedding of Charles and Diana. Diana was in many ways a conventional young woman, without much education or major career ambitions. She sought a traditional role as wife and mother; her primary mission was to produce heirs. And like many other young women, she was interested in fashion and glamour in ways that were considered superficial and frivolous by intellectuals and media cynics at the time. But the mass audience adored her, and she inspired among young women a widespread return to the romance and regalia of weddings. I avidly followed the Diana phenomenon throughout the 1980s. It made me see how disjunct feminist thinking had become from the sensibilities of ordinary women, whom feminism should be serving. Now in 1997, after the staggering response to her tragic death only three months ago, no one can be in any doubt about Diana's impact, which crossed lines of race and nationality. One has to ask, could any *man* have aroused such feeling? Diana demonstrates the elusive mystique of sex differences, which we should be interested in studying again. Diana's appeal was from a level of subliminal, primal emotion that we have no language for outside of art.

Now let us return to feminist history in this century. Women's great push forward onto the public stage in the 1920s and 1930s was terminated by the disasters of World War Two, when Western civilization itself fought for survival. Following that war, there was in Europe exhaustion and recovery, a gray period even for the victors. And in America, which was untouched physically by the war but which paid dearly in lives and treasure on two distant fronts, there was a period of surface tranquility with repressed inner disturbances. This very conformist, domestic era, into which my so-called baby-boom generation was born, returned sex roles to their traditional strict polarization. We young people did not understand the traumas that our parents suffered, since around us there were no physical signs of war, like the devastation in southern England and Europe. Our parents, born in the 1920s, had experienced the Depression and witnessed the rise of fascism and Nazism. They were recuperating, and they wanted something better for their children. Hence we were raised in an artificially "normal" environment that many of us found unbearable.

The women's movement that erupted in the 1960s was only one of many responses to the social repression of the 1950s. Feminist activism had so disappeared after the winning of suffrage that when Simone de Beauvoir was writing her great book, *The Second Sex*, in Paris after World War Two, her project was already regarded as somewhat quaint and scarcely of pressing concern. The reemergence of the organized women's movement happened after the publication in 1963 of Betty Friedan's *The Feminine Mystique*, which was certainly inspired by de Beauvoir's example. Friedan spoke of the malaise of white middle-class suburban housewives and exposed their dissatisfactions, their inability to express their creative talents outside the home. Friedan was simply calling for greater opportunities for women. She would always remain grounded in the everyday life of mainstream housewives and mothers.

But Betty Friedan represented an older generation. My 1960s generation had its own story and its own battles, early signs of which came in the Free Speech Movement at the University of California at Berkeley in 1964. Popular culture—Elvis Presley, the Beatles, the Rolling Stones—was our native expression. Histories of feminism credit Friedan with more than she did, for there was a brand-new spirit already at work in my rebellious generation, which not incidentally profited from the development of the first reliable contraceptive pill.

When we survey the twentieth century, it would be quite wrong to say that the feminist movement is entirely responsible for the modern transformation in sex roles. Far more consequential was the role of popular culture, Hollywood in particular, in disseminating a new image of women in movies shown around the world from the mid-1920s on. Just to give one example of an alternate genealogy: in the early 1960s, before Friedan's book was published, I myself as a teenager had been obsessively pursuing a research project on the aviatrix Amelia Earhart, whom I celebrated, to the bafflement of my schoolmates, as a model of assertive womanhood. And in the mid-1960s, I felt, from the vast wintry landscape of upstate New York, that I had two spiritual homes: Andy Warhol's Manhattan studio, the Factory, with its decadent gay aesthetes and drag queens, and second, Swinging Sixties London, with its Mods and dandies. The innovations of Mary Quant, Vidal Sassoon, and David Bailey made me see fashion and fashion photography as the essence of modernity. And the electrifying Diana Rigg in *The Avengers* prefigured feminism before it made news. Hence I have fiercely resisted the majority opinion in feminist theory, coming from outmoded paradigms of the old left, that fashion and popular culture are politically retrograde, an exploitative system of commodification devised by heterosexist, capitalist imperialists. Such clichéd ways of thinking, in my view, are hopelessly inadequate for dealing with the complexities of contemporary life.

The leading feminists have mostly come from the Anglo-American tradition. Even a Jewish thinker like Betty Friedan shares what I have called the word-fetishism of Anglo-American culture, which confuses language with reality and leads to an inability to understand images, which are the pagan essence of Babylonian Hollywood. Both Madonna and I, as lapsed Catholics, have brought a Mediterranean point of view to late-twentieth-century feminism. We respect sensuality and the Dionysian, with its deep, dark earth rhythms, as well as the more Apollonian phenomena of glamour, fashion, and the idolatry of stars, a taste we share with gay men.

After Betty Friedan co-founded the National Organization for Women in 1966, the group was almost immediately riven by internal dissension, eventually so intense that it would drive Friedan herself out of the group. There was a conflict between the older women, who, like the liberal Friedan, were mothers and wives, and the younger women coming out of the radical student protest movement, who were far more confrontational. The latter would be joined by militant lesbians, who forced an argument about what status lesbianism should have in the movement. Some felt that the lesbian should be hailed as the ultimate liberated woman, who did not need men. Friedan thought the movement must remain close to the lives of ordinary women, and that polemical lesbianism would be an inflammatory distraction threatening the mainstream success of the movement. With the success of the gay liberation movement after the Stonewall riots in New York in 1969, this argument increased in ferocity.

A spate of books in 1970 and 1971 demonstrated both the positive and the negative in the new feminism. First was Kate Millett's book, *Sexual Politics*, which created what I call the Stalinist style of feminist criticism, a form of vandalism. It strides into great literature and art with jackboots on and red pen in hand, checking off "racist," "sexist," "homophobic," peremptorily decreeing what should remain and what should be discarded. That one book drove away from the still-nascent feminist movement many serious women thinkers and scholars. Millett's book offered sanctuary to those who were looking for dogma, who longed for a religion to supplant the one they had abandoned.

Then Germaine Greer burst on the scene in 1970 with her

marvelous book, *The Female Eunuch*, with its blistering attack on the exploitation of the female body in popular culture and advertising. Greer's international tour to promote that book was for me the zenith of twentieth-century feminism. Everything has been downhill ever since! Greer's impact in America was enormous. She was formidable—witty, learned, stylish, and sexy, the charismatic superstar that feminism wanted and needed at that time. Within a few short years the exhilaration of that moment was over. Greer herself was no longer the same person, and her positions seemed to harden against sex, men, and art. It would be unfair to blame Greer for what happened, because there was an enormous cultural shift that remains to be understood. The 1960s, flowing into the early 1970s, seem to have imploded from their own excesses. We are still sorting through the political fallout of that period, which marked the beginning of the disintegration and retraction of the old left.

If I were asked what or whom should be put into a time capsule as a legacy of the twentieth century, I would name three emblematic women: Amelia Earhart, who conquered the world of masculine adventure; Katharine Hepburn, who embodied in life and film an enormous range of authoritative female personae; and Germaine Greer at her debut and high point. These three would symbolize the new twentieth-century woman.

However, having said that, I must note what is missing from this triad. All these women were childless. Here is one of the great dilemmas facing women at the end of the century. Second-wave feminist rhetoric placed blame for the female condition entirely on men, or specifically on "patriarchy," an overused and nebulous term that might well apply to Republican Rome or Victorian England but is historically specious and should be discarded. The exclusive focus of feminism was on an external social mechanism that had to be smashed or reformed. It failed to take into account women's intricate connection with nature—that is, with procreation.

In this era of the career woman, there has been a denigration or devaluing of the role of motherhood. Feminism must not become over-absorbed with expanding the privileges of upper-middle-class professional women. Feminist activism of the past decade has become increasingly focused on office politics. My position is that women must enter the arena of power without asking for special protections that are not accorded to men. Hence I have strongly opposed preferential quotas. And I call for moderate sexual harassment guidelines that must not infringe on other people's rights in the workplace or create a reactionary double standard that defines women as somehow weaker, frailer, or purer than men. The secondary "hostile workplace" clause in sexual harassment policy is, I think, inhibiting women's progress and guaranteeing that men will treat them with suspicion rather than full collegiality. *Every* workplace is hostile for both women and men; testing, challenge, and potential sabotage are everywhere. Women must learn how to maneuver and negotiate for their own territory from the moment they arrive on the scene of any office or schoolroom.

The focus on the professional career ladder has led to a neglect of the problems facing mothers. From the start, second-wave feminists vigorously lobbied for improvements in women's health care and have recently succeeded in expanding U.S. government support for medical research into female ailments such as breast cancer. But too many feminists now seem interested in motherhood only as it relates to day care, private or government-supported—in other words, child-rearing is seen as merely an adjunct to success in the workplace.

I dedicated my first book to my two grandmothers, because

I felt that these women of the Italian countryside, with their roots in a village life that had not substantially changed in a thousand years, had an awesome majesty and power and a greater stature than that of any feminist I have yet met. Yet they rarely left the kitchen, the warm shrine of the home, from dawn to midnight. Their slow, pre-modern rhythms were mesmerizing.

Feminist ideology has never dealt honestly with the role of the mother in human life. Its portrayal of history as male oppression and female victimage is a gross distortion of the facts. There was a rational division of labor from the hunter and gatherer period that had its roots not in the male desire to subjugate and imprison but in the procreative burden which has fallen on woman from nature. It is woman who bears most of the responsibility in the process of procreation. The male contribution to procreation is momentary, a mere pinprick, but the human female makes an enormous investment in the nine months of pregnancy, which could formerly not be forestalled or controlled as it can today. Even now, pregnancy is a risky business that can still result in the death of the mother. Anything can go wrong and often does. Before modern medicine, the mortality rate in childbirth was enormous. In early history, women in advanced pregnancy or just after childbirth were extraordinarily vulnerable; they could not fend for themselves and required the protection of men. Feminist theory has been grotesquely unfair to men in refusing to acknowledge the enormous care that most men have provided to women and children. The atrocious exceptions have been used by feminist theorists to blame all men, when over the whole of human history, men have given heroically of their energy and labor and indeed their lives to benefit and protect women and children. Feminism has been very small-minded in the way it has treated male history. Feminism cannot continue with this poisoned rhetoric—it is disastrous for young women to be indoctrinated to think in that negative way about men.

When men step out of line, women should deal with it on the spot. Most men are cowed by women! Any woman worth her salt should know how to deal with men and put them in their place. Women must demand respect, and over time they will get it. It is foolish to think that substantial change in human psychology or sexual relationships can be achieved through legislation and regulation, that is, through authoritarian intrusion into private life.

Motherhood has become so secondary to professional ambitions in the American middle class that it is impossible to imagine a second-year undergraduate at an Ivy League university, for example, announcing to her friends that she plans to drop out, get married, and have a baby. She would be treated as a traitor to her class. "You're wasting your life," she would be told. "You're throwing away your expensive education. You are a future leader!" So these girls of 18, 19, and 20 are coerced not to listen to their bodies but to suppress natural instinct for some ultimate professional goal, which they may or may not be interested in and which may take a decade or more to come to fruition. It is no coincidence that these elite schools have suffered an epidemic of eating disorders, which originate not with fashion magazines, as some have falsely claimed, but with a deep disturbance in female sexual identity rooted in ambitious, demanding, and overprotective middle-class families.

The male undergraduates at these campuses where feminist rhetoric is at its most intense are a sad, puny lot, routinely portrayed as rapists, but in fact they are men on the leash, intimidated by female demands. Often the products of professional homes where the mother worked, these boys accept women taking positions of power in the world. But what is the result? Is it a new paradise of sexual relations? Are these new, evolved males desirable in terms of social history? These boys have nothing to offer women; many seem to be graduating at 21 with the mental age of 13. The irony is that the more that men accept the feminist line on what women want, the less women want them. In the professional white middle class, the sizzle is going out of sexual relations. It could well be that testosterone levels are stimulated by testing and swagger, by conflict and challenge—in other words, by some unpleasant degree of sex war, without which boys do not become men.

I fear very much for the state of sexual relations in America, and I want to warn England and the world that as feminism goes global, as it surely must, it should not make the mistakes of American feminism. There has been a disastrous institutionalization of feminism on college campuses, where it has become insular and autocratic, virtually a state religion, distorting course content and faculty hiring in collusion with the paternalistic pampering of students by a caretaker class of overpaid, social-welfare-oriented administrators.

Again, the question of motherhood is central. I have tried to bring the missing term of nature back onto the feminist agenda after a quarter century when the dominant ideology has been social constructionism, which alleges that we are born blank slates and that we become male and female not via biology but through social conditioning or environmental influences. I have argued, in *Sexual Personae*, that sexuality is "the intricate intersection of nature and culture" and that we need to understand *both* in order to understand ourselves. Beginning in the 1970s, there was an irrational pressure in feminism to deny any kind of hormonal basis to sex differences, a scientifically illiterate fantasy that still flourishes today in postmodern culture studies.

Because of my childhood revolt against the restrictive

codes of the 1950s, I leaned early toward sexual relativism and initially thought that sex roles are entirely fictive and that they change from culture to culture and period to period. However, once I began to study the subject systematically in graduate school, in doing the research for what became *Sexual Personae*, my investigations into anthropology and medicine began to convince me that this was wrong. The more I learned, the more I realized that despite many superficial differences of sexual behavior and sexual rituals, there is an amazing underlying congruence. I found more agreement than disagreement in sexual definitions over time and concluded that there are certain fundamental principles of human life that return again and again. In my work I have characterized shamans and artists as an exceptional class whose inner sexual fluidity is inseparable from their prophetic gift. But I have serious doubts about whether androgyny can usefully be extended as a master plan for the human race.

Although I am an historian of the arts, I have always deeply respected science. What teaching about gender can there possibly be at the university level without a foundation in science?—which the majority of those currently teaching in women's studies utterly lack. So this is the second of the major deficiencies that I find in feminist theory that simply must be remedied as the millennium approaches. We cannot have a feminism that is hostile to great art, and we cannot have a feminism that is hostile to science.

The women's studies programs on American college campuses that began to be established in the early 1970s and increased exponentially by the end of that decade were thrown together without regard for scholarly integrity or oversight. They began as political cells, and they continue as political cells, untouchable and sacrosanct. Women's studies should have been constructed with required coursework in science—genetics, anatomy, neurology, endocrinology—accompanied by rigorous training in high-level historical analysis. Instead, the need for a missing technical grammar would be fulfilled by pernicious poststructuralism, which invaded American universities in that decade. Arcane, bombastic wordplay became a substitute for common observation and deep learning.

The one place nature impinged on early feminist theory was in the sentimental goddess cult, which began outside the academy but swept into it with one poorly researched book after another claiming there once was a happy, pacifist, agrarian age ruled by goddesses, an Arcadia overthrown by nasty men, who introduced war and invented male gods to make rigid rules circumscribing sexuality. A trace of this fantasy can be found in the flimsy books of a lionized psychologist and professor of gender studies at Harvard that assert woman's moral superiority to man. Of course there never was such a paradise in human history. Only the smallest, most isolated tribal cultures were free of recurrent war and conflict, and they tended to be stagnant and intellectually repressive, making no major, lasting contribution to art or thought.

The great goddesses were always dual, like the Hindu Kali both cruel and kind. In trying to reconnect female identity to nature, I am not saying that we must yield to nature. On the contrary, I have constantly maintained in my work that everything great in human history has come from resisting nature and protesting against it. I call art itself a line drawn against nature. But nevertheless, every woman inhabits a mysterious, complex, procreative mechanism, which science still does not fully understand because female hormonal chemistry changes from hour to hour and day to day.

Much of female identity, from puberty on, is occurring below the level of consciousness—which we were taught to plumb by Freud, the seminal theorist of the twentieth century

and another male genius whom callow feminists have sought
to overthrow. From the moment of puberty, a woman is out of
control of her own body. Something else takes over, something
greater than you. The more a woman tries to fight it, the more
stressed she is, the more her hormonal system will misfire.
It's like riding a wave in the night. The oceanic metaphor is
built into female experience. Early in second-wave feminism,
overlapping the hippie 1960s, there was much more talk about
exploring and rediscovering your own body, including the
menstrual flow. There was a grittily physical quality to much
early feminist writing. But by the 1970s, academic abstraction
arrived, a clinical removal from the squalid facts of nature.

I want to return to first principles. In the office, women
must be treated exactly like men, as the equals of men. But
women are much more than men. There is one place where
men can never equal women and where female power is at its
height—the realm of procreation. More honor must be given
to it. Maternity, in fact, is where sex war begins. All misunderstanding between the sexes begins there. We become social
or political beings later, long after we emerge from a woman's
body. It may be that technology will eventually mimic and
usurp conception and fetal development, but until that hap-
pens, we're stuck with the present system, with its incredible
psychological complexity. I believe there is something magical
about procreative power, which proves that woman is in mysterious tune with natural rhythms. It's no coincidence that the
word "menstruation" is related to the words for month and
moon. Woman's yoking to celestial cyclic pattern remains
unnerving.

Many would object to the identification of woman with
nature, on the grounds that it consigns her to a lower realm.
But this is a Judeo-Christian way of interpreting and scorning
nature. I want to recover metaphors from the older traditions

of paganism and even Hinduism. The effort by feminist theorists to detach woman from nature, or to admit nature only by sanitizing it, has over the long run diminished woman's status and power. And it has made it difficult if not impossible to understand human sexual psychology, which begins in early, murky family relationships.

I view a great deal of criminal behavior by men against women as related to an obscure memory of or fixation on the mother figure. There is a kind of sexual theater going on, produced by the fear of being reabsorbed by the mother. I see a shadowy image of the mother behind many sex crimes. It's no coincidence, for example, that Alfred Hitchcock's 1960 film *Psycho* took such hold of the popular imagination. It is about the vampiric maternal domination of a son's psyche. Separation from the mother is a crucial stage in male development. I view many cases of rape as a form of attack on mother-power. I speak here not of individual mothers, who are usually blameless, but of the inescapable priority of maternity in every male life. Woman possesses the greatest power that exists. In my system, woman is strong, and man is weak. Most successful heterosexual women know this and have pity on and compassion for men. They like men. They want men to be strong, and they know that the only way to make them strong is to pay attention to them. What most men are looking for is female attention and female approval. How simple men are! When women are encouraged to think that they are powerless, we are destroying their ability to recognize reality and to triumph in their own terms.

At the end of the century, we are in enormous sexual confusion, thanks partly to the homogenization of middle-class professional roles, which can be performed equally well by either sex. Going to war or to sea or taking up manual trades used to give men a natural sense of masculine identity. I am old enough to remember the very masculine men who had just come home from the battlefields of World War Two. Most of my college students have never seen such men and must try to imagine them via pumped-up action-adventure films. My high opinion of men certainly dates from my early admiration for those veterans and what they had achieved.

My confidence in women's inevitable advance is tempered by the fact that history moves in cycles and that permanence and continuity are never assured. If there is ever a serious destabilization of the world's economies, perhaps through some sudden climate change that affects food production and leads to a breakdown of law and order, history shows that everything will regress. We will have to rely on men once more to protect us and to put things back together again.

We also must be cautious about the complacency with which we export Western feminism. There are serious psychological stresses in the Western world, which impel so many people to medicate themselves with legal and illegal drugs. Where women are treated like chattel in the Third World, we must improve educational opportunities and provide legal support. But Western feminism is not a perfect instrument. Untempered, it can be arrogant and destructive of traditional local beliefs and practices. It suffers from an evangelical secularism. The old leftist roots of contemporary feminism are clearest in its hostility to religion. This is one of the primary areas where feminist leaders have become woefully out of touch with the masses of ordinary women, who tend to be religious as well as to identify strongly with conventional family life. Though I am an atheist, I am profoundly respectful of religion, which I recognize as far more spiritually sustaining to culture and helpful to child-rearing than anything that the intellectual elite has yet produced. People need gods. The academics who pushed Jehovah and Jesus out the window ended up throwing open the door to Marx and Foucault. A purely secular culture risks hollowness and, paradoxically, sets itself up for the rise of fundamentalist movements that ominously promise to purify and discipline.

In some ways, contemporary feminism is a house built on sand, because its ideology is so removed from practical reality. One of the signs of current instability in sexual relations is a rise in the incidence of homosexuality. As an open lesbian and libertarian, I feel that every person should be free to express his or her sexuality in private consensual relationships and that the state has no business intruding. But at the same time I reject the simplistic formulas that the gay movement has learned from feminism. First of all, the idea that anyone is born gay is ridiculous. This is a misreading of very sparse and contradictory evidence. Homosexuality is an adaptation to social conditions. The present spread as well as openness of homosexuality is coming from a fatigue or discontent with the failing traditional sex roles. Homosexuality is a rejection of the conflicted state of heterosexual relations, which is also evidenced in the soaring divorce rate of the past 30 years.

There is an enormous bitterness among contemporary heterosexual women toward men, whom they blame for not understanding them, for not communicating well, for shirking responsibility, for exchanging their aging wives at midlife for younger trophy wives. Here is nature's injustice once again. A man can sire children until his seventies, but nature removes women from the sexual race relatively early. In the old days of the rural village, women gained power by moving into the grandmother role, where they could boss around their sons' young wives from the apex of the extended family. But today aging women are edged off the map. Isolated by the nuclear family, scattered in the suburbs, surrounded by strangers with no sense of their past role or contribution, aging women now experience cultural abandonment.

Another area in which feminism has misplayed its hand

is in the abortion rights campaign, as it was conducted in the United States. I favor unrestricted access to abortion. As a member of the two major pro-choice organizations in America, I strongly feel that no one may intervene in a woman's control of her own body. Nevertheless, this issue has become inflamed in the United States because of the clumsiness with which feminist leaders pursued the pro-choice argument, falsely portraying pro-life proponents as fundamentalist, "anti-woman" fanatics. Again, there was needless disrespect shown toward religious values, which after all were making the highly ethical argument that the fetus is a fully human individual with a right to life.

Thus as we assess sexual relations at the present moment, we see many areas that require rigorous rethinking and a general redress of grievances. Though I have often spoken of the need for a bisexual responsiveness to life and art, I don't think that bisexuality per se is necessarily the answer to our problems. This is another area where civilizations have gone through recurrent cycles. There are many parallels between our time and that of the Roman empire. Whenever you get cosmopolitan cultures that are very tolerant and permissive, where women begin to move forward, where there is open homosexuality, it seems to be the case that such cultures are ripe for collapse! So we must negotiate a very fine line here. Too much tolerance too fast can produce a puritanical or fascist backlash. The creative drive in great cultures has often been religious or spiritual. Romanticism, for example, in rebelling against organized religion, reverently embraced nature and art. But contemporary feminism and poststructuralism, in discarding religion, have rejected nature and defamed art. In my view, the intellectual elites, in both Europe and America, have become corrupt. I want a more practical and less theoretical feminism that helps women achieve personal responsibility. I don't want a situation, particularly in regard to date rape, where women are relying on the protection of nanny figures of the state, of grievance committees and law courts. Each woman must fight for her place in the social hierarchy.

If it is true, for example, as reported in the United States, that new women members of the House of Commons were recently so distressed by sexist jeers from male members of the opposing party that they appealed to Madame Speaker to intervene, then we are going backwards fast in feminism. I think the opposite: strong women leaders must nourish themselves on the brilliant British tradition of raillery and push the men back with their own weapons. Good heavens, women, use your wits! Find the scathing riposte to impugn your opponent's manhood, ancestry, or tatty receding hairline!

My mission as an Amazon feminist is to strengthen the will power of the individual woman to show her how far she can go on her own. Political organization and legislative reform are necessary, but we must beware of the depressive cultural effect of authoritarian bureaucracy. Women must not feel that they can only be strong under the aegis of the all-seeing state.

As for men, they must learn that the genie will not go back in the bottle. Women are here to stay. But women must be prudent in their demands. And they must be more honest about men. Until feminism can admit the great things men have done in art, science, and technology in creating the modern industrial world that liberated women from the home and thus made feminism possible in the first place, the sexes will not be reconciled. We will remain at war, and it is young people who will pay the price.

18

AMERICAN GENDER STUDIES TODAY

WOMEN: A CULTURAL REVIEW ASKED FOUR LEADING, VERY DIVERSE, AMERICAN FEMINIST CRITICS FOR THEIR PERSONAL VIEW OF THE SIGNIFICANCE OF PRESENT TRENDS IN GENDER STUDIES.

CAMILLE PAGLIA: At present, the women's movement is in radically different stages in different regions of the world. Hence many misunderstandings exist, even between British and American feminism, despite their mutual influence and support in the historical campaign for suffrage.

There are, in my analysis, two primary spheres of future action: first, basic civil rights and educational opportunity must be secured for Third World women; second, the education and training of Western women must be better designed to prepare them for leadership positions in business and politics. Women's studies programs, as structured in the United States, have not proved that feminist ideology helps women to understand life or to function in the real world, where men must be dealt with as friends or foes.

As a classroom teacher of nearly thirty years, I am committed to identifying and developing the factual material

[From "Symposium" in *Women: A Cultural Review* (U.K.), vol. 10, no. 2, 1999]

and practical strategies that the next generation of women will need to exercise power and, one hopes, to head nations. Military history, not feminist theory, is required: without an understanding of war, few women will ever be entrusted with topmost positions in government. In the United States, for example, the president also serves as Commander-in-Chief and thus must win the confidence of the armed forces.

American feminism has experienced cataclysmic changes in the 1990s. My wing of pro-sex feminism, which was ostracized and silenced through the long period ruled by anti-pornography activists like Andrea Dworkin and Catharine MacKinnon, has made a stunning resurgence. As a free speech militant, my thinking is grounded in the 1960s sexual revolution. Most of the positions for which I was pilloried when I came on the scene a decade ago, with the publication of my long-delayed first book, are now scarcely controversial at all, so sweeping has been the victory of libertarian feminism, which is in tune with a younger, sassier generation of feminists.

Popular culture, particularly rock 'n' roll, is no longer the enemy—as it was when I was at war with fellow feminists in the late 1960s for my admiration of the "sexist" Rolling Stones. Fashion and beauty are of interest again, instead of being automatically labeled as oppressive tools of patriarchy. Hormones and biological sex differences are slowly returning to the agenda, after a quarter century of rigid social constructionism. Labyrinthine poststructuralist feminism is increasingly recognized as an ahistorical dead end. The disintegration of the Soviet Union undermined the fashionable Marxism of bourgeois intellectuals like the propagandist Susan Faludi. Capitalism's central role in the modern emancipation of women is starting to be seen.

American campus feminists, who rode high for twenty years, have been gradually marginalized in this decade: few played much role in the public debates that have raged about sexual harassment in the workplace, a vital issue that swept away the victim-obsessed date-rape hysteria of the late 1980s. From the 1991 Clarence Thomas/Anita Hill hearings to today's bitter quarrel over the president's affair with a young intern, the prominent campus feminists have been irresponsibly silent, demonstrating the inadequacies of conventional feminist theory when grappling with thorny contemporary questions.

The Clinton scandals have also exposed the political biases of women's groups like the National Organization for Women: the obtrusive collusion of present and past presidents of NOW (plus Gloria Steinem) with the most liberal wing of the Democratic Party has seriously damaged the women's movement, which should in my view be a big tent that gathers in women of every political and religious affiliation. As a registered Democrat and a member of pro-choice groups like Planned Parenthood, I contend that the women's movement should have no ideological litmus test about abortion or any other issue.

Most feminists abroad have little conception of the way American feminism veered toward tyranny after its early successes in the late 1960s. What looks like "anti-feminism" has really been a rebellion here by insurgents like myself who are equity feminists: that is, we believe that only equality of the sexes before the law will guarantee women's advance. We vigorously oppose all special protections of women (as in anti-pornography legislation) as inherently infantilizing. This is an old argument within feminism: Susan B. Anthony, for example, promoted the temperance movement (which demanded prohibition of the public sale of alcohol because drunken men impoverished and endangered women), thus endorsing a puritanical intrusion of the state into private life.

Even though recent polls show that most American

women refuse to describe themselves as feminists and often have a negative view of movement leaders, I am convinced that feminism, for all its internal dissension, is alive and well and will continue to be a major cultural force around the world in the twenty-first century.

19

THE CRUEL MIRROR:
BODY TYPE AND BODY IMAGE
AS REFLECTED IN ART

Last year, I had the great honor and pleasure of being the Art Libraries Society of North America's closing speaker at its annual conference in Baltimore. My subject was the dramatic fluctuations in female body type in Western art, demonstrated by a discussion of 66 slides drawn from the Visual Resources Collection of Greenfield Library at the University of the Arts in Philadelphia.

My title, "The Cruel Mirror," was inspired by Walt Disney's classic animated film, *Snow White and the Seven Dwarfs* (1937), where the elegant witch-queen, with her Marlene Dietrich-like glamour, is obsessively preoccupied with her brutally candid mirror. I was thinking also of Oscar Wilde's use of the artwork as magic mirror in *The Picture of Dorian Gray* (1890), where a young man retains his charismatic beauty while the effects of age and corruption are shifted to his painted portrait.

Young people today in industrialized nations, from North and South America to Europe and Japan, come to consciousness amid a constant shower of media messages glorifying

[*Art Documentation*, vol. 23, no. 2, Fall 2004]

perfect beauty and perpetual youth. While there is reason for serious concern about the quality or realism of images our students see, I find unhelpful and moralistic the standard set of academic terms like "commodification" applied to modern commercial culture. In a careerist era of dreary, word-oriented office routine, sensual appeals to the eye need to be valorized. The media supply what is missing from prevailing social codes.

As a free-speech proponent, I oppose regulation of the media (or the Web). Forms of cultural expression have their own dynamic, whose evolution can never be fully foreseen. But it is educators' obligation to diagnose and supply what is missing in their students' experience. This is especially critical in the portrayal of female body type in advertisements and celebrity photojournalism. Since the rise of coed health clubs in the 1980s, a trim, aerobicized silhouette has been projected as the ideal for white middle-class girls. In the 1990s, the outlandishly pneumatic superheroines of animated science-fiction video games gave enormous impetus to the vogue for breast augmentation. Thus, for the past decade a strange and perhaps impossible amalgam has emerged: the thin, sleek, toned female figure with a flat, exposed midriff but startlingly large breasts. This silhouette is difficult enough to maintain during the hormonal teenage years, but its imposition on older women requires a manic regime of exercise and dieting as well as a costly maintenance program of plastic surgery and liposuction.

The massive power of commercial media can only be countered by alternative images from world art and culture. Unfortunately, the venerable survey course in art history, with its invigorating chronological sweep, is slowly losing ground in the United States to narrowly specialized courses, which means that the responsibility for acquiring and organizing representative images will fall more and more on art librarians, with their broad view of university collections present and future. What is needed is not just a complete time range of objects from fine art and archaeology but a record of media images. After the triumph of avant-garde abstraction, movies and advertising became the primary arena for contemplation of the human figure.

From my classroom experience with slide lectures, I find that contemporary students are astonished and fascinated by the mercurial metamorphoses in standards of female beauty over the centuries. My materials thus far have been chosen mainly from Western art, simply because of the centrality it gives to the nude. What follows is a reconstruction (from my podium notes) of my lecture at last year's conference.

As a general rule, large, ample women have preferred status in agrarian or subsistence periods, while a thin, linear silhouette becomes fashionable for women in urban or courtly societies. When food is in short supply, a plump wife advertises a man's wealth and property. But there were also biological reasons why, when both pregnancy and childbirth could be difficult and dangerous, fleshy women with wide hips were seen as better prospects for motherhood than thin women with narrow hips. Today we know that body-fat level is connected to fertility: women runners who become too lean may develop amenorrhea, since nature interprets low weight as a sign of famine, insufficient to support pregnancy. With today's media focus on thinness, young women are torn between nature and society: when fat is the enemy, young women are at war with their own fragile, life-creating physiology.

In the Stone Age, fat was beautiful because it meant vitality and fertility. The Venus of Willendorf (ca. 30,000 B.C.), a tiny limestone statuette found in a riverbank above the Austrian Danube in 1908, has become one of the most popular objects in world art. The sac-like breasts, bulging belly, and padded hips conflate woman with her procreative function. She symbolizes health and abundance. But the masked face and withered arms disturbingly show that she has no sight, speech, or reach—no identity as an individual.

Less well-known are other Stone Age objects also ironically named after the Roman Venus. The Venus of Laussel, found in 1911, was carved into the rounded wall of a limestone rock shelter in the Dordogne. Once again we see the blank face, protuberant belly, and dwindling, knock-kneed legs with their lack of feet, which may sometimes have been ritually broken off, perhaps to keep fertility from leaving. The Venus of Laussel holds a bison horn, an early cornucopia. Shaped like a crescent moon, it is incised with a calendar of lunar months.

The Venus of Lespugue, found in 1922 in the Pyrenees foothills, is carved of ivory (mammoth tusk). Here for the first time we see a major change in female body type. The suave, streamlined linearity of this object strikes us as modernist. The doll head is blank and the arms pencil-thin, so that the balloon-like breasts and buttocks hang like waistline pouches—possessions rather than body parts.

Continuing this long process of female stylization were the marble "idols" (3000–2200 B.C.) found in graves in the Cyclades islands in the mid-Aegean. Cycladic faces are blank, as in Stone Age cult objects, but they are lifted, as if communing with invisible forces. Now the female silhouette is elongated and geometric. The sex organs are treated schematically—a pubic delta and surprisingly small breasts. The violin shape of early Cycladic idols prefigures the Western analogy between woman's body and stringed instruments that can be seen all the way down to Picasso and Man Ray.

In ancient Egypt, woman is projected as a *visual* object, a sophisticated work of art. Svelte, body-revealing garments of sheer linen can be seen as early as the Old Kingdom tomb sculptures of Prince Rahotep and his wife Nofret (ca. 2660 B.C.), where there is also an interesting disparity in skin color. The affluent woman, with the luxury to stay out of the desert sun, is paler than her husband or servants. The famous bust of Nefertiti (ca. 1350 B.C.), found in 1912, has a mathematical severity that is new in portraits of women. She is all head, while the Venus of Willendorf was all body. Nefertiti's chiseled cheekbones have a mannequin's high-fashion hauteur. (I analyzed Nefertiti's relation to the Egyptian cult of beauty in my book, *Sexual Personae*.) Aristocratic Egyptian style became increasingly linear and elongated, as illustrated in my lecture by several chic New Kingdom princesses (18th and 19th dynasties).

The mysterious Minoan statuettes of snake priestesses (ca. 1500 B.C.) found at Knossos on Crete combine the prior traditions. We see bursting, bare, nursing breasts set off by ornate, highly structured clothing—a wasp-waisted corset, double apron, flounced hoop skirt, and symbolic hat crowned by a wild animal. Serpents, presumably symbolizing earth power, wind around the figures' raised arms. I also showed crude Minoan vases where the upraised, prophesying arms are perched on bell-like bases: the female body here is a vessel—like Mary as the chosen vessel inseminated by the Holy Spirit.

A striking segue can be made between Egyptian princesses, draped in pleated linen, and the columnar Archaic Greek *korai* (7th–early 5th centuries B.C.), holding out their devotional plates. I like to contrast the plain Attic style of the sprightly Peplos Kore with a demure kore from Chios in a rippling blue chiton—fancy Ionian dress. Here we spot an early sense of fashion, associated with the cultivated western coast of Asia Minor, notorious for its "feminine" lyricism in music and poetry. The *korai* ("maidens") were ingénues, suggesting an innocent, springtime femininity. They became more statuesque in the graceful caryatids of the Erechtheum's Porch of the Maidens (ca. 415 B.C.) on the Athenian Acropolis. These grand constructions show both power and composure as they literally hold the roof up on their heads.

There are no large-scale female nudes in high classic Greek art: such depictions weren't considered respectable. (The rollicking nudes in pornographic pottery are prostitutes.) Instead, heavy, clinging drapery (the "wet look") reveals the female torso and thighs, as in the three intertwined, banqueting goddesses from the Parthenon's east pediment (ca. 438–32 B.C.). The common claim that the Athenians were misogynistic or exclusively homosexual is undercut by these voluptuous sculptures, with their relaxed, regal womanliness.

My examples of Hellenistic nudes (4th–1st centuries B.C.) were the Aphrodite of Syracuse, with her pear-like buttocks, and the Venus de Milo, whose robes are provocatively slipping down her hips as she prepares to step into her bath. The motif of the bathing woman, turning the viewer into a Peeping Tom, can also be seen in the canonical Cnidian Aphrodite and Capitoline Venus (Venus Pudica, the "modest Venus"). The Venus de Milo's precipitous decline in reputation over the past half century demonstrates the evanescence of style. A symbol of female perfection since 1820, when she was found on the island of Melos, the Venus de Milo is still touted by drawing pencils or hair salons as a paragon of beauty. But tastes have so changed that she now seems stolid and broad in the beam, and she has vanished from art books.

Even mutilated, the Winged Nike ("Victory") of Samothrace (ca. 190 B.C.) wonderfully illustrates muscular female power, like that of the caryatids. Nike is woman in action, her great wings beating as the sea spray plasters her filmy robes against her curvaceous torso. Most published photographs of the statue, which commands the Daru Staircase at the Louvre, do not show that she is landing on the prow of a war ship. But the entire brilliant drama was that Nike is a female energy entering and dominating male space—a naval battle where she is the arbiter of victory and defeat.

Had I had more time, I would have liked to show Etruscan enthroned goddesses (ca. 5th century B.C.), where woman was defined by her lap and embracing arms, and also ancient Roman portrait busts where aging matrons flaunted their wrinkles and double chins. But I moved on to the Middle Ages with a fifteenth-century German carved-wood *Vierge ouvrante* ("opening Virgin") from the Musée National du Moyen-Age (Cluny): the hinged tabernacle doors swing out to reveal Mary's body as internal space. These popular devotional items, sometimes called Shrine Madonnas, were finally banned by the Pope. They show Mary as a cosmic cathedral containing Jehovah and the crucified Jesus, as if she were a Great Mother goddess like the winged Isis. A fruitful comparison would be to Piero della Francesca's *Misericordia* (Madonna of Mercy, ca. 1460), where a giant Mary spreads her bat-like cape to shelter humanity.

Standing in the elegant S-curve posture of the courtly High Middle Ages, the silver-gilt Golden Virgin (1339) from the Abbey Church of Saint-Denis can be juxtaposed with her descendant, Botticelli's blonde goddess in *The Birth of Venus* (ca. 1485). The sinuous linearity of these figures is an enduring type of female beauty. In his excellent book, *The Nude: A Study in Ideal Form,* Kenneth Clark contrasts the ideal women of Renaissance Florence and Venice as the Crystalline versus the Vegetable Venus. The former—tall, small-breasted, and intellectual—is like Botticelli's reserved Venus, while the latter is languid, vapid, and opulent, her organic figure resembling the rolling hills. As examples of Venetian style I chose Titian's lush *Venus of Urbino* (1538) and *Venus with a Mirror* (1555), the latter introducing the themes of narcissism and self-scrutiny. Correggio's naughtily rear-view *Jupiter and Io* (1532) demonstrates how Venetian artists saw full-figured fleshiness (and even "problem area" cellulite) as sexy. The line is clear to Rubens, who studied Titian's work in Italy. My examples from Rubens were *The Toilet of Venus* (1612–15), *Venus at a Mirror* (1655), *The Fur* (bare-breasted Helene Fourment as Venus Pudica; 1635–40), and *The Three Graces* (1636–38), in which Botticelli's sylphlike nymphs have become big, beefy, good-humored women with assertive peasant feet. Amusing examples of Rubens's physically imposing women are the lusty, biceps-popping rowers of the allegorical Ship of State in his *Life of Marie de' Medici* series (panel XVI; 1622–25) for the Luxembourg Palace. To demonstrate the extremes of rococo eroticism, I suggest juxtaposing Boucher's paintings of two of Louis XV's mistresses: the pearly, splayed *L'Odalisque* (Mlle. O'Murphy; 1745) and *Madame de Pompadour* (1758, National Galleries of Scotland), the latter showing the king's meddling confidante as the epitome of high fashion in her beribboned, décolleté gown as she archly lounges with—shock!—a book in her hand.

Nineteenth-century Romantic and realist painting offers a dazzling variety of body types. I showed Ingres's *Grand Odalisque* (1814) and Manet's *Olympia* (1863) as nudes in the Venetian tradition of recumbent, lewdly accessible beauty. The first, with her zucchini shape and perversely unmarked foot-pads, is a doped and sullen Turkish sex slave, while the second (a homage to Titian's *Venus of Urbino*), with its bleak dawn light, shows a shrewd Parisian businesswoman with a slightly bored, scandalously direct gaze. Alternative nineteenth-century styles are represented by Ingres's coolly self-contained *Portrait of Mlle. Rivière* (1805), with her Greek-inspired Empire dress, ermine boa, and mustard gloves, and Whistler's moody *Symphony in*

White, no. 1 (1862), the "White Girl" with her unpinned hair and unstructured Pre-Raphaelite dress.

In the twentieth century, the seductive female figure remained a central inspiration for Matisse, with his bold lyricism, and Picasso, a master of mutating styles. A superb example is Picasso's *Girl Before a Mirror* (1932), where his mistress's breasts and belly become apples and hanging pear, while the hatched Matisse wallpaper evokes a paradise thicket. Another modern artist who saw the female body mythologically was the sculptor Henry Moore, whose monumental, reclining earth mothers (inspired by Mayan art) follow the landscape or, hollowed out, expose woman's creative inner space.

Western art's ambivalent love affair with the female body was taken up by studio-era Hollywood after World War One. My final slides came from the collection of media images that I have helped build at the University of the Arts over the past fifteen years. Jean Harlow, with her loose, slatternly breasts, broke from hyperactive 1920s flappers who had bound their bosoms for a flat, androgynous look. At exactly the same moment (the early 1930s), Mae West was sporting her flamboyant signature costume as Diamond Lil—the corseted hourglass figure of the long-gone Belle Époque, clearly a nostalgic dream to many in her vast audience. Meanwhile, Norma Shearer was modeling Madame Vionnet's new, simple, elegantly streamlined evening dress, daringly exposing the small of the back.

Claudette Colbert as the empress Poppaea in Cecil B. DeMille's *The Sign of the Cross* (1932) illustrated how ancient archetypes of the femme fatale were used to costume Hollywood vamps. The same can be seen in the controversial poster for *Suddenly, Last Summer* (1959), where Elizabeth Taylor, barely contained in a tight white bathing suit, emerges from the waves like Aphrodite. My other examples from Hollywood history included Betty Grable's famed 1943 pin-up, which demonstrates how radically ideal female proportion has changed. Grable's once-perfect "million-dollar legs" now look a bit stumpy because our eye has been retrained by the long-legged models of the sports era inaugurated in the 1970s by Cheryl Tiegs's "California girl" look. Today's coltish models and actresses (like Nicole Kidman and Gwyneth Paltrow) would have been considered miserably scrawny and gawky before World War Two.

Big-breasted blondeness (a cardinal modern category) can be traced from Harlow to Marilyn Monroe and her more bosomy disciples like Jayne Mansfield, who plays her cartoonishly exaggerated figure for laughs. Monroe has the sleepy look and moist, parted lips of French odalisques. The "missile cone" 1950s brassiere (parodied by Jean Paul Gaultier's lethally pointy stage costume for Madonna) deployed the breast as a social weapon. A composite slide showed the Monroe/Mansfield constellation still flourishing in that Rubensian Texan, Anna Nicole Smith.

In the late 1990s, Jennifer Lopez made history by mainstreaming the black and Latino "booty": buttocks had never before been a focus of white Anglo-American eroticism. But this advance in acceptance of women's natural contours was overshadowed by a deceptive editorial trend over the past decade for using Photoshop software to thin out women's faces and bodies on magazine covers. I showed a 2002 *Rolling Stone* cover that flatteringly elongated Britney Spears's squat legs and blocky torso. A slide of a skanky, whip-lean Christina Aguilera illustrated the child-harlot or Lolita syndrome.

My final slide was of the current St. Pauli Girl beer carton ("Germany's fun-loving beer"). It shows a merry beer-hall maid, her bosom overflowing her peasant bodice and each hand effortlessly hefting three foaming beer steins—quite a feat! Her arms are flung wide in the embracing posture of medieval Madonnas. The St. Pauli Girl is in the Rubens line of powerful, exuberant, life-affirming women. But St. Pauli is Hamburg's red-light district, where sailors carouse. Hence, one suspects, she too may be on the menu.

The body, for good or ill, has become a primary marker of identity in this transient society where the extended family and old community ties have broken down. Style is cyclic: all standards will eventually change. But that may not be soon enough for young people (increasingly male as well as female) barraged by images of "better" bodies than the ones they have been dealt. By encouraging historical exploration, we can reduce pressure and anxiety. There are companions and competitors beyond number in the great image book of the past.

20

THE PITFALLS OF PLASTIC SURGERY

THE ABILITY TO RESCULPT OUR BODIES AND FACES CAN BE EMPOWERING. BUT IS IT ALSO ROBBING US OF OUR OWN UNIQUE BEAUTY AND KILLING SEXUAL ALLURE?

Plastic surgery is living sculpture, a triumph of modern medicine. As a revision of nature, cosmetic surgery symbolizes the conquest of biology by human free will. With new faces and bodies, people have become their own works of art.

Once largely confined to the entertainment and fashion industries, plastic surgery has become routine in the corporate workplace in the United States, even for men. A refreshed, youthful look is now considered essential for job retention and advancement in high-profile careers. As cosmetic surgery has become more widespread and affordable, it has virtually become a civil right, an equal-opportunity privilege once enjoyed primarily by a moneyed elite who could fly to Brazil for a discreet nip and tuck.

The questions raised about plastic surgery often have a moralistic hue. Is cosmetic surgery a wasteful frivolity, an exercise in narcissism? Does the pressure for alteration of face and body fall more heavily on women because of endemic sexism?

[*Harper's Bazaar*, May 2005]

And are coercive racist stereotypes at work in the trend among black women to thin their noses or among Asian women to "Westernize" their eyes?

All these ethical issues deserve serious attention. But nothing, I submit, will stop the drive of the human species toward beauty and the shimmering illusion of perfection. It is one of our deepest and finest instincts. From prehistory on, tribal peoples flattened their skulls, pierced their noses, elongated their necks, stretched their earlobes, and scarred or tattooed their entire bodies to achieve the most admired look. Mutilation is in the eye of the beholder.

Though cosmetic surgery is undoubtedly an unstoppable movement, we may still ask whether its current application can be improved. I have not had surgery and have no plans to do so, on the theory that women intellectuals, at least, should perhaps try to hold out. (On the other hand, one doesn't want to scare the horses!) Over the past fifteen years, I have become increasingly uneasy about ruling styles of plastic surgery in the United States. What norms are being imposed on adult or aging women?

I would suggest that the current models upon which many American surgeons are basing their reworking of the female face and body are far too parochial. The eye can be retrained over time, and so we have come to accept a diminished and even demeaning view of woman as ingénue, a perky figure of ingratiating girliness. Neither sex bomb nor dominatrix, she is a cutesy sex kitten without claws.

In the great era of the Hollywood studio system, from the 1920s to the early '60s, pioneering makeup techniques achieved what plastic surgery does now to remold the appearance of both male and female stars. For example, the mature Lana Turner of *Imitation of Life* or *Peyton Place* was made to look like a superglamorous and ravishingly sensual version of a woman of Turner's own age. The problem today is that Hollywood expects middle-aged female actors to look 20 or even 30 years younger than they are. The ideal has become the bouncy Barbie doll or simpering nymphet, not a sophisticated woman of the world. Women's faces are erased, blanked out as in a cartoon. In Europe, in contrast, older women are still considered sexy: women are granted the dignity of accumulated experience. The European woman has a reserve or mystique because of her assumed mastery of the esoteric arts of love.

Why this cultural discrepancy? Many of the founders of Hollywood, from studio moguls to directors, screenwriters, makeup artists, and composers, were European émigrés whose social background ranged from peasant to professional. European models of beauty are based on classical precedents—on luminous Greek sculpture, with its mathematical symmetry and proportion, or on Old Master oil paintings with their magnificent portraiture of elegant aristocrats and hypnotic femmes fatales. As an upstart popular form with trashy roots in nickelodeons and penny arcades, Hollywood movies strove to elevate their prestige by invoking a noble past. The studios presented their stable of stars as a Greek pantheon of resurrected divinities, sex symbols with an unattainable grandeur.

But Hollywood's grounding in great art has vanished. In this blockbuster era of computerized special effects and slam-bang action-adventure films, few producers and directors root their genre in the ancestry of the fine arts. On the contrary, they are more likely to be inspired by snarky television sitcoms or holographic video games, with their fantasy cast of overmuscled heroes and pneumatic vixens. The profound influence of video games can be seen in the redefining of today's ultimate female body type, inspired by Amazonian superheroines like Lara Croft: large breasts with a flat midriff and lean hips, a hormonally anomalous profile that few women can attain without surgical intervention and liposuction.

Maximizing one's attractiveness and desirability is a justifiable aim in any society, except for the most puritanical. But it is worrisome that the American standard of female sexual allure may be regressing. In the post-1960s culture of easy divorce on demand, middle-aged women have found themselves competing with nubile women in their 20s, who are being scooped up as trophy second wives by ambitious men having a midlife crisis. Cosmetic surgery seems to level the playing field. But at what cost?

Good surgery discovers and reveals personality; bad surgery obscures or distorts it. The facial mask should not be frozen or robotic. We still don't know what neurological risks there may be in long-term use of nonsurgical Botox, a toxin injected subcutaneously to paralyze facial muscles and smooth out furrows and wrinkles. What is clear, however, is that unskilled practitioners are sometimes administering Botox in excessive amounts, so that even major celebrities in their late 30s and 40s can be seen at public events with frighteningly waxen, mummified foreheads. Actors who overuse Botox are forfeiting the mobile expressiveness necessary to portray character. We will probably never again see "great faces" among accomplished older women—the kind of severe, imperious, craggy look of formidable visionaries like Diana Vreeland or Lillian Hellman.

The urgent problem is that today's cosmetic surgeons are drawing from too limited a repertoire of images. Plastic surgery is an art form: therefore surgeons need training in art as well as medicine. Without a broader visual vocabulary, too many surgeons will continue to homogenize women, divesting them of authority and reducing them to a generic cookie-cutter sameness. And without a gift for psychology, surgeons cannot intuit and reinforce a woman's unique personality.

For cosmetic surgery to maintain or regain subtlety and nuance, surgeons should meditate on great painting and sculpture. And women themselves must draw the line against seeking and perpetuating an artificial juvenility that obliterates their own cultural value.

21

FEMINISM PAST AND PRESENT: IDEOLOGY, ACTION, AND REFORM

Feminism is back in the news. After a long period when feminist debate has been mainly confined to websites and to books that, however well reviewed, did not find a readership beyond that of other feminists, the current presidential campaign has restored gender war to the center ring. There has been an explosion of international publicity and acrimony over the candidacy of Hillary Clinton. Hillary is not, as is too often alleged, the first woman to run for president: she has a long line of strong-willed precursors beginning with Victoria Woodhull in 1872 and Belva Lockwood in 1884 and extending to Margaret Chase Smith, Patsy Mink, Bella Abzug, Shirley Chisholm, Patricia Schroeder, Lenora Fulani, and Elizabeth Dole. However, Hillary, as she collects state primaries like trophies, has progressed much farther than any woman candidate before her, and, win or lose, she is blazing a trail for ambitious women who come after her.

Controversy will continue for many years over the degree

[Keynote address of The Legacy and Future of Feminism, a conference at Harvard University, April 10, 2008. Published in *Arion*, Spring/Summer 2008] to which sexism has or has not hindered Hillary's campaign. Has she been treated more severely by the media than her male opponents? Has she herself opportunistically played the gender card? There can be no doubt that Hillary, for complex reasons, has attracted archaic mythic stereotypes—the witch, the crone, the bitch, the shrew, the ball-busting nutcracker. The National Organization for Women, which has languished in relative obscurity for almost a decade, recently seized the moment to proclaim, in a press release about Hillary entitled "Ignorance and Venom: The Media's Deeply Ingrained Sexism," that "Media misogyny has reached an all-time high"—a statement that, as a professor of humanities and media studies, I quite frankly find ridiculous.

Earlier this year, there was a major intervention by Gloria Steinem, the doyenne of American feminism for nearly four decades, who in an incendiary *New York Times* op-ed defending Hillary declared that "gender is probably the most restricting force in American life"—another highly questionable generalization. Steinem portrayed Hillary as a noble victim of sexism and in effect lobbied for all women to vote for her merely because she is a woman. In the blogosphere and in reader letters on news sites, women Democrats like me who are supporting Barack Obama have been called "traitors" who are undermining feminism. My defense would be that women have been advancing so rapidly in politics—we have female mayors, senators, governors, and even a woman Speaker of the House—that there is no longer a need, if there ever was one, for lockstep gender solidarity. Women are rational creatures who can vote in each election on the merits.

In any case, it can be argued that Hillary is an imperfect feminist candidate insofar as her entire public life has been tied to her husband's career; her past professional performance, furthermore, notably in regard to health care reform, has been uneven. The United States has embarrassingly lagged behind other nations in never having a woman leader, but this is partly due to the special demands of the presidency. It has been much easier for women to become prime minister, the leader of a party who assumes office when her party wins an election. The U.S. president symbolizes and unifies a vast nation and must also serve as Commander-in-Chief of the armed forces, which puts special pressure on women seeking that role. Education, fractured by identity politics, has inadequately prepared women for seeking the presidency—which is why for nearly 20 years I have been calling for young feminists to study military history.

Hillary Clinton's candidacy has done more to awaken and re-energize feminism than anything since the enormous controversy over Anita Hill, who testified against Clarence Thomas's nomination for the Supreme Court in 1991. Hence it's time to reassess. Where has feminism been, and where is it going? And why did feminism recede after its high visibility during the culture wars of the 1980s and early '90s—when feminist leaders were routinely consulted by the media on every issue facing women? Ironically, it was during the two Clinton presidencies that feminists began to lose ground as key players in the public arena. Throughout the 1990s, news stories regularly reported how few young women were then willing to identify themselves as feminists.

Two technological innovations—cable TV and the World Wide Web—broke the hold that American feminist leaders had had on media discourse about gender for twenty years. Suddenly, there was a riot of alternative points of view. Most unexpectedly, a new crop of outspoken conservative women arrived on the scene in the '90s—Laura Ingraham, Barbara Olson, Monica Crowley, Ann Coulter, Michelle Malkin—who blurred conventional expectations about female self-assertion.

These women, who had attended elite colleges and in some cases had worked in the Republican administrations of Richard Nixon and Ronald Reagan, were aggressive, articulate, funny, and startlingly sexier and more glamorous than their dour feminist adversaries. The old Pat Nixon stereotype of conservative women as dowdy, repressed, soft-spoken, and deferential was annihilated. Old-guard feminists, who came across as humorless and dogmatic, were losing the TV wars to a spunky new breed of issues-oriented women. Barbara Olson, who died in the attack on the Pentagon on 9/11, was a co-founder of the Independent Women's Forum, an association of conservative and libertarian women that was first formed as a response to liberal media bias in reporting during the Anita Hill case, in which Northeastern women journalists were directly and perhaps inappropriately involved.

After 9/11 and the invasion of Iraq, gender issues were even further sidelined by questions of life and death and the clash of civilizations in an era of terrorism. There was a resurgence of popular interest in military regalia and history and in traditional masculinity, showing up even in children's toys. Feminist commentary on this development—which was predictably labeled "reactionary"—has seemed out of touch with the times. Perhaps whenever survival is at stake, we need to unite as human beings rather than quarreling genders. The legacy of 9/11 has presented a problem for Hillary Clinton in her political aspirations. The necessity at this time for a woman candidate to look strong and to show command of military issues certainly led Hillary to vote for the fateful war resolution authorizing President Bush to use military force in Iraq—a decision that has come back to haunt her and that has made her a constant target of that audacious and ingenious female guerrilla group, Code Pink.

What precisely *is* feminism? Is it a theory, an ideology, or a praxis?—that is, a program for action. Is feminism perhaps so Western in its premises that it cannot be exported to other cultures without distorting them? When we find feminism in medieval or Renaissance writers, are we exporting modern ideas backwards? Who is or is not a feminist, and who defines it? Who confers legitimacy or authenticity? Must a feminist be a member of a group or conform to a dominant ideology or its subsets? Who declares, and on what authority, what is or is not permissible to think or say about gender issues? And is feminism intrinsically a movement of the left, or can there be a feminism based on conservative or religious principles?

While there are scattered texts, in both prose and poetry, which protest women's lack of rights and social status, from Christine de Pisan to Anne Bradstreet and Mary Wollstonecraft, feminism as an organized movement began in the mid-nineteenth century, inspired by the movement to abolish slavery—just as the resurgence of feminism in the 1960s was stimulated by the civil rights movement, which targeted segregation and the disenfranchisement of African-Americans in the Jim Crow South. Feminism was therefore keyed to the expansion of liberty to an oppressed group. And feminism was always linked to democracy: it is no coincidence that feminism was born in America and that it became the early model for British feminism.

In general, feminist theory has failed to acknowledge how much it owes to the Western tradition of civil liberties grounded in ancient Greece, not simply in the flawed democracy of classical Athens, with its slave economy and its severe circumscription of women's lives, but much earlier in the first appearance of the individual voice in Archaic poetry, one of whose finest practitioners was the world's first major woman writer, Sappho of Lesbos. Second, feminist theory has failed

to acknowledge how much the emergence of modern feminism owes to capitalism and the industrial revolution, which
transformed the economy, expanded the professions, and gave
women for the first time in history the opportunity to earn
their own living and to escape dependency on father or husband. Capitalism's emancipation of women is nowhere clearer
than in those magical labor-saving appliances such as auto-
matic washers and dryers that most middle-class Westerners
now take for granted.

Third, feminist history has insufficiently acknowledged
the degree to which the founders of the woman suffrage
movement—that is, the drive to win votes for women—were
formed or influenced by religion. It is no coincidence that
so many early American feminists were Quakers: Susan B.
Anthony, for example, was the daughter of a Quaker farmer,
and Lucretia Mott was a Quaker minister. It was in Quaker
meetings, where men and women were treated as equals, that
women first learned the art of public speaking. The quest for
suffrage, motivated by religious idealism and paradigms, cannot therefore automatically be defined as a movement of the
left. Indeed, the social conservatism of most of the suffrage
leaders was shown in their attraction to the temperance movement, whose goal of banning alcohol in the United States
finally led to the fourteen socially disruptive years of Prohibition after World War One. In the nineteenth century, alcohol
was seen as a woman's problem: that is, working-class men
were alleged to waste the meager family income on alcohol,
which led in turn to the neglect or physical abuse of wives and
children. Temperance, flaring into public view in the 1870s,
was called the "Women's Crusade" or "Women's Holy War."
Temperance women gathered in groups outside saloons,
where they prayed, sang hymns, obstructed entry, and generally made nuisances of themselves. Many saloons had to move

or close. It was one of the first examples in history of women mobilizing for social action.

However, the impulse to regulate private behavior that can be seen here was a persistent element in feminism that would resurface in the virulent anti-pornography crusade of the 1970s and '80s. The nineteenth-century suffrage leaders reacted punitively to Victoria Woodhull, who espoused free love—an issue that Susan B. Anthony and others felt would tar the entire movement and doom it politically. They were motivated by a contrary goal to rescue women from "vice," that is, the clutches of prostitution. Sexuality outside of traditional marriage was seen as a danger that had to be curtailed by moral norms. The preeminence of ideology over the personal can also be seen in Anthony's nun-like devotion to the cause and in her prickly resentment of the way her colleagues were pulled in another direction by the needs of family and children. By the end of her life, Anthony was revered and universally honored, but her obsessive focus on one issue was perhaps not a model for the balanced life.

There are other omissions or elisions in the standard feminist narrative: Margaret Sanger, who was the foster mother of Planned Parenthood and a bold pioneer of reproductive rights and who was jailed in 1916 for opening a birth control clinic in New York, was a public adherent of eugenics, the philosophy of selective breeding that was adopted by the Nazis as part of their brutal campaign to purify the human race of undesirables.

Huge sacrifices were made by the first-wave feminists, who showed enormous courage and daring in their demand not just for the vote but for reform of laws preventing women from entering contracts or owning property. Nineteenth-century satirical cartoons portrayed suffrage leaders as mutant pseudo-males, flaunting male trousers and cigars and threatening to dethrone men from their positions at home and in the public sphere. When women suffragists first gave speeches in the streets, it was considered a scandalous affront to propriety. It is intriguing that the first states to give American women the right to vote after the Civil War were in the Western territories. But the Northeast, the nation's intellectual and cultural capital, held out. Even in 1915, the state governments of Massachusetts, New York, Pennsylvania, and New Jersey rejected the woman suffrage amendment. It was the frontier states, where men and women worked side by side doing manual labor, that first viewed women as equals, whereas the East was still ruled by the genteel persona of the "lady," with her code of delicacy and decorum. Ladies and gentlemen in the East and Deep South seemed not to belong to the same species.

The 19th Amendment to the Constitution granting women the right to vote was finally passed in 1920 after a series of increasingly intense protests: beginning in 1907, there were massive parades in New York and Washington with horses, banners, and floats, a lavish pageantry that American feminists had borrowed from their British counterparts. British feminists, led by Emmeline Pankhurst, were paradoxically more aggressive, more drawn to militant confrontation and direct action. Feminists in London broke windows and barged into government meetings. In 1910, they tried to force their way into the House of Commons. There was a six-hour fracas, followed by mass arrests and imprisonment. Barbaric methods of forced feeding were later employed against jailed feminists in both England and the United States.

In 1917, the public image of American feminism was damaged by the tactics of women protestors outside the White House. Holding placards demanding votes for women, they kept a silent, dignified vigil for months. But male passersby turned abusive and then violent when the messages, in that time of war, became more provocative. One sign called then president Woodrow Wilson "Kaiser Wilson." Hostile crowds began to gather daily; the signs were immediately ripped to pieces and the women themselves buffeted. The demonstrations were finally banned by the police as a threat to public safety and order. Dismayingly, feminists had begun to seem like unpatriotic subversives. Hence it can be argued that the upsurge of anti-feminist rhetoric before, during, and after World War One in both England and the United States was not necessarily anti-woman per se but in some cases may have been a comprehensible response to what had become an ideological extremism and fanaticism in some suffragists.

Many of the lively, sexually adventurous women of the Roaring Twenties who drank, smoke, cursed, and did wild dances like the Charleston disassociated themselves from the feminist label. And indeed, the suffrage movement was only partly responsible for the revolutionary change in women of that decade. The disillusionment following the cataclysmic First World War produced a flood of anti-authority sentiment, which weakened the prestige of father figures in government, religion, and the family. Second, there was a mammoth cultural impact from African-American jazz as well as from Hollywood movies, a new medium that so transformed sexual expectations and behavior that demands for the regulation of the industry came from ministers, teachers, journalists, city officials, and women's civic groups. Out of that protest movement would come the infamous studio production code, which ruled Hollywood with an iron hand until the early 1960s.

The 1920s and '30s were a glory period for exceptional, accomplished women, such as Dorothy Parker, Dorothy Thompson, Clare Boothe Luce, Amelia Earhart, Babe Didrikson, and Katharine Hepburn. Feminism may have dissipated as a political movement, but women's achievement and public visibility were very strong. It is depressing that second-wave feminism would initially dismiss those enterprising, path-breaking women as "male-identified" and allegedly indifferent to the needs of women as a group. I would maintain that inspiring female role models are always crucial to demonstrate what personal ambition and initiative can accomplish and to model an attitude of pride and self-respect that may be invaluable to other, less outspoken women struggling to establish their independence from domineering parents or spouses as well as from capricious or dictatorial bosses and co-workers.

The beckoning promise of that period in women's history was canceled by the Great Depression, the rise of fascism in Europe, and the outbreak of World War Two. While men were at the front, women had to take over their factory jobs: this was the heyday of Rosie the Riveter, flexing her biceps. But when the veterans returned, women were expected to step aside. That pressure was unjust, but after World War Two, there was a deep longing shared by both men and women for the normalcy of family life. Domestic issues came to the fore, and gender roles repolarized. With so many weddings, there was an avalanche of births—the baby-boomers who are now sliding downhill toward retirement. In the late 1940s and '50s, movies, television, and advertisements promoted motherhood and homemaking as women's highest goals. It was this homogeneity that second-wave feminism correctly and admirably rebelled against. But too many second-wave feminists extrapolated their discontent to condemn all men everywhere and throughout history. In other words, the ideology of second-wave feminism was or should have been time- and place-specific. Post-war domesticity was a relatively local phenomenon. The problem was not just sexism; it was the postindustrial social evolution from the working-class extended family to the middle-class nuclear family, which left women

painfully isolated in their comfortable homes. They had lost
the companionship, instruction, and shared labor of the joy-
ous, centuries-old, multi-generational community of women.

Second-wave feminism was launched by Betty Friedan's
book, *The Feminine Mystique*, published in 1963. Its analysis of
the anomie felt by suburban housewives struck a chord with
a broad audience. Three years later, Friedan co-founded the
National Organization for Women, the first political group
devoted to women's issues since suffrage had been won nearly
fifty years before. Two major points were missing in early
assessments of Friedan: she was not simply a housewife, as
she had portrayed herself, but had been a leftist labor activist in the 1950s. Second, Friedan's debt to Simone de Beauvoir's magisterial 1949 book, *The Second Sex*, was obscured
by herself and others. When Friedan died two years ago, the
outpouring of testimonials in the American and British media
rightly acknowledged her importance but exaggerated the role
she had played in women's lives. It is categorically untrue that
Friedan single-handedly opened the door for my baby-boom
generation of professional women, who were already head-
ing with determination toward college and careers when she
arrived on the scene. We had been animated from childhood
by the can-do spirit inherited from our parents, who had lived
through the Depression and war. For example, Friedan did not
produce Germaine Greer, who was already a firebrand in her
native Australia. Nor did Friedan produce me in the snow belt
of upstate New York: in the early 1960s, before Friedan's book
was published, I was an adolescent absorbed in an eccentric,
three-year research project on my feminist idol, Amelia Earhart. The organized women's movement of the late 1960s was
only one important strain among many other elements that
characterized my feisty generation.

Almost immediately, a split opened within NOW which

would force Betty Friedan out of the group she had co-founded. Younger, more militant women, alienated by the sexism of their male fellow radicals in the anti-war movement, clashed with the older, married women of Friedan's generation, who were often uncomfortable with homosexuality. Like the nineteenth-century suffragists who feared that sexual issues would derail the movement, Friedan felt that militant lesbians ("the lavender menace," in her words) would drive mainstream women away from feminism. Friedan herself was pitifully marginalized when Gloria Steinem, a journalist whom she had brought into the movement, stole the media spotlight because of her telegenic good looks. Steinem, who had made her name through infiltrating a Playboy Bunny club for an exposé for *New York* magazine, played a crucial early role in normalizing the image of feminists. With her flowing blonde tresses, hip aviator glasses, and soothing voice and manner, she made feminism seem reasonable and unthreatening. In 1972, Steinem founded *Ms.*, the first glossy, mass-market magazine devoted to feminist issues. Its name would enter the language and transform how women are addressed to this day.

Despite her Smith College education, however, Steinem was neither an intellectual nor a theorist. She was a tireless, peripatetic activist, but virtually from the start, she played the role of stern guardian of a victim-centered ideology that did not permit alternate viewpoints. *Playboy*, for example, which Steinem excoriated, had laid the groundwork for the sexual revolution; Hugh Hefner, a descendant of New England Puritans, had been progressively forward-thinking in refining the post-war macho image of the American male toward a more sophisticated European model of pleasure-loving connoisseur of food, wine, sex, and jazz. Steinem's male-bashing was overt: she famously said, "A woman needs a man like a fish needs a bicycle." Meanwhile, she kept from public view how vital a role men played in her private life in Manhattan. Steinem also unapologetically aligned feminism with partisan Democratic politics, thus limiting its reach over time.

In the first ferment over the revived feminism, women athletes such as Billie Jean King played a central role. Like Martina Navratilova after her, the blunt, hot-tempered King adopted a startlingly aggressive style on the tennis court that inspired a generation of women to play competitive sports. The passage by the U.S. Congress in 1972 of Title IX, a section of the Educational Amendments, radically expanded campus sports programs for women but sometimes at the expense of men's programs like wrestling, which were too often cut by ruthless college administrators.

In the 1970s, women's studies courses and programs were created in profusion. There has been no honest study of the institutionalization of women's studies and of the effects it has had on feminism. Women's studies was assembled haphazardly and piecemeal, without due consideration of what the scholarly study of gender ought to entail. The victim-centered agenda of the current women's movement was adopted wholesale, an ideological bias that neither women's studies nor its successor, gender studies, has been able to shed. Furthermore, because so many of the first women's studies professors came from literature departments, science was completely excluded. But without a grounding in basic biology, neither students nor teachers can negotiate the tangle of nature and culture that produces human sex differences.

As a new field, eager to gain a reputation for seriousness, women's studies, like the equally new film studies, was woefully vulnerable to European poststructuralism, which began to infiltrate American humanities departments via Johns Hopkins and Yale universities in the early 1970s. Poststructuralism is uniformly social constructionist, denying that gender has any basis in biology and bizarrely attributing all sex differences to language alone. Academic feminists at the elite schools soon devoted volumes of labyrinthine theory to their interrogation of gender assumptions—a project that they mistook for revolutionary action which would have utopian social results.

In the real world, however, two major events marked 1970s feminism. First was the Supreme Court's Roe v. Wade ruling in 1973, which legalized abortion in all 50 states. This was an epochal expansion of women's reproductive rights, which I support without qualification. Unfortunately, abortion would come to dominate American feminism and eventually, I submit, would distort and weaken it. The second event was the creation by Phyllis Schlafly, a lawyer, Republican activist, and mother of six, of STOP ERA, a group devoted to defeating the Equal Rights Amendment, which was slowly wending its way through state legislatures. This was a watershed moment in American politics, because Schlafly's grassroots organizing would lay the foundation for the future revival of conservatism. Feminist leaders, trapped by their own ideology, which was becoming increasingly dogmatic, demonized Schlafly without adequately responding to the concerns that she had raised—which included basic questions about whether women would be drafted or whether unisex toilets would be mandated. After a ten-year struggle, the Equal Rights Amendment failed in 1982 to pass the requisite number of states, and it died. But this defeat did not stimulate self-analysis among feminist leaders; on the contrary, it hardened their oppositional attitudes. They now saw the world simplistically divided between feminist and anti-feminist.

By the 1980s, a chasm had opened up between academic feminism, then under the fashionable spell of Jacques Lacan, and mainstream feminism, which was geared to action.

Central to the women's studies curriculum were the polemical writings of Catharine MacKinnon and Andrea Dworkin, who asserted that pornography causes rape and that it should therefore be banned. Here is a typical sample of their pronouncements: "The pornographers rank with Nazis and Klansmen in promoting hatred and violence." What hysterical agitprop, unworthy of modern women thinkers. MacKinnon and Dworkin's activism led to the passage of anti-pornography ordinances in Indianapolis and Minneapolis that were later declared unconstitutional. MacKinnon's cultural dominance was shown by the way she was virtually canonized in a 1991 cover story of *The New York Times Magazine*. A parallel phenomenon in the late 1980s and early '90s was an increasing campus focus on rape, and specifically date rape. News magazines and TV talk shows took up the theme with a vengeance. This was an important social issue, yet the way it was promoted on campus and off was turning women once again into helpless victims.

But a sea change was coming in feminism. In the mid-1980s, the explicit sexual imagery and semi-nudity used by Madonna in her pioneering music videos, broadcast to the world through the new medium of cable TV, electrified a younger generation of women. Madonna started the process of liberalization that led to what many commentators, on both the left and the right, have been recently lamenting as the "pornification" of America. Within feminism, a revolt against the MacKinnon-Dworkin tyranny began in the 1980s in San Francisco, where there were pitched battles over lesbian sadomasochism and butch-femme role-playing. By the early '90s, "lipstick" lesbianism had gained national attention—a drastic switch from the image of the lesbian feminist as a drab, granola-eating, earth-shoe-wearing political ideologue. The third-wave feminists of the '90s—a term first used by Rebecca Walker—took different stances on these issues. Despite her early puritanism about beauty, Naomi Wolf eventually espoused a pro-sex position close to my own, while Susan Faludi adopted the Steinem party line about the systemic anti-feminism of popular culture.

While both academic and mainstream feminists have always claimed to foster a diversity of viewpoints, the reality was far from that. I came close to fistfights with other feminists in the early 1970s over hard rock music, which was then dubbed sexist, and over the question of hormones, which I saw as a factor in sex differences. In the late 1980s, Christina Hoff Sommers, then a philosophy professor at Clark University, hit a wall at academic conferences when she tried to initiate debate with other feminists on fundamental issues. When my first book, *Sexual Personae*, was published by Yale University Press in 1990, that 700-page tome on art and culture was compared by Gloria Steinem, who clearly had not bothered to read it, to Hitler's *Mein Kampf*. When an op-ed I wrote on date rape for New York *Newsday* in January 1991* was reprinted via syndication across the United States, there was a huge reaction, including what was clearly an organized campaign of vilification: the president of my university in Philadelphia was besieged with calls from around the country calling for me to be fired from my teaching job. Fortunately, the president took the enlightened line that faculty members have the right to express themselves freely on all public issues. I was also lucky enough to have tenure. Younger teachers, then and now, would be far more hesitant to express heterodox views. When, three years later, Katie Roiphe published her 1994 book, *The Morning After*, on campus rape ideology, the vicious attacks on her by the older women of the feminist establishment were

* Reprinted in this volume on page 52.

outrageous and unconscionable. That, in my view, was one of
the lowest, most amoral moments in contemporary feminism.

The stridency of old-guard feminism was intensifying
even as feminism was losing the war. The Web, which became
a near-universal tool by the mid-1990s, thrives on diversity.
When pornography moved to the Web, feminists also lost
the ability to track and stop it. While the Web is a spectacular resource for feminist networking and discussion, it may
also be one reason that feminism has seemed to fall below the
radar, because websites can become far-flung niches attracting
only true believers.

There was one last grand act for mainstream feminist leaders in the 1990s: their staunch defense of Bill Clinton, from
the lawsuit filed by Paula Jones in 1994 through the Monica
Lewinsky scandal in 1998. Suddenly, the arguments presented
about sexual harassment during Anita Hill's testimony were
dropped and reversed—even though Jones, a former Arkansas
state employee, was making far more serious charges against
Clinton than Hill ever did against Clarence Thomas. Although
I had voted for him twice, I was appalled by President Clinton's
exploitation of the young Monica Lewinsky, a furtive series of
squalid encounters in taxpayer-funded office space in which
there was a gross disparity of power, which feminists usually
claim makes informed consent impossible. The openly partisan tactics and special pleading of feminist leaders during
Clinton's impeachment crisis killed their credibility and damaged core feminist issues.

One thing is clear: the feminism of the future will be created by women who are young now. The doctrinal disputes
and turf wars of the older generation (including me) must be
set aside. I reject the term "postfeminism," which became a
glib media tag line in the 1990s and is often attached to me.
There is no such animal. Feminism *lives* but goes through

cycles of turmoil and retreat. At present, there is no one leading issue that can galvanize women across a broad spectrum.
Feminism certainly has an obligation to protest and, if possible, correct concrete abuses of women and children in Third
World nations. But feminism might look very different in
more traditional or religious societies, where motherhood and
family are still valorized and where the independent career
woman is less typical or admired.

In conclusion, my proposals for reform are as follows.
First of all, science must be made a fundamental component
of all women's or gender studies programs. Second, every
such program must be assessed by qualified faculty (not
administrators or politicians) for ideological bias. The writings
of conservative opponents of feminism, as well as of dissident
feminists, must be included. Without such diversity, students
are getting indoctrination, not education. Certainly among
current dissident points of view is the abstinence movement,
as an evangelical Protestant phenomenon and also as an
argument set forth in Wendy Shalit's first book, *A Return to
Modesty*, which created a storm when it was published nine
years ago but whose influence can be detected in today's campus chastity clubs, including here at Harvard. As a veteran of
pro-sex feminism who still endorses pornography and prostitution, I say more power to all these chaste young women who
are defending their individuality and defying groupthink and
social convention. That is true feminism!

My final recommendation for reform is a massive rollback
of the paternalistic system of grievance committees and other
meddlesome bureaucratic contrivances which have turned
American college campuses into womb-like customer-service
resorts. The feminists of my baby-boom generation fought
to tear down the intrusive *in loco parentis* rules that insult-
ingly confined women in their dormitories at night. College

administrators and academic committees have no competence whatever to investigate crimes, including sexual assault.
If an offense has been committed, it should be reported to the
police, so that the civil liberties of both the accuser and the
accused can be protected. This is not to absolve young men
from their duty to behave honorably. Hooliganism cannot be
tolerated. But we must stop seeing everything in life through
the narrow lens of gender. If women expect equal treatment in
society, they must stop asking for infantilizing special protections. With freedom comes personal responsibility.

22

NO SEX PLEASE, WE'RE MIDDLE CLASS

Will women soon have a Viagra of their own? Although a Food and Drug Administration advisory panel recently rejected an application to market the drug flibanserin in the United States for women with low libido, it endorsed the potential benefits and urged further research. Several pharmaceutical companies are reported to be well along in the search for such a drug.

The implication is that a new pill, despite its unforeseen side effects, is necessary to cure the sexual malaise that appears to have sunk over the country. But to what extent do these complaints about sexual apathy reflect a medical reality, and how much do they actually emanate from the anxious, overachieving, white upper middle class?

In the 1950s, female "frigidity" was attributed to social conformism and religious puritanism. But since the sexual revolution of the 1960s, American society has become increasingly secular, with a media environment drenched in sex.

The real culprit, originating in the nineteenth century, is bourgeois propriety. As respectability became the central middle-class value, censorship and repression became the norm. Victorian prudery ended the humorous sexual candor of both men and women during the agrarian era, a ribaldry chronicled from Shakespeare's plays to the eighteenth-century novel. The priggish 1950s, which erased the liberated flappers of the Jazz Age from cultural memory, were simply a return to the norm.

Only the diffuse New Age movement, inspired by nature-keyed Asian practices, has preserved the radical vision of the modern sexual revolution. But concrete power resides in America's careerist technocracy, for which the elite schools, with their ideological view of gender as a social construct, are feeder cells.

In the discreet white-collar realm, men and women are interchangeable, doing the same, mind-based work. Physicality is suppressed; voices are lowered and gestures curtailed in sanitized office space. Men must neuter themselves, while ambitious women postpone procreation. Androgyny is bewitching in art, but in real life it can lead to stagnation and boredom, which no pill can cure.

Meanwhile, family life has put middle-class men in a bind; they are simply cogs in a domestic machine commanded by women. Contemporary moms have become virtuoso super-managers of a complex operation focused on the care and transport of children. But it's not so easy to snap over from Apollonian control to Dionysian delirium.

Nor are husbands offering much stimulation in the male display department: visually, American men remain perpetual boys, as shown by the bulky T-shirts, loose shorts, and sneakers they wear from preschool through midlife. The sexes, which used to occupy intriguingly separate worlds, are suffering from over-familiarity, a curse of the mundane. There's no mystery left.

The elemental power of sexuality has also waned in American popular culture. Under the much-maligned studio production code, Hollywood made movies sizzling with flirtation and romance. But from the early 1970s on, nudity was in, and steamy build-up was out. A generation of filmmakers lost the skill of sophisticated innuendo. The situation worsened in the '90s, when Hollywood pirated video games to turn women into cartoonishly pneumatic superheroines and sci-fi androids, fantasy figures without psychological complexity or the erotic needs of real women.

Furthermore, thanks to a bourgeois white culture that values efficient bodies over voluptuous ones, American actresses have desexualized themselves, confusing sterile athleticism with female power. Their current Pilates-honed look is taut and tense—a boy's thin limbs and narrow hips combined with amplified breasts. Contrast that with Latino and African-American taste, which runs toward the healthy silhouette of the bootylicious Beyoncé.

A class issue in sexual energy may be suggested by the apparent striking popularity of Victoria's Secret and its racy lingerie among multiracial lower-middle-class and working-class patrons, even in suburban shopping malls, which otherwise trend toward the white middle class. Country music, with its history in the rural South and Southwest, is still filled with blazingly raunchy scenarios, where the sexes remain dynamically polarized in the old-fashioned way.

On the other hand, rock music, once sexually pioneering, is in the dumps. Black rhythm and blues, born in the Mississippi Delta, was the driving force behind the great hard rock bands of the 1960s, whose cover versions of blues songs were filled with electrifying sexual imagery. The Rolling Stones' hypnotic recording of Willie Dixon's "Little Red Rooster," with its titillating phallic exhibitionism, throbs and shimmers with sultry heat.

But with the huge commercial success of rock, the blues receded as a direct influence on young musicians, who simply imitated the white guitar gods without exploring their roots. Step by step, rock lost its visceral rawness and seductive sensuality. Big-ticket rock, with its well-heeled middle-class audience, is now all superego and no id.

In the 1980s, commercial music boasted a beguiling host of sexy pop chicks like Deborah Harry, Belinda Carlisle, Pat Benatar, and a charmingly ripe Madonna. Late Madonna, in contrast, went bourgeois and turned scrawny. Madonna's dance-track acolyte, Lady Gaga, with her compulsive overkill, is a high-concept fabrication without an ounce of genuine eroticism.

Pharmaceutical companies will never find the holy grail of a female Viagra—not in this culture driven and drained by middle-class values. Inhibitions are stubbornly internal. And lust is too fiery to be left to the pharmacist.

23

THE STILETTO HEEL

The stiletto high heel is modern woman's most lethal social weapon. First imagined in the 1930s but not realized until post-war technology made it possible in the early 1950s, the stiletto is a visual slash born to puncture and pierce.

While platform shoes increased stature for both men and women from Greco-Roman actors to Venetian sophisticates on flooded walkways, the slanted structure of current high heels descends from the boots of early medieval horsemen seeking traction in the stirrup. Hence high heels have a masculine lineage, latent in their use by emancipated women eager to rise to men's level.

But this quest for equality, dominance, or merely assertive presence at work and play is contradicted by a crippling construction: no item of female dress since the tight-laced Victorian corset is so mutilating. Pain and deformation are the price of high-heeled beauty. The high heel creates the illusion of a lengthened leg by shortening the calf muscle, arching the foot, and crushing the toes, forcing breasts and buttocks out in a classic hominid posture of sexual invitation.

[*Design and Violence* project, The Museum of Modern Art website,
October 25, 2013. Published in the book *Design and Violence*,
Paola Antonelli, James Hunt, and Michelle Fisher, eds.,
New York: The Museum of Modern Art, 2015]

The eroticization of high heels (still at medium height) was sped along in the 1920s by the rising hemlines of flappers showing off their legs in scandalously hyperkinetic dances like the Charleston. Alfred Hitchcock's fetishistic focus on high heels can be seen throughout his murder mysteries, from his early silent films in London to his Technicolor Hollywood classics like *Vertigo* and *The Birds*, where Tippi Hedren (a former fashion model) demonstrates the exquisite artifice of high-heel wearing as well as its masochistic vulnerability, chronicled in a thousand low-budget horror movies. A woman in high heels, unable to run, is a titillating target for attack.

But the high heel as an instrument of sex war can be witnessed in action in a stunning face-off in *Butterfield* 8 (1960), where Elizabeth Taylor as a glossy call-girl, her wrist painfully gripped by Laurence Harvey at a chic Manhattan bar, implacably grinds her phallic spike heel into his finely leathered foot. This was at a time when stiletto heels, which concentrate enormous pressure in a tiny space, were banned from buildings with susceptible linoleum or hardwood floors.

It was already being rumored in those pre-Stonewall days that drag queens, harassed on the street, would whip off their high heels and ferociously wield them against assailants. In 2006, noted New York drag queen Flotilla DeBarge was jailed after a bar-room fracas where she swung her black high heels (impounded by the police as evidence) to inflict wounds requiring stitches upon an insulting straight man and his date (an online headline: "Meatpacking District Drag Queen High-Heel Beatdown").

Reports of high-heeled crime were on the increase in 2013. In Washington, D.C., a man complained to the police that a petite woman had hit him in the head with her shoe outside the Ibiza nightclub. After a fight at a Washington 7-Eleven, three women were arrested for stabbing their opponents; one wielded a knife, but the other two used their shoes, leading to the charge, "assault with a dangerous weapon." In Houston, Texas, a 44-year-old woman was charged with murder after a bloody clash in a condominium tower during which her professor boyfriend died after being struck in the head, face, and neck by 30 blows from her stiletto heels.

The dagger later called a stiletto began as a needle-like medieval tool to finish off a fallen knight by a thrust through chain mail or between plate armor. During the Renaissance, the stiletto became the favorite weapon of Italian assassins, jabbing from behind through heavy fabric or leather and killing invisibly while barely leaving a drop of blood. The stiletto's historic association with deception and treachery thus gives an aura of sadistic glamour to the modern high heel, whose stem contains a concealed shaft of steel. Woman as seducer or seduced can also lance and castrate.

Helmut Newton, whose superb fashion photography was suffused with the perverse world-view of his native Weimar Berlin, captured the disturbing complexities of the high heel in *Shoe*, a picture taken in Monte Carlo in 1983. Here we see the fashionable shoe in all its florid delicacy and dynamic aggression. The stance, with shifted ankle, seems mannish. Is this a dominatrix poised to trample her delirious victim? Or is it a streetwalker defiantly defending her turf? Or a drag queen scornfully pissing in an alley? The shoe, shot from the ground, seems colossal, a pitiless totem of pagan sex cult.

The luxury high heel as status marker is directed not toward men but toward other women—both intimate confidantes and bitter rivals. The high heel in its dazzlingly heraldic permutations (as dramatized in *Sex and the City*) is beyond the comprehension of most men: only women and gay men can tell the difference between a Manolo Blahnik and a Jimmy Choo. In full disclosure, I never wear these shoes and indeed deplore their horrifying cost at a time of urgent social needs. Nevertheless, I acknowledge and admire the high heel as a contemporary icon and perhaps our canonical objet d'art.

At the Neiman Marcus department store at the King of Prussia Mall in suburban Philadelphia, a visitor ascending the escalator to the second floor is greeted by a vast horizon of welcoming tables, laden with designer shoes of ravishing allure but staggering price tags (now hovering between $500 and $900 a pair but soaring to $6000 for candy-colored, crystal-studded Daffodile pumps by Christian Louboutin). Despite my detestation of its decadence, this theatrical shoe array has for years provided me with far more intense aesthetic surprise and pleasure than any gallery of contemporary art, with its derivative gestures, rote ironies, and exhausted ideology.

Designer shoes represent the slow but steady triumph of the crafts over the fine arts during the past century. They are streamlined works of modern sculpture, wasteful and frivolous yet elegantly expressive of pure form, a geometric reshaping of soft and yielding nature. An upscale shoe department is a gun show for urban fashionistas, a site of ritual display where danger lurks beneath the mask of beauty.

24

SCHOLARS IN BONDAGE

DOGMA DOMINATES STUDIES OF KINK

REVIEW OF MARGOT WEISS, *TECHNIQUES OF PLEASURE*;
STACI NEWMAHR, *PLAYING ON THE EDGE*;
AND DANIELLE J. LINDEMANN, *DOMINATRIX*

Once confined to the murky shadows of the sexual underworld, sadomasochism and its recreational correlate, bondage and domination, have emerged into startling visibility and mainstream acceptance in books, movies, and merchandising. Two years ago, E. L. James's *Fifty Shades of Grey*, a British trilogy that began as a reworking of the popular *Twilight* series of vampire novels and films, became a worldwide bestseller that addicted its mostly women readers to graphic fantasies of erotic masochism. Last December, Harvard University granted official campus status to an undergraduate bondage-and-domination club. In January, *Kink*, a documentary produced by the actor James Franco about a successful San Francisco–based company specializing in online "fetish entertainment," premiered at the Sundance Film Festival.

[Cover story, "The Chronicle Review," *The Chronicle of Higher Education*, May 24, 2013]

Three books from university presses dramatize the degree to which once taboo sexual subjects have gained academic legitimacy. Margot Weiss's *Techniques of Pleasure: BDSM and the Circuits of Sexuality* (Duke University Press, 2011) and Staci Newmahr's *Playing on the Edge: Sadomasochism, Risk, and Intimacy* (Indiana University Press, 2011) record first-person ethnographic explorations of BDSM communities in two large American cities. (The relatively new abbreviation "BDSM" incorporates bondage and discipline, domination and submission, and sadomasochism.) Danielle J. Lindemann's *Dominatrix: Gender, Eroticism, and Control in the Dungeon* (University of Chicago Press, 2012) documents the world of professional dominatrixes in New York and San Francisco.

These books embody the dramatic changes in American academe over the past 40 years, propelled by social movements such as the sexual revolution, second-wave feminism, and gay liberation. It seems like centuries ago that, as a graduate student in 1970, I was vainly searching for a faculty sponsor for my doctoral dissertation, later titled *Sexual Personae*, which was—hard to imagine now—the only project on sex being proposed or pursued at the Yale Graduate School. (Rescue finally came in the *deus ex machina* of Harold Bloom, whose classes I had never taken. Summoning me to his office, Bloom announced, "My dear, I am the *only* one who can direct that dissertation!") Finding a teaching job in that repressive climate proved even more difficult. By the mid- to late 1970s, however, the gold rush was on, as women's studies programs mushroomed nationwide, partly as a quick-fix administrative strategy to increase the number of women faculty on embarrassingly male-heavy campuses.

Today's market for sex topics is wide open. Major university presses balk at little these days, short of apologias for pedophilia or bestiality, and even those may be looming. However, despite the refreshing candor displayed by the three books under review, a startling prudery remains in the way their provocative subjects have been buried in a sludge of opaque theorizing, which will inevitably prevent these books from reaching a wider audience. Weiss, Newmahr, and Lindemann come through as smart, lively women, but their natural voices have been squelched by the dreary protocols of gender studies.

It is unclear whether the grave problems with these books stemmed from the authors' wary job maneuvering in a depressed market or were imposed by an authoritarian academic apparatus of politically correct advisers and outside readers. But the result is a deplorable waste. What could and should have been enduring contributions to both scholarship and cultural criticism have been deeply damaged by the authors' rote recitation of theoretical clichés.

Margot Weiss, a product of the department of cultural anthropology and the women's studies program at Duke University, is an assistant professor of American studies and anthropology at Wesleyan University. In her absorbing portrait of San Francisco as "a queer Sodom by the sea," Weiss surveys the gradual transformation of BDSM from the "more outlaw" era of gay leathermen in Folsom Street bars of the pre-AIDS era to today's largely heterosexual scene in affluent Silicon Valley, where high-tech workers congregate at private parties or convivial "munches" at chain restaurants with convenient parking lots. During her three-year fieldwork, Weiss became an archivist for the Society of Janus, which was founded in San Francisco in 1974 as America's second BDSM-support group. (The first was the Eulenspiegel Society, founded three years earlier in New York.) She also enrolled in "Dungeon Monitor" training, where she learned safety guidelines for "play parties," including proper use of whips and floggers and the adoption of a "safe word" to terminate scenes.

Weiss's colorful cast of characters includes Lady Thendara and her husband, Latex Mustang, who spend virtually all their spare time and considerable income on an elaborate BDSM lifestyle. Mustang insists, "It's no different than owning a boat." We meet "Francesca, a white, bisexual pain slut bottom in her late 40s," and "heteroflexible" Lily, age 29, who "identifies as a bottom/sub." Uncle Abdul, an electrical engineer in his 60s, "identifies as a bi techno-sadist."

Weiss lists but avoids detailing BDSM practices, which range from the benign (spanking, "corsetry and waist training") to the grisly ("labial and scrotal inflation"). We also hear about "incest play" and the baffling "erotic vomiting." Weiss attended workshops in "Beginning Rope Bondage," "Hot Wax Play," and "Interrogation Scenes" (Spanish Inquisition, Salem witch trials, uniformed Nazis). Her "all-time favorite workshop title": "Tit Torture for an Uncertain World."

Equipment for BDSM activities can be acquired as pricey customized gear at specialty shops. Quality handcrafted floggers run from $150 to $300, while a zippered black-leather body bag goes for $1,395. But even ordinary objects, such as table-tennis paddles, can be adapted as "good pervertables." Home Depot is sometimes dubbed "Home Dungeon" for its tempting offerings, such as rope, eye bolts, and wooden paint stirrers, which we are told make "great, stingy paddles." The thrifty take note: rattan to make canes can be cheaply purchased in bulk at garden-supply stores.

A recurrent problem with Weiss's book is that, despite its claim to be merely descriptive, it is full of reflex judgments borrowed wholesale from the current ideology of gender studies, which has become an insular dogma with its own priesthood and god (Michel Foucault). Weiss does not trust her own fascinating material to generate ideas. She detours so often into nervous quotation of fashionable academics that she short-shrifts her 61 interview subjects, who are barely glimpsed except in a list at the back.

One feels the pressure on her to bang the drum of a pretentious theorizing for which she has little facility and perhaps no real sympathy. There are clunkers: "These binaries rely on the social construction of risk." And howlers: "In what follows, I unfold the thickness of such loadedness." Or this résumé of the circular thinking of Judith Butler, the long overrated doyenne of gender studies: "In Butler's work, intelligibility provides a horizon of recognition for subjectivity itself, within which all subjects are either recognizable or unrecognizable as subjects." Weiss speaks of her own "positionality" and "Foucauldian framework," but she seems unaware that Foucauldian analysis is based on Saussurean linguistics, a system of contested and indeed dubious validity for interpreting the untidy realm of physical experience. As for Butler, there are few signs in her work that she has yet done the systematic inquiry into basic anthropology and biology that academe should expect from theorists of gender.

Furthermore, Weiss is lured by the reflex Marxism of current academe into reducing everything to economics: "With its endless paraphernalia, BDSM is a prime example of late-capitalist sexuality"; BDSM is "a paradigmatic consumer sexuality." Or this mind-boggling assertion: "Late capitalism itself produces the transgressiveness of sex—its fantasized location as outside of or compensatory for alienated labor." Sex was never transgressive before capitalism? Tell that to the Hebrew captives in Babylon or to Roman moralists during the early Empire!

The constricted frame of reference of the gender studies milieu from which Weiss emerged is shown by her repeated slighting references to "U.S. social hierarchies." But without a comparative study of and allusion to *non*-American hierarchies, past and present, such remarks are facile and otiose. The collapse of scholarly standards in ideology-driven academe is sadly revealed by Weiss's failure, in her list of the 18 books of anthropology that most strongly contributed to her project, to cite any work published before 1984—as if the prior century of distinguished anthropology, with its bold documentation of transcultural sexual practices, did not exist. Gender-theory groupthink leads to bizarre formulations such as this, from Weiss's introduction: "SM performances are deeply tied to capitalist cultural formations." The preposterousness of that would have been obvious had Weiss ever dipped into the voluminous works of the Marquis de Sade, one of the most original and important writers of the past three centuries and a pivotal influence on Nietzsche. But incredibly, none of the three authors under review seem to have read a page of Sade. It is scandalous that the slick, game-playing Foucault (whose attempt to rival Nietzsche was an abysmal failure) has completely supplanted Sade, a mammoth cultural presence in the 1960s via Grove Press paperbacks that reprinted Simone de Beauvoir's seminal essay, "Must We Burn Sade?"

Weiss is so busy with superfluous citations that she ignores what her interviewees actually tell her when it doesn't fit her a priori system. Thus any references to religion or spirituality are passed by without comment. She also refuses to consider or inquire about any psychological aspect to her subjects' sexual proclivities, no matter how much pain is inflicted or suffered. She declares that she rejects the "etiological approach": any search for "the causation of or motivation for BDSM desires" would mean that "marginalized sexualities" must be "explained and diagnosed as individual deviations." To avoid any ripple in the smooth surface of liberal tolerance, therefore, flogging, cutting, branding, and the rest of the menu of consensual torture must be assumed to be meaning-free—no different than taking your coffee with cream or without. (These books approvingly quote BDSM players comparing what they do to extreme but blatantly nonsexual sports like rock climbing and sky diving.) Weiss's neutrality here would be more palatable if she were indeed merely recording or chronicling, but her own biases are palpably invested in her avoidance of religion and her moralistic stands on economics.

Staci Newmahr, an assistant professor of sociology at Buffalo State College, did her ethnographic research in a "loud, large Northeastern metropolis" that she mysteriously calls "Caeden." The city has five SM organizations, three public "play spaces," and three private dungeons for play parties. Newmahr went "deeply immersive" in Caeden: while informing everyone that she was a researcher, she also became a participant, taking the alias "Dakota" and logging over a hundred hours a week in the SM scene. (Newmahr prefers the term "SM" to "the newer and trendier" BDSM.) Members of the SM community in Caeden are less affluent than those in Weiss's Bay Area sample but just as overwhelmingly white. Newmahr did 20 "loosely structured" interviews, which included off-topic conversation. Her portraits are sharply observed and represent a significant contribution to contemporary sociology.

Newmahr captures how her subjects, even before they entered SM, viewed themselves as "outsiders" who lived "on the fringe of social acceptance." Most are overweight, but it's never remarked on. Several women are over six feet tall, generally a social disadvantage elsewhere. Newmahr gets answers from her subjects to questions about the past that Weiss never asked: some men are small-statured or have vivid, angry memories of being bullied at school. Newmahr notes the "pervasive social awkwardness" in the scene, the "ill-fitting, outdated clothing" and the women's lack of makeup and jewelry. The men often lack interest in sports and own cars of middling quality.

In describing her subjects' style of "blunt speaking" and boasting, as well as their disconcerting invasion of personal space in conversation, however, Newmahr does not mention social class, about which she says little in her book. I would hazard a guess that she was uncovering the difference between lower-middle-class and upper-middle-class manners—the latter characterizing the world she customarily inhabits as an academic. These fine distinctions are insufficiently observed in the United States, where liberal political discourse too often employs a simplistic dichotomy between rich and poor. Both Weiss and Newmahr observe how often their subjects' casual conversations focus on science fiction or computer software. But Newmahr shows superior deductive skills when she connects this to the Caeden community's "affinity for complicated techniques and well-made toys." Where Weiss sees only rank consumerism, Newmahr recognizes an operative aesthetic of "geekiness as cool."

Despite her wealth of assembled data, Newmahr still stumbles into the weeds of academic theory. We get "hermeneutic" this and "hegemonic" that and trip over showy obstacles like "discursive inaccessibility." There are empty phrases ("As Foucault illustrated so powerfully") as well as a lockstep parade of the usual suspects, like the automatically venerated Butler. Even more troublesome are Newmahr's semifictionalized sections, which she posits as intrinsic to the genre of "auto-ethnography": "The postmodern view of ethnography as a jointly constructed narrative rather than an accurate objective depiction of social reality has gained support in recent years." Her accounts are "not necessarily verbatim" but "edited or blended, resulting in representations not entirely true to time and space simultaneously"; they are "creative representations of authentic experiences."

But is this questionable practice defensible in scholarly terms? The postmodernist slide away from the search for factual truth undermines the entire raison d'être of universities and the professors who ought to serve them. It is cringe-making that students are being fed this postmodernist gruel: history is a narrative; every narrative is a fiction; objectivity is impossible, so who cares what's real and what's not? Newmahr declares, "All ethnographic work is on some level 'about' the ethnographer" (a claim that begs for refutation). Peculiarly, she then decides to exclude her own personal responses to her SM experiences because it might invite voyeurism. But she can't have it both ways, fictionalizing her material (inescapably "about" her) and yet arbitrarily concealing herself.

Where this diffidence becomes unsettling and even alarming is in Newmahr's graphic descriptions of scenes she witnessed or participated in. The first night she enters an SM club, she sees a woman in a nurse's uniform "quietly nailing a man's scrotum to a wooden board," as he "hissed and screamed." Newmahr was "taken aback" by this horrific spectacle but tells us nothing more.

Newmahr's refusal of comment on this activity, to which I would apply a term like "barbaric" (a concept evidently falling outside the anesthetized world of academic theory), becomes even more glaring when the object of abuse is herself. On one occasion, she lies on a bed in a deserted apartment, where a stranger straddles her and presses a thick cord on her throat until her breathing nearly stops; he smashes her in the face again and again with the back of his hand and draws a razor blade across her cheek. Except for a momentary panic at her isolation and potential danger, we learn nothing of her reaction. Newmahr's flat affect, always disconcerting, becomes positively chilling when she says of a sadist and masochist indulging in "edgeplay": "Only the bottom is risking her life, and only the top is risking a prison sentence."

Despite its defects, this book contains tantalizing pos-
sibilities for a more flexible approach to gender studies. At
times, Newmahr uses theater metaphors like "social scripts,"
derived from Erving Goffman, the great Canadian-American
sociologist whose work in such pioneering books as *The Pre-
sentation of Self in Everyday Life* (1959) was one of Foucault's
primary and deviously unacknowledged sources. Newmahr
intriguingly describes SM as "improvisational theater," where
"observers drift from scene to scene" and where the perform-
ers must act as if the audience is not there. But this excellent
train of thought is not followed or developed.

Like Weiss, Newmahr tries to evade making judgments:
she shies away from "the ultimately unhelpful questions about
whether SM is or is not deviant sex." Nevertheless, she comes
close to a breakthrough at the very end of her book, when quot-
ing a Caeden resident who sees SM play as a way "to connect
with the animalistic part of our beings." But because nature
and biology are erased from the Foucauldian worldview, with
its strict social constructionism, that hint is not followed up
on. Poststructuralism is myopically obsessed with modern
bourgeois society. It is hopelessly ignorant of prehistoric or
agrarian cultures, where tribal rituals monitored and invoked
the primitive forces of nature.

When she acutely declares that "issues of power are at the
core of SM play," Newmahr is unable to progress, because
the only power that exists for poststructuralism resides in
society—which every major religion teaches is limited and
evanescent. In the absence of knowledge of the historical origin and evolution of social hierarchies, Newmahr ends up with
strained conclusions—for instance, that in the structured play
of SM "the erotic is desexualized," which is absurd on the face
of it. Her own hunches are more reliable, as when she rightly
calls SM "a carnal experience"—without realizing she has bro-

ken a law of the claustrophobic Foucauldian universe, where nothing exists except refractions of language and where the body is merely a passive recipient of oppressive social power.

Danielle Lindemann, who earned her doctorate in sociology from Columbia University, is a research scholar at Vanderbilt University. *Dominatrix* has vibrant passages of sparkling writing that demonstrate Lindemann's talent and promise as a culture critic. Her personality charmingly surfaces even in the acknowledgments, where she hails the "giant, cheap margaritas" at the Dallas BBQ chain as "influential in the successful completion of this project." Her knack for compelling scene-setting is shown at the start of the very first chapter:

> One night, I realize I've accidentally stepped on a man rolled up in a carpet. We're at a Scene party in the basement of a restaurant in New York's East Village. I approach the bar and put my foot on what I assume is a step, when I hear a faint "Oof!" The man is laid out in front of the bar, fully submerged in the rug, his face peering out of a roughly cut hole. I step off and apologize, but I am immediately "corrected" by a nearby domme.
>
> "That's okay, sweetie—he likes it!" She proceeds to kick the carpet repeatedly and with great force in her platform boots, while the other people at the bar look on with a mixture of nonchalance and delight. The man in the rug beams the whole time. I return to the table where I've been sitting.
>
> "I just accidentally stepped on a guy rolled in a rug," I tell the group of people who've brought me to the party.
>
> "Carpet Guy's here?" one responds.

Lindemann adroitly positions herself as a respectful but bemused observer, like Alice in a perverse Wonderland. Unlike Weiss and Newmahr, she maintains her professional objectivity and attunement to ordinary social standards by preserving her outsider's stance and declining to become a participant in the world she is studying. Lindemann is brisk and discerning as she explores the world of professional dominatrixes ("pro-dommes"), mainly in New York but also in San Francisco. Pro-dommes, who call their work spaces "dungeons" or "houses" (short for "houses of pain"), are rarely "full service," that is, providing sex. Instead they cater to a broad range of tastes and desires, which Lindemann organizes into three types: "pain-producing dominant, non-pain-producing dominant, and fetishistic."

Requested scenarios include smothering (categorized with choking as "breath play"), mummification (encasing in plastic wrap and duct tape), infantilism (a man put in diapers), "splash" (playing with messy food like creamed corn or pies), animal transformation (a man becoming a puppy or pony), "French-maid servitude" (a man donning a maid's uniform to clean house), "prison/interrogation fantasies," and "secret-agent/hostage fantasies." Rarities reported by Lindemann include a "leprechaun fetishist" and a client "aroused by a Hillary Clinton mask."

The audacious voices of Lindemann's pro-dommes fairly leap off the page. These fierce women have a haughty sense of métier. "I will not recite dialogue," they proclaim on their websites. To bossy customer demands, one pro-domme replies, "*I* am dominant. *You* are submissive. You serve *me*." Another instantly rejects any client who says, "I want." She insists on "etiquette, protocols" and hangs up on callers who fail to show due respect. It is proper for prospective clients to begin, "Mistress, I want to serve you. My enjoyments are . . ."

Pro-dommes often call their payment a "tribute" rather than a fee, as if they were sovereign nations or celestial divinities. In written correspondence with Lindemann, some pro-dommes habitually capitalized "Me." What comes strongly across is the mystique surrounding pro-dommes, with their special expertise and their disdainful separation from the world of prostitution. The Internet, rather than magazines, has become the preferred advertising medium. One pro-domme says flatly, "Print is dead. Nobody who can afford to see me doesn't have a computer."

Another of Lindemann's disarming chapter openings: "I'm sitting in a basement dungeon in Queens, and the first thing I notice is the cheerleading outfit emblazoned with the word 'SLUT' hanging on the back of the door." What a marvelous book this would have made had Lindemann sustained that clear, engaging, reportorial style! But as in everything blighted by poststructuralism these days, we soon hit the obscurantist shallows. We hear about the "dialectical process," "instantiation," "discursive constitutions," and that dread phenomenon, "normative, gendered tropes." Insights about drag are credulously attributed to Butler that were basic to discussions 40 years ago of transvestism in Shakespeare's comedies and that were soon superseded by David Bowie's avant-garde experiments with androgyny in music and fashion.

As this book began to veer astray, I felt that Lindemann's mind was like a sleek yacht built for exhilarating grace and speed but commandeered by moldy tyrants for mundane use as a sluggish freighter. Her book is woefully burdened by the ugly junk she is forced to carry in this uncertain climate, where teaching jobs are so scarce. The very first paragraph of her acknowledgments shows what has happened to this and countless other academic books: Lindemann effusively thanks a Princeton professor "for giving me the idea that Bourdieu may have had something to say about pro-dommes' claims to artistic purity." Well, the dull Pierre Bourdieu, another pumped-up idol forced on American undergraduates these days, had little useful to say about that or anything else about art, beyond his parochial grounding in French literature and culture. (No, Bourdieu did not discover the class-based origin of taste: that was established long ago by others, above all the Marxist scholar Arnold Hauser in his magisterial 1951 study, *The Social History of Art*.) The leaden Bourdieu chapters bring Lindemann's momentum to a humiliating halt and effectively destroy the reach of this valuable book beyond the dusty corridors of academe.

Lindemann stays cautiously neutral about the acrimonious, long-running debate among feminists over whether sado-masochism is progressive or reactionary. But she so distracts herself with paying due homage to academic shibboleths that she doesn't pursue her own leads—as when a San Francisco pro-domme describes what she does as "performance art." Lindemann should have investigated the genre of performance art as it developed from the 1960s and '70s on (thanks to Joseph Beuys, Yoko Ono, Eleanor Antin, and Bowie), which would have given her a superb cultural analogue. She notes pro-dommes' ability to "create environments" and separately draws a very striking parallel to the Stanislavski theory of actors' total identification with their characters. But neither of these exciting ideas is fleshed out.

Buried in a footnote at the back is a glimmer of what could have made a sensational book: Lindemann says that pro-dominance "may have more in common with other theatrical pursuits than with prostitution." "I was recently struck to find, during a visit to the Barnard College library," she writes, "that the books about strippers were sandwiched between texts relating to pantomime and vaudeville, while the texts about prostitutes inhabited a different aisle." Yes, modern burlesque was in fact born in the 1930s and '40s in vaudeville houses that had gone seedy because of competition from movies. Lindemann was poised to place pro-dommes' work into theater history—a tremendous advance that did not happen.

The lamentable gaps in the elite education that Lindemann received at Princeton and Columbia are exposed in her two-page "Appendix C: Historical Context," which is an unmitigated disaster. Two millennia since ancient Rome are surveyed in the blink of an eye, and we are confidently told, on the basis of no evidence, that the professional dominatrix is "a fundamentally postmodern social invention." Sade and Leopold von Sacher-Masoch (author of the 1870 SM novel *Venus in Furs*) are mentioned in passing, but only via an academic book published less than a decade ago. There is no reference to the immense prostitution industry in nineteenth-century Paris, where flagellation was called *"le vice anglais"* (the English vice) because of its popularity among brothel-haunting Englishmen abroad.

All three books under review betray a dismaying lack of general cultural knowledge—most crucially of so central a work as Pauline Réage's infamous novel of sadomasochistic fantasy, *Story of O*, which was published in 1954 and made into a moody 1975 movie with a groundbreaking Euro-synth score by Pierre Bachelet. The long list of items missing from the research backgrounds and thought processes of these books is topped by Luis Buñuel's classic film *Belle de Jour* (1967), in which Catherine Deneuve dreamily plays a bored, affluent Parisian wife moonlighting in a fetish brothel. Today's formalized scenarios of bondage and sadomasochism belong to a tradition, but poststructuralism, with its compulsive fragmentations and dematerializations, is incapable of recognizing cultural transmission over time.

These three authors have not been trained to be alert to historical content or implications. For example, they never notice the medieval connotations of the word "dungeon" or reflect on the Victorian associations of corsets and French maids (lauded even by Oscar Wilde's Lady Bracknell). It never dawns on Weiss to ask why a San Francisco slave auction is called a "Byzantine Bazaar," nor does Newmahr wonder why the lumber to which she is cuffed for flogging is called a "St. Andrew's cross."

To analyze the challenging extremes of contemporary sexual expression, one would need to begin in the 1790s with Sade, Gothic novels, and the Romantic femme fatale, who becomes the woman with a whip in Swinburne's poetry and Aubrey Beardsley's drawings and turns into the vampires and sphinxes of late-nineteenth-century Symbolist art, leading directly to movie vamps from Theda Bara to Sharon Stone. And where is Weimar Berlin in these three books? Christopher Isherwood's autobiographical *The Berlin Stories*, set in a doomed playground of sexual experimentation and decadent excess, was transformed into a play, a musical, and a major movie, *Cabaret* (1972), which has had a profound and enduring cultural influence (as on Madonna's videos and tours). The brilliant Helmut Newton, born in Weimar Berlin, introduced its sadomasochistic sensibility and fetish regalia to high-fashion photography, starting in the 1960s. Weimar's sadomasochism and transvestism as portrayed in Luchino Visconti's film *The Damned* (1969) helped inspire British glam rock. Nazi sadomasochism was also memorably re-dramatized by Dirk Bogarde and Charlotte Rampling in Liliana Cavani's *The Night Porter* (1974).

Where is the Velvet Underground? The menacing song,

"Venus in Furs," based on Sacher-Masoch's novel, was a high-light of the group's debut 1967 album. On tour with the Velvets that same year, Mary Woronov did a dominatrix whip dance with the poet Gerard Malanga in Andy Warhol's psychedelic multimedia show, the Exploding Plastic Inevitable. Other SM motifs have woven in and out of pop music: a brutal bondage billboard on Los Angeles's Sunset Strip for the Rolling Stones' 1976 album, *Black and Blue*, was taken down after fierce feminist protests; dominatrix gear and attitude were affected onstage by Grace Jones, Prince, Pat Benatar, and heavy-metal "hair" groups like Mötley Crüe.

I was very disappointed to see Xaviera Hollander go unmentioned. That vivacious Dutch madame's feisty memoir, *The Happy Hooker* (1971), detailing her bondage and fetish services, sold 15 million copies worldwide. But there is no excuse whatever for the absence in these books of Tom of Finland, whose prolific drawings of priapic musclemen formed the aesthetic of gay leathermen following World War Two. And the most shocking omission of them all: Tom's devotee Robert Mapplethorpe, whose luminous homoerotic photos of the sadomasochistic underworld sparked a national crisis over arts funding in the 1980s. Yet our three authors and their army of advisers found plenty of time to parse the meanderings of every minor gender theorist who stirred in the past 20 years.

These books never manage to explain sadomasochism or sexual fantasies of any kind. In addition to its rejection of biology, poststructuralism has no psychology, because without a concept of the coherent, independent individual (rather than a mass of ironically dissolving subjectivities), there is no self to see. One of the numerous flaws in Foucault's system (as I argued in my attack on poststructuralism, "Junk Bonds and Corporate Raiders," published in *Arion* in 1991) is his inability

to understand symbolic thought—which is why poststructuralism is such a clumsy tool for approaching art. But without
a grasp of symbolism, one cannot understand the dream process, poetic imagination, or the ritual theater of sadomasochism, with its symbolic psychodramas. Freud's analysis of guilt
and repression, as well as his theory of "family romance,"
remains indispensable, in my view, for understanding sex
in the modern Western world. Surely current SM paradigms
carry some psychological baggage from childhood, imprinted
by parents as our first, dimly felt authority figures.

The mystery of sadomasochism was one of the chief
issues I investigated in *Sexual Personae* (Yale University
Press, 1990). My interest in the subject began with my childhood puzzlement over lurid scenes of martyrdom in Catholic iconography, notably a polychrome plaster statue in my
baptismal church of a pretty St. Sebastian pierced by arrows.
I traced the theme everywhere from flagellation in ancient
fertility cults through Michelangelo's neoplatonic bondage
fantasy, *Dying Slave,* to the surreal poems of Emily Dickinson, whom I called "Amherst's Madame de Sade." I speak
simply as a student of sexuality: I have had no direct contact
of any kind with sadomasochism—except that I once had an
author photo taken in front of a purple velvet curtain in the
waiting room of a dungeon in a midtown Manhattan office
building (which may be the very one where Lindemann's book
begins).

In researching sadomasochism, I did not begin with
a priori assumptions or with the desire to placate academic
moguls. I let the evidence suggest the theories. My conclusion, after wide reading in anthropology and psychology, was
that sadomasochism is an archaic ritual form that descends
from prehistoric nature cults and that erupts in sophisticated "late" phases of culture, when a civilization has become

too large and diffuse and is starting to weaken or decline. I state in *Sexual Personae* that "sex is a far darker power than feminism has admitted," and that its "primitive urges" have never been fully tamed: "My theory is that whenever sexual freedom is sought or achieved, sadomasochism will not be far behind."

Sadomasochism's punitive hierarchical structure is ultimately a religious longing for order, marked by ceremonies of penance and absolution. Its rhythmic abuse of the body, which can indeed become pathological if pushed to excess, is paradoxically a reinvigoration, a trancelike magical realignment with natural energies. Hence the symbolic use of leather—primitive animal hide—for whips and fetish clothing. By redefining the boundaries of the body, SM limits and disciplines the overexpanded consciousness of "late" phases, which are plagued by free-floating doubts and anxieties.

What is to be done about the low scholarly standards in the analysis of sex? A map of reform is desperately needed. Current discourse in gender theory is amateurishly shot through with the logical fallacy of the appeal to authority, as if we have been flung back to medieval theology. For all their putative leftism, gender theorists routinely mimic and flatter academic power with the unctuous obsequiousness of flunkies in the Vatican Curia.

First of all, every gender studies curriculum must build biology into its program; without knowledge of biology, gender studies slides into propaganda. Second, the study of ancient tribal and agrarian cultures is crucial to end the present narrow focus on modern capitalist society. Third, the cynical disdain for religion that permeates high-level academe must end. (I am speaking as an atheist.) It is precisely the blindness to spiritual quest patterns that has most disabled the three books under review.

The exhausted poststructuralism pervading American universities is abject philistinism masquerading as advanced thought. Everywhere, young scholars labor in bondage to a corrupt and incestuous academic establishment. But these "mind-forg'd manacles" (in William Blake's phrase) can be broken in an instant. All it takes is the will to be free.

25

GENDER ROLES: NATURE OR NURTURE

CAMILLE PAGLIA V. JANE FLAX

CAMILLE PAGLIA, OPENING STATEMENT: Nature or nurture? The question informs many pressing issues of our time—from the origins of criminality to the legitimacy of intelligence tests to definitions of gender. The quarrel over nature and nurture can be traced to Romanticism in the late eighteenth century, when Jean-Jacques Rousseau and his follower, the poet William Wordsworth, defined nature as good and society as bad, the source of oppressive fictions that cloud our thought and distort our behavior. Rousseau is ultimately responsible for the approach still current among postmodernists and poststructuralists today, who believe that we are born blank slates and that prejudices, including normative gender assumptions, are "inscribed" upon us by social pressures conveyed through arbitrary and slippery verbal constructs.

My own thinking on this issue of innate versus

[Janus Forum Debate, Political Theory Institute, American University, Washington, D.C., October 8, 2013] learned traits is heavily indebted to Romanticism. But I take the Late Romantic view, associated with mid- to late-nineteenth-century Decadents like Charles Baudelaire and Oscar Wilde, who saw nature as a beautiful but tyrannically mechanical force that we are obligated to resist and defy through the ever-evolving permutations of culture. The precursor in this strain of perverse Romanticism was not Rousseau but the Marquis de Sade, whose voluminous writings had vast influence, including on Nietzsche, whom Michel Foucault, the deity of poststructuralism, claimed as his model.

I have argued, as in my first book, *Sexual Personae*, which was an expansion of my doctoral dissertation, that the historical and mythological identification of woman with nature is true—based on biological facts that we may find unpalatable in these emancipated times but that cannot be wished away or amended as of yet by science. But arriving at that highly controversial position was the result of a long process of observation, investigation, and reflection. Indeed, during my adolescence in upstate New York, I had angrily held a completely opposite point of view, which I was eventually forced to relinquish after the extensive research I did into both biology and anthropology for my dissertation.

I had been raised as a baby-boomer during the stiflingly conformist 1950s, when gender roles were rigidly polarized. Men were men, and women were women, with a draconian dress code and rules of conduct for each gender. Much later, I became more sympathetic to the longing for a comforting stability on the part of our parents' generation, who had endured the traumatic stresses and sacrifices of the Depression and World War Two. But the options for girls in the 1950s were very limited. They were expected to date and become wives and mothers, and there were few suitable careers for women aside from that of secretary, public-school teacher, or Roman Catholic nun. The atmosphere was claustrophobic for any girl with ambition or a spirit of competition, which was viewed as grossly unfeminine.

A biological paradigm certainly shaped those attitudes. For example, girls were constantly given dolls—on the assumption that girls needed and welcomed exercise of their innate nurturing instincts. I myself regarded this shower of dolls as a plague or infestation. I wanted swords and spears and knights in armor! And I telegraphed my rebellion by a series of transgender Halloween costumes that were highly eccentric for children in the 1950s.

Biological assumptions were enforced at school. Girls were discouraged from taking drum lessons in music class on the presumption that they did not have the strength to wield the sticks or carry a snare drum across the football field. (Thus I was stuck with the clarinet, which I played very badly for eight years in the school band until graduation.) In gym class, girls were thought to be too fragile for extreme exercise. Hence we were not allowed to play full-court basketball but had to stop (with great difficulty) at the center line and pass off the ball to another player on the other side. So if, as a guard, I stole the ball at one end of the court, I couldn't bomb down to the other end to make a basket. These paternalistic protections were infuriating.

Biological doctrine was explicit in an incident at my elementary school, when we fifth-grade girls got in a rumble with the sixth-grade girls at recess (from which I emerged in defeat with a chipped tooth). In grounding me for two weeks, my classroom teacher sternly reprimanded me for having punched another girl in the stomach, a grave and dangerous offense because, I was told, I could have damaged her delicate reproductive organs—a claim which, over time, seemed medically questionable.

Rescue from this gender hell came through *research*—my mantra! In 1961, just before entering high school, I saw an article about Amelia Earhart in the local newspaper, which propelled me into an obsessive three-year project delving into her life and times. Exploring the old volumes of decaying newspapers and magazines in the sooty basement of the Syracuse public library, I discovered an entirely different era, the 1920s and '30s, when first-wave feminism had inspired an extraordinary series of women achievers in the public realm—from Earhart herself to Dorothy Parker, Dorothy Thompson, Lillian Hellman, Margaret Bourke-White, Clare Boothe Luce, and Katharine Hepburn, whom I had already spotted on then-neglected old movies on late-night TV. It was a revelation. It seemed to prove that standards of gender are mutable and dependent on social conditions. Later, I would understand more about the larger forces at work in that period, above all a rebellion against authority that energized the impudent Jazz Age after the institutional failures that led to the catastrophe of the First World War. The adventurous careerism of those singular women was in many cases a calculated reversal of Victorian conventions, which had exalted prudery and propriety and sanctified motherhood.

However, throughout the early to mid-1960s, I was simultaneously observing the complex process of puberty in myself and my friends, both male and female, and also the operations of pregnancy, childbirth, and infant care among my extended family and others. There seemed to me significant, troubling, and even intractable issues in human physiology over which we have little or no control. Hence the relationship between nature and nurture was becoming increasingly problematic to me. My earlier dismissive attitude toward biology was proving untenable.

By the time second-wave feminism began in 1966, with Betty Friedan's co-founding of the National Organization for Women, I found myself, as a college student, already out of sync with the views of most feminists. The situation worsened in graduate school, where, at a 1970 feminist conference held at the Yale Law School, I had a disillusioning close encounter with the celebrity feminists Kate Millett and Rita Mae Brown. Any appeal to biology was denounced as reactionary heresy. Passions ran high: in 1973, as a young teacher in Vermont, I nearly came to blows with a table of early academic feminists in Albany when I casually alluded to a hormonal element in sex differences. They unanimously declared that I had been "brainwashed" and hoodwinked by generations of sexist male scientists. Hormones, in their view, played no role whatever in human life. It was not simply that they were questioning hormones' level of impact on personality and behavior; they were surreally denying the very existence of hormones. I felt as if I had fallen down a rabbit hole in *Alice in Wonderland*.

Women's studies programs were rushed into existence in the 1970s partly because of national pressure to add more women to faculties that were often embarrassingly all-male. Administrators diverting funds to these new programs were less concerned with maintaining scholarly rigor than with solving a prickly public relations problem. Hence women's studies was from the start flash-frozen at that early stage of ideology, which might be described as militant social environmentalism. In my view, biology and endocrinology should have been built as required courses into the curriculum of every women's studies program in the country. Theorizing about gender must begin from that foundation, even if biology is eventually minimized or rejected altogether. Rather than encouraging scholarly inquiry and free thought, women's studies programs began in an a priori way from an already crystallized agenda. No deviation was permitted from the party line, which was that all gender differences are due to patriarchy, with its monolithic enslavement and abuse of women by men.

The arrival of more sophisticated approaches, such as poststructuralist French feminism in the mid-1970s and "difference" feminism in the early '80s, brought little change, because both skirted biological facts or omitted them altogether. Male academics, sensing which way the wind was blowing, were reluctant to challenge the new power structure and shrank back out of fear of being labeled sexist and retrograde. History will not be kind to their timidity and cowardice. There was a kind of contemptuous indifference in it—"Let the women make their own sandbox and play in it." Thus the women's studies and later gender studies curriculum grew autonomously, battening on itself and creating its own insular canon, protected from challenge from outside voices and even from dissident feminists like myself.

But the real-life consequences of this wholesale exclusion of biology from contemporary social thought continue to multiply. For example, second-wave feminism had been habitually guilty of a callous and to me counterproductive denigration of motherhood. The tone for this was set by Betty Friedan's bestselling 1963 exposé, *The Feminine Mystique,* a somewhat sensationalistic and suspiciously unsourced portrait of the miserable lives of bored, affluent suburban housewives. Second-wave feminism glorified the career woman and dismissed the stay-at-home mom as a traitor to the cause. This eventually made Friedan herself uncomfortable, and she vainly tried to steer feminism back toward the concerns of mainstream women. She suffered an acrimonious split from NOW, partly over what she dubbed the "lavender menace"—that is, radical young lesbians taking over the women's movement and alienating it, she believed, from the general population.

What I conclude from my own research is that despite the transformation in gender roles at certain colorful moments in history, such as Shakespeare's London, when Puritan preachers inveighed against a fad for cross-dressing, there is eventually and predictably a return to a polarized norm. Gender experimentation, while very intriguing to us today, has usually remained an exceptional practice that was not embraced by the majority in any given society. Finally, a volatility in gender roles is usually symptomatic of tensions and anxieties about larger issues. That is, sexual identity becomes a primary focus only when other forms of identification and affiliation—religious, national, tribal, familial—break down. Furthermore, while androgyny or transgender fluidity is currently regarded as progressive, such phenomena have at times helped trigger a severe counter-reaction that could last for centuries. For example, the permissiveness of imperial Rome, with its empty, ritualistic religion, created an ethical vacuum soon filled by a massive spiritual movement from the eastern Mediterranean—Christianity, which two millennia later remains a powerful global presence. Elite Romans vacationing in Pompeii or Capri undoubtedly felt that their relaxed, hedonistic world would go on forever.

The overflow of gender theory into real life can conceal developing problems. For example, what are the long-term consequences of the disruption of biologic patterns in our imposing on young women a male-centered career path that occupies women's optimal years of fertility with a prolonged sequence of undergraduate and postgraduate education? By the time our most accomplished young women are ready to marry, they may be in their 30s, when pregnancy carries more risks and when their male peers suddenly have an abundant marital choice of fresher, more nubile girls in their 20s. The TV series *Sex and the City*, which was a huge surprise hit internationally as well, dramatized the quandary of young career women as an unsettling mix of comedy and tragedy.

I consider it completely irresponsible that public schools offer sex education but no systematic guidance to adolescent girls, who should be thinking about how they want to structure their future lives: do they want children, and if so, when should that be scheduled, with the advantages and disadvantages of each option laid out. Because of the stubborn biologic burden of pregnancy and childbirth, these are issues that will always affect women more profoundly than men. Starting a family early has its price for an ambitious young woman, a career hiatus that may be difficult to overcome. On the other hand, the reward of being with one's children in their formative years, instead of farming out that fleeting and irreplaceable experience to day care centers or nannies, has an inherent emotional and perhaps spiritual value that has been lamentably ignored by second-wave feminism.

Right now in the United States, young mothers are automatically regarded as déclassé; they are pitied for "wasting" their talents. This animus, shot through with social snobbery, must end. Colleges and universities that claim to support women's rights must adapt to a more humane recognition of biologic needs and patterns. The presence of mothers—or married students in general—in the classroom would be of enormous benefit in bringing campus discourse about gender back to reality. Campuses should provide and promote flexible programs of part-time study with long leaves of absence permitted for parents to complete their degrees over many years or even decades.

Similarly, our present system of primary and secondary education should be stringently reviewed for its confinement of boys to a prison-like setting that

curtails their energy and requires ideological renun-
ciation of male traits. By the time young middle-class
men emerge from college these days, they have been
smoothed and ground down to obedient clones. The
elite universities have become police states where
an army of deans, subdeans, and faculty committees
monitor and sanction male undergraduate speech
and behavior if it violates the establishment feminist
code. The now routine surveillance of students' dating
lives on American campuses would be unthinkable in
Europe. Campus gender theorists can merrily wave
their anti-male flag, when every man within ten miles
has fled underground.

In conclusion, I do believe that gender roles are
malleable and dynamically shaped by culture. However, the frequency with which gender roles return
to a polarized norm, as well as the startling similar-
ity of gender roles in societies separated by vast dis-
tances of time and space, does suggest that there is
something fundamentally constant in gender that is
grounded in concrete facts. A modern democracy,
based on concepts of individual liberties, has an obligation to protect all varieties of personal expression.
But the majority of earthlings do seem to find clear
gender roles helpful compass points in the often conflicted formation of identity. Gender questioning has
always been and will remain the prerogative of artists
and shamans, gifted but alienated beings.

Extravaganzas of gender experimentation sometimes precede cultural collapse, as they certainly did
in Weimar Germany. Like late Rome, America too is
an empire distracted by games and leisure pursuits.
Now as then, there are forces aligning outside the

borders, scattered fanatical hordes where the cult of heroic masculinity still has tremendous force. I close with this question: is a nation whose elite education is increasingly predicated on the neutralization of gender prepared to defend itself against that growing challenge?

26

ARE MEN OBSOLETE?

RESOLVED: MEN ARE OBSOLETE

PRO: HANNA ROSIN, MAUREEN DOWD

CON: CAITLIN MORAN, CAMILLE PAGLIA

CAMILLE PAGLIA, OPENING STATEMENT: If men are obsolete, then women will soon be extinct—unless we rush down that ominous Brave New World path where females will clone themselves by parthenogenesis, as famously do Komodo dragons, hammerhead sharks, and pit vipers.

A peevish, grudging rancor against men has been one of the most unpalatable and unjust features of second- and third-wave feminism. Men's faults, failings, and foibles have been seized on and magnified into gruesome bills of indictment. Ideologue professors at our leading universities indoctrinate impressionable undergraduates with perilously fact-free theories alleging that gender is an arbitrary, oppressive fiction with no basis in biology.

[The Munk Debate, Roy Thomson Hall, Toronto, November 15, 2013. Published by Time.com, December 16, 2013, and by the House of Anansi Press in *Are Men Obsolete?: The Munk Debate on Gender*, Toronto, 2014]

Is it any wonder that so many high-achieving young women, despite all the happy talk about their academic success, find themselves in the early stages of their careers in chronic uncertainty or anxiety about their prospects for an emotionally fulfilled private life? When an educated culture routinely denigrates masculinity and manhood, then women will be perpetually stuck with *boys*, who have no incentive to mature or to honor their commitments. And without strong men as models either to embrace—or for dissident lesbians to resist—women will never attain a centered and profound sense of themselves *as* women.

From my long observation, which predates the sexual revolution, this remains a serious problem afflicting Anglo-American society, with its Puritan residue. In France, Italy, Spain, Latin America, and Brazil, in contrast, many ambitious professional women seem to have found a formula for asserting power and authority in the workplace while still projecting sexual allure and even glamour. This is the true feminine mystique, which cannot be taught but flows from an instinctive recognition of sexual differences. In today's punitive atmosphere of sentimental propaganda about gender, the sexual imagination has understandably fled into the alternate world of online pornography, where the rude but exhilarating forces of primitive nature rollick unconstrained by religious or feminist moralism.

It was always the proper mission of feminism to attack and reconstruct the ossified social practices that had led to wide-ranging discrimination against women. But surely it was and is possible for a progressive reform movement to achieve that without stereotyping, belittling, or demonizing men. History must be seen clearly and fairly: obstructive traditions arose not from men's hatred or enslavement of women but from the natural division of labor that had developed over thousands of years during the agrarian period and that once immensely benefited and protected women, permitting them to remain at the hearth to care for helpless infants and children.

Over the past century, it was labor-saving appliances, invented by men and spread by capitalism, that liberated women from daily drudgery. What is troubling about too many books and articles by feminist journalists in the United States, despite their putative leftism, is an implicit privileging of bourgeois values and culture. The particular focused, clerical, and managerial skills of the upper-middle-class elite are presented as the highest desideratum, the ultimate evolutionary point of humanity. Yes, there has been a gradual transition from an industrial to a service-sector economy in which women, who generally prefer a safe, clean, quiet work environment, thrive.

Hanna Rosin's triumphalism [in her book, *The End of Men*] about women's gains seems startlingly premature, as when she says of the sagging fortunes of today's working-class couples that they and we had "reached the end of a hundred thousand years of human history and the beginning of a new era, and there was no going back." This sweeping appeal to history somehow overlooks history's far darker lessons about the cyclic rise and fall of civilizations, which as they become more complex and interconnected also become more vulnerable to collapse. The earth is littered with the ruins of empires that believed they were eternal.

After the next inevitable apocalypse, men will be desperately needed again! Oh, sure, there will be the odd gun-toting Amazonian survivalist gal, who can rustle game out of the bush and feed her flock, but most women and children will be expecting men to scrounge for food and water and to defend the home turf. Indeed, men are absolutely indispensable right now, invisible as it is to most feminists, who seem blind to the infrastructure that makes their own work lives possible. It is overwhelmingly men who do the dirty, dangerous work of building roads, pouring concrete, laying bricks, tarring roofs, hanging electric wires, excavating natural gas and sewage lines, cutting and clearing trees, and bulldozing the landscape for housing developments. It is men who heft and weld the giant steel beams that frame our office buildings, and it is men who do the hair-raising work of insetting and sealing the finely tempered plate-glass windows of skyscrapers 50 stories tall.

Every day along the Delaware River in Philadelphia, one can watch the passage of vast oil tankers and towering cargo ships arriving from all over the world. These stately colossi are loaded, steered, and off-loaded by *men*. The modern economy, with its vast production and distribution network, is a male epic, in which women have found a productive role—but women were not its author. Surely, modern women are strong enough now to give credit where credit is due!

27

PUT THE SEX BACK IN SEX ED

WHEN PUBLIC SCHOOLS REFUSE TO ACKNOWLEDGE GENDER DIFFERENCES, WE BETRAY BOYS AND GIRLS ALIKE

Fertility is the missing chapter in sex education. Sobering facts about women's declining fertility after their 20s are being withheld from ambitious young women, who are propelled along a career track devised for men.

The refusal by public schools' sex-education programs to acknowledge gender differences is betraying both boys and girls. The genders should be separated for sex counseling. It is absurd to avoid the harsh reality that boys have less to lose from casual serial sex than do girls, who risk pregnancy and whose future fertility can be compromised by disease. Boys need lessons in basic ethics and moral reasoning about sex (for example, not taking advantage of intoxicated dates), while girls must learn to distinguish sexual compliance from popularity.

Above all, girls need life-planning advice. Too often, sex education defines pregnancy as a pathology, for which the cure is abortion. Adolescent girls must think deeply about their ultimate aims and desires. If they want both children and a career, they should decide whether to have children early or late. There are pros, cons, and trade-offs for each choice.

Unfortunately, sex education in the United States is a crazy quilt of haphazard programs. A national conversation is urgently needed for curricular standardization and public transparency. The present system is too vulnerable to political pressures from both the left and the right—and students are trapped in the middle.

Currently, 22 states and the District of Columbia mandate sex education but leave instructional decisions to school districts. Sex-ed teachers range from certified health educators to volunteers and teenage "peer educators" with minimal training. That some instructors may import their own sexually permissive biases is evident from the sporadic scandals about inappropriate use of pornographic materials or websites.

The modern campaign for sex education began in 1912 with a proposal by the National Education Association for classes in "sexual hygiene" to control sexually transmitted diseases like syphilis. During the AIDS crisis of the 1980s, Surgeon General C. Everett Koop called for sex education starting in third grade. In the 1990s, sex educators turned their focus to teenage pregnancy in inner-city communities.

Sex education has triggered recurrent controversy, partly because it is seen by religious conservatives as an instrument of secular cultural imperialism, undermining moral values. It's time for liberals to admit that there is some truth to this and that public schools should not promulgate any ideology. The liberal response to conservatives' demand for abstinence-only sex education has been to condemn the imposition of "fear and shame" on young people. But perhaps a bit more self-preserving fear and shame might be helpful in today's hedonistic, media-saturated environment.

My generation of baby-boom girls boldly rebelled against the cult of virginity of the Doris Day 1950s, but we left chaos in our wake. Young people are now bombarded with premature sexual images and messages. Adolescent girls, routinely dressing in seductive ways, are ill-prepared to negotiate the sexual attention they attract. Sex education has become incoherent because of its own sprawling agenda. It should be broken into component parts, whose professionalism could be better assured.

First, anatomy and reproductive biology belong in general biology courses taught in middle school by qualified science teachers. Every aspect of physiology, from puberty to menopause, should be covered. Students deserve a cool, clear, objective voice about the body, rather than the smarmy, feel-good chatter that now infests sex-ed workbooks.

Second, certified health educators, who advise children about washing their hands to avoid colds, should discuss sexually transmitted diseases at the middle-school or early-high-school level. But while information about condoms must be provided, it is not the place of public schools to distribute condoms, as is currently done in the Boston, New York, and Los Angeles school districts. Condom distribution should be left to hospitals, clinics, and social service agencies.

Similarly, public schools have no business listing the varieties of sexual gratification, from masturbation to oral and anal sex, although health educators should nonjudgmentally answer student questions about the health implications of such practices. The issue of homosexuality is a charged one. In my view, anti-bullying campaigns, however laudable, should not stray into political endorsement of homosexuality. While students must be free to create gay-identified groups, the schools themselves should remain neutral and allow society to evolve on its own.

28

IT'S TIME TO LET
TEENAGERS DRINK AGAIN

THE AGE-21 RULE PUSHES KIDS TOWARD PILLS
AND OTHER ANTISOCIAL BEHAVIOR

The National Minimum Drinking Age Act, passed by Congress 30 years ago this July, is a gross violation of civil liberties and must be repealed. It is absurd and unjust that young Americans can vote, marry, enter contracts, and serve in the military at 18 but cannot buy an alcoholic drink in a bar or restaurant. The age-21 rule sets the United States apart from all other advanced Western nations and lumps it with small or repressive countries like Sri Lanka, Pakistan, Indonesia, Qatar, Oman, and the United Arab Emirates.

Congress was stampeded into this puritanical law by Mothers Against Drunk Driving, who with all good intentions wrongly intruded into an area of personal choice exactly as did the hymn-singing nineteenth-century temperance crusaders, typified by Carry Nation smashing beer barrels with her hatchet. Temperance fanaticism eventually triumphed and gave us 14 years of Prohibition. That in turn spawned the crime syndicates for booze smuggling, laying the groundwork for today's global drug trade. Thanks a lot, Carry!

[*Time*, May 19, 2014]

Now that marijuana regulations have been liberalized in Colorado, it's time to strike down this dictatorial national law. Government is not our nanny. The decrease in drunk-driving deaths in recent decades is at least partly attributable to more uniform seat-belt use and a strengthening of DWI penalties. Today, furthermore, there are many other causes of traffic accidents, such as the careless use of cell phones or prescription drugs like Ambien—implicated in the recent trial and acquittal of Kerry Kennedy for driving while impaired.

Learning how to drink responsibly is a basic lesson in growing up—as it is in wine-drinking France or in Germany, with its family-oriented beer gardens and festivals. Wine was built into my own Italian-American upbringing, where children were given sips of my grandfather's homemade wine. This civilized practice descends from antiquity. Beer was a nourishing food in Egypt and Mesopotamia, and wine was identified with the life force in Greece and Rome: *In vino veritas* (in wine, truth). Wine as a sacred symbol of unity and regeneration remains in the Christian Communion service. Virginia Woolf wrote that wine with a fine meal lights a "subtle and subterranean glow, which is the rich yellow flame of rational intercourse."

What the cruel 1984 law did is deprive young people of safe spaces where they could happily drink cheap beer, socialize, chat, and flirt in a free but controlled public environment. Hence in the 1980s we immediately got the scourge of crude binge drinking at campus fraternity keg parties, cut off from the adult world. Women in that boorish free-for-all were suddenly fighting off date rape. Club drugs—ecstasy, methamphetamine, ketamine (a veterinary tranquilizer)—surged at raves for teenagers and on the gay-male circuit scene.

Alcohol relaxes, facilitates interaction, inspires ideas, and promotes humor and hilarity. Used in moderation, it is quickly flushed from the system, with excess punished by a hangover. But deadening pills, such as today's massively overprescribed anti-depressants, linger in the body and brain and may have unrecognized long-term side effects. Those toxic chemicals, often manufactured by shadowy firms abroad, have been worrisomely present in a recent uptick of unexplained suicides and massacres. Half of the urban professional class in the United States seems doped on meds these days.

As a libertarian, I support the decriminalization of marijuana, but there are many problems with pot. From my observation, pot may be great for jazz musicians and Beat poets, but it saps energy and willpower and can produce physiological feminization in men. Also, it is difficult to measure the potency of plant-derived substances like pot. With brand-name beer or liquor, however, purchased doses have exactly the same strength and purity from one continent to another, with no fear of contamination by dangerous street additives like PCP.

Exhilaration, ecstasy, and communal vision are the gifts of Dionysus, god of wine. Alcohol's enhancement of direct face-to-face dialogue is precisely what is needed by today's technologically agile generation, magically interconnected yet strangely isolated by social media. Clumsy hardcore sexting has sadly supplanted simple hanging out over a beer at a buzzing dive. By undermining the art of conversation, the age-21 law has also had a disastrous effect on our arts and letters, with their increasing dullness and mediocrity. This tyrannical infantilizing of young Americans must stop!

29

CLIQUISH, TUNNEL-VISION INTOLERANCE AFFLICTS TOO MANY FEMINISTS

INTERVIEW WITH DEBORAH COUGHLIN, *FEMINIST TIMES*

When the *Daily Mail* described our interviewee as a "dissident feminist" last December we knew we had to talk to this outsider of mainstream feminism, professor and writer Camille Paglia. I wanted to know why it's not easy to slot her into a "camp," what we can learn from her dissidence, and whether, looking back, she would consider acting differently in the public sphere. Has Paglia mellowed with age? Erm, that would be a big, bellowing NO!

The Daily Mail *described you as a "dissident feminist" and then went on to list a series of counterintuitive opinions you are reported as having. Why is it important for a feminist to be "dissident"? Do you ever play devil's advocate, and do we need feminists who are "controversial"?*

I am a dissident because my system of beliefs, worked out over the past five decades, has been repeatedly attacked, defamed, and rejected by feminist leaders and their acolytes across a wide spectrum, both in and out of academe. This punitive style of mob ostracism began from the very start of second-wave feminism, when Betty Friedan was pushed out of the National Organization for Women by younger and more radical women, including fanatical lesbian separatists.

As a graduate student in 1970, I quietly clashed with future bestselling lesbian novelist Rita Mae Brown at an early feminist conference held at the Yale Law School. Brown said, "The difference between you and me, Camille, is that you want to save the universities and I want to burn them down." The next year, I nearly got into a fistfight with the New Haven Women's Liberation Rock Band over my defense of the Rolling Stones. Two years after that, as a Bennington College teacher at dinner at an Albany restaurant, I had an angry confrontation with the founding faculty of the pioneering women's studies program of the State University of New York when they sweepingly dismissed any role of hormones in human development. They accused me of being "brainwashed by male scientists," a charge I still find stupid and contemptible. (I walked out before dessert, thereby boycotting the feminist event we were all headed to.)

There was a steady stream of other such unpleasant incidents, but everything paled in comparison to the international firestorm of lies and libel that greeted me after the publication in 1990 of my first book, *Sexual Personae* (a 700-page expansion of my Yale dissertation). It's all documented and detailed in the back of my two essay collections, but let me give just one example. In 1992, Gloria Steinem, the czarina of U.S. feminism, sat enthroned with her designated heirs, Susan Faludi and Naomi Wolf, on the stage of New York's 92nd Street Y and, when asked a question about me from the floor, replied: "We don't give a shit what she thinks." The moment was caught by TV cameras and broadcast by CBS's 60 *Minutes* program. Faludi has monotonously insisted over the years that I am not a feminist but "only play one on TV." Well, who made Faludi pope? Neither she nor any other feminist has the right to canonize or excommunicate.

I remain an equal-opportunity feminist. That is, I call for the removal of all barriers to women's advance in the professional and political realms. However, I oppose special protections for women (such as differential treatment of the names of accuser and accused in rape cases), and I condemn speech codes of any kind, above all on university campuses. Furthermore, as a libertarian, I maintain that our private sexual and emotional worlds are too mercurial and ambiguous to obey the codes that properly govern the workplace. As I recently told *The Village Voice*, I maintain that everyone has a bisexual potential and that no one is born gay. We need a more flexible psychology, as well as an end to the bitter feminist war on men. My feminist doctrine is completely on the record in four of my six books.

As for playing "devil's advocate," I can't imagine a committed feminist engaging in that kind of silly game. The real problem is the cliquish, tunnel-vision intolerance that afflicts too many feminists, who seem unprepared to recognize and analyze ideas. In both the United States and Britain, there has been far too much addiction to "theory" in poststructuralist and postmodernist gender studies. With its opaque jargon and elitist poses, theory is no way to build a real-world movement. My system of pro-sex feminism has been constructed by a combination of scholarly research and everyday social observation.

The infamous faxes between you and Julie Burchill in The Modern Review *are still very much the stuff of legend in the U.K.'s media. Any regret about the whole thing? If you were mentoring a young Camille today, how would you tell her to deal with that kind of situation? All guns blazing, take her down, and combative, or would you be recommending some mindfulness, meditation, and understanding?*

There is not a single thing I would change in my handling of that acrimonious 1993 episode. British journalist Julie Burchill gratuitously attacked and insulted me, and I responded in kind. Our exchanges continued, with my replies getting longer and hers getting shorter, until she realized she had misjudged her opponent and "bottled out" (a British locution for beating a hasty retreat that I heard for the first time from an amused *Times* reporter commenting on the battle).

I learned how to jab and parry from my early models, Oscar Wilde, Dorothy Parker, and Mary McCarthy. Germaine Greer, whom I deeply admire, has always been glorious in combat. As for mentoring a young Camille Paglia, I would tell her to study my martial arts moves and do likewise!

We have found ourselves in the midst of many similar battles of wits online, as Twitter is effectively publishing everyone's faxes. As someone who can give as good as you get, how do you feel about some prominent feminists and writ-

ers being hounded off Twitter by other feminists? What do you think Twitter is doing for feminism—making it narcissistic, polarized, and too noisy, or democratic, pluralist, and a thriving community?

It's a sad comment on the current state of feminism that the movement has been reduced to the manic fragments and instant obsolescence of Twitter. Although I adore the Web and was a co-founding contributor to Salon.com from its very first issue in 1995, I have no interest whatever in social media. My publisher maintains an informational Facebook page for me on the Random House site, but I don't do Facebook or Twitter and wouldn't even know how.

It is difficult to understand how a generation raised on the slapdash jumpiness of Twitter and texting will ever develop a logical, coherent, distinctive voice in writing and argumentation. And without strong books and essays as a permanent repository for new ideas, modern movements eventually sputter out for lack of continuity and rationale. Hasty, blathering blogging (without taking time for reflection and revision) is also degrading the general quality of prose writing.

As for feminists being hounded off Twitter by other feminists, how trivial and adolescent that sounds! Both sides should get offline and read more—history, sociology, psychology, and the big neglected subject, biology. How can the greater world, much less men, ever take feminism seriously if its most ardent proponents behave like catty sorority girls throwing hissy fits at the high-school cafeteria?

The two feminist issues that create the most noise on Twitter, and generate backlash whichever way you side, are the sex industry and gender, the latter especially in relation to transgenderism. What are your thoughts on both?

I support, defend, and admire prostitutes, gay or straight. They do important and necessary work, whether moralists of the left and right like it or not. Child prostitution and sexual slavery are of course an infringement of civil liberties and must be stringently policed and prohibited.

Feminists who think they can abolish the sex trade are in a state of massive delusion. Only a ruthless, fascist regime of vast scale could eradicate the rogue sex impulse that is indistinguishable from the life force. Simply in the Western world, pagan sexuality has survived 2000 years of Judeo-Christian persecution and is hardly going to be defeated by a few feminists whacking at it with their brooms.

Transgenderism has taken off like a freight train and has become nearly impossible to discuss with the analytic neutrality that honest and ethical scholarship requires. First of all, let me say that I consider myself a transgender being, neither man nor woman, and I would welcome the introduction of "OTHER" as a gender category in passports and other government documents. I telegraphed my gender dissidence from early childhood in the 1950s through flamboyantly male Halloween costumes (a Roman soldier, a matador, Napoleon, etc.) that were then shockingly unheard of for girls.

As a libertarian, I believe that every individual has the right to modify his or her body at will. But I am concerned about the current climate, inflamed by half-baked postmodernist gender theory, which convinces young people who may have other unresolved personal or family issues that sex-reassignment surgery is a golden road to happiness and true identity.

How has it happened that so many of today's most daring and radical young people now define themselves by sexual identity alone? There has been a collapse of perspective here that will surely have mixed consequences for our art and culture and that may perhaps undermine the ability of Western societies to understand or react to the vehemently contrary beliefs of others who do not wish us well. As I showed in *Sexual Personae*, which began as a study of androgyny in literature and art, transgender phenomena multiply and spread in "late" phases of culture, as religious, political, and family traditions weaken and civilizations begin to decline. I will continue to celebrate androgyny, but I am under no illusions about what it may portend for the future.

30

SOUTHERN WOMEN:
OLD MYTHS AND NEW FRONTIERS

Young women today face a multitude of choices about their future lives. The career system is open to them, and many barriers of discrimination have fallen, through a combination of state regulation and social change. Yet challenges remain for women who would like to combine a career with marriage and motherhood. From the perspective of the past 5,000 years of civilization, this territory truly remains a new frontier.

Since the incendiary culture wars of the 1980s and early '90s, which received heavy media coverage, feminism has mostly receded to online blogs and sporadic street theater. Surveys have shown that a majority of young women, here and abroad, no longer identify with feminism—and surely that is at least partly due to the unnecessarily punitive anti-male tone that still pervades too much feminist discourse. While sexual minorities have been central to my work since graduate school, I am more concerned here with the majority of women who seek life partnerships with men. I have felt for a very long time that Southern women, for a variety of cultural reasons, have achieved a formula of cordial yet confident

[Honors College Convocation Lecture, Sally McDonnell Barksdale
Honors College, University of Mississippi, September 16, 2014]

self-presentation that seems superior to the more militant and sometimes hectoring persona of Northern women, which may descend from New England Puritanism. For this lecture, I read widely in Southern history and tried to answer these questions for myself. Do Southern women, both white and black, have a personal power that Northern women have lost or never had? And if so, what is it, and how can it be preserved and redefined for the future?

Later in my talk, I will present three major examples of old myths about Southern women that have been bitterly contested and even rejected outright but that remain very much alive because they are so embedded in novels, movies, TV, and advertising. My argument is that each of these antiquated stereotypes does in fact contain a residue of authentic power that can be extracted, salvaged, and reincorporated in new models of contemporary selfhood to inspire and motivate. All three myths have some basis in historical reality. They are: the fierce old Appalachian mountain woman with her dirt boots and corncob pipe; the nurturing mammy of antebellum plantation households, whose edited image controversially persists in the logo for Aunt Jemima pancake mix; and the Southern belle, an idealized symbol of the white planter elite before and after the Civil War.

A crucial point is the agrarian roots of these three myths. In my opinion, second-wave feminism, for all its professed concern for mainstream, working-class, or disenfranchised women, has drifted toward privileging the concerns and complaints of upper-middle-class career women, who seek the lofty status and material rewards of an economic system built by and for men. Despite the rapid growth of urban centers like Atlanta over the past 40 years, the American South remains strongly rural in its traditions and assumptions. I am particularly alert to this theme because I am only one generation removed from the farm; my mother and all four of my grandparents were born in the Italian countryside, and many branches of the family still reside there. In grade school, furthermore, I lived for a while on a working dairy farm when my father was teaching high school in the village of Oxford in upstate New York. It is my thesis that country women were and are stronger both physically and mentally than most of today's affluent, successful professional women obsessively doing their Pilates in fancy urban gyms.

Beyond that, I am specifically concerned about what I feel to be a regression in speech style among elite Northern women who give lip service to feminism but whose speaking voice in college and early career seems increasingly weak, bland, and sometimes annoyingly juvenile, which may be a product of the bourgeois gentility with which they were raised in the sterile landscape of the shopping-mall suburbs. The pampered overprotection of middle-class girls at home is prolonged in expensive Northern colleges by the intrusive paternalism of an ever-expanding campus administrator class, who now routinely use unconstitutional speech codes to enforce political correctness about sex and gender.

For example, three years ago, a raucous incident at Yale University caused a firestorm that led to the suspension of the Delta Kappa Epsilon fraternity for five years. The Yale Women's Center protested that pledges were required to chant pornographically explicit verses on the hallowed Old Campus, which is ringed by freshman dormitories. These admittedly vulgar lines (which I cannot repeat here) were dubbed "hate speech," but they were actually satirizing the feminist mantra, "No always means no." When the Yale administration was slow to respond, sixteen Yale students and recent graduates filed a complaint with the U.S. Department of Education Office for Civil Rights, and Yale buckled. Predictably, it laid on yet another layer of bureaucracy—a new committee special-izing in complaints about sexual misconduct.

This now nationally accepted system of academic surveil-lance and control of students' private lives is virtually unheard of in Europe. In my opinion, while reasonable sexual harassment guidelines should indeed govern the supervisory relationship of teachers to students, college administrations should not be interfering in students' lives outside the classroom—unless a crime has been committed, in which case the police should be called. But more germane to our present theme, why are self-described feminists instantly turning to authorities for help—especially over a clownish incident involving mere words being boisterously flung into the outdoor air at night? My 1960s generation of women fought to get authority figures *out* of our lives in that era of strict parietal rules, when colleges claimed the duty to operate *in loco parentis*—that is, "in place of the parent." And far from running to the authorities about a bunch of chanting men, we would have mounted a prank-ish counterattack, responding with even more lurid language about the lapses and follies of men. Here is where Northern feminists have much to learn from the Tennessee-born Dixie Carter's brilliant performances as Julia Sugarbaker in the CBS TV hit series *Designing Women,* which was set in Atlanta and ran from 1986 to 1993. It was a recurrent set piece that brought down the house when Dixie would gather herself up and unleash a rhythmic gale of tongue-lashing force against a hapless miscreant—without ever losing the poise and dignity of a true Southern lady. In a democracy, offensive speech must be countered by stronger speech, not by infantilizing appeals to authority.

Impressions of the South for Northerners like myself have been refracted through art and media and are therefore nec-essarily half-fictional and unreliable—but so were the heroic lays out of which Homer fashioned the *Iliad* and the *Odyssey!*

So let me chronicle the formative highlights of my exposure to things Southern. The very first movie star who enamored me on sight and converted me to my lifelong pagan worship of Hollywood was Ava Gardner, playing the mulatto singer Julie in *Show Boat*, which I saw at the age of four at the movie's release in 1951. Ava's magnetic power of personality filled the screen in the opening scenes, set at a dock in Natchez, where she sang "Can't Help Lovin' That Man of Mine." Much later, I learned that Ava was a country girl from Smithfield, North Carolina, where she had run around barefoot on her father's small, struggling tobacco farm. The youngest of seven, she was of mixed Scots-Irish, French Huguenot, and Tuscarora Indian heritage. When she got to Hollywood, her rural Southern accent was so heavy and incomprehensible that she was sent for emergency voice training. Ava was an untamable free spirit with a superhuman energy level. She knocked out her first husband, Mickey Rooney, by beaning him with a marble ashtray. Friends of her third husband, Frank Sinatra, whose heart she broke, said she was the only woman whom the arrogant Sinatra never conquered. Ava's country girl indifference to convention was typified by her constantly kicking off her shoes in public places, which was simply not done at the time. That habit of hers certainly influenced the title of one of her best movies, *The Barefoot Contessa*. Throughout her career, Ava's closest friend remained Reenie Jordan, an African-American woman who began as her maid and became her inseparable personal assistant and companion, even in Ava's expatriate years in Madrid and London. Reenie, who died last year at the age of 92, wrote an affectionate memoir called *Living with Miss G*, where she describes how Ava fiercely defended her against racism in their travels. In this respect, Ava Gardner was an admirable role model; she didn't simply espouse progressive principles—she lived them.

The next Southern woman who had a major impact on

my consciousness was Tallulah Bankhead, whose sensational appearance on *The Lucy-Desi Comedy Hour* in 1957 practically blew up the TV set. At the peak of the conformist 1950s, when girls were universally expected to become docile wives and homemakers, the lordly, swashbuckling Tallulah seemed to throw back a curtain on a radically different time and place. She carried with her all the irrepressible scintillation and daring impudence of the 1920s flapper era, when she was the toast of the New York and London stage. Tallulah was born to wealth and social position in Huntsville, Alabama. After the early death of her mother, a classic Southern belle, Tallulah often lived with family in Montgomery, where she became a childhood friend of another famously independent Southern woman, Zelda Sayre, who would marry novelist F. Scott Fitzgerald and become a symbol of the Roaring Twenties. Tallulah's father, William Brockman Bankhead, was an Alabama politician who rose to become Speaker of the U.S. House of Representatives. Her grandfather, John Hollis Bankhead, was a U.S. senator who had been a planter and a captain of the Alabama Infantry during the Civil War. With her wickedly outspoken flamboyance and flagrantly libertine lifestyle, Tallulah represented a new archetype of the emancipated woman after American women had won the right to vote in 1920. But after World War Two, that daring, assertive style had completely vanished. With her grandiloquent manner, rich Alabama accent, and rumbling chesty voice, Tallulah would end up playing a satirical version of herself on TV shows in the 1950s, when she became a cult idol for gay men and campy female impersonators.

In that same period, my family and I, then living in Syracuse, New York, began to notice and exclaim about the Southern women competing in the Miss America pageant, which was then an annual televised event in the United States of immense importance. From the moment they walked onstage, the Southern contestants exuded a stunningly intense wattage of molten warmth and dazzling charisma that was instantly recognizable. What *is* it that Southern women have, we would wonder? Indeed, from 1951 to 1964, when I graduated from high school, the Miss America crown was repeatedly won by Southern contestants—Miss Alabama, Miss Georgia, Miss South Carolina, Miss Mississippi (winning back-to-back years in 1959 and 1960), Miss North Carolina, Miss Arkansas. If that pace slowed over the following years, it is surely because other contestants studied the Southern secret and began to imitate that radiant style of self-presentation, which continues to flourish in beauty pageants influenced by Miss America all over the world.

As an adolescent, I saw the classic 1939 Hollywood movie *Gone with the Wind* in rerun theaters four times and bought Margaret Mitchell's original novel—an 862-page paperback (then costing 95 cents) that I still own, though the pages have severely yellowed. As the decades passed, I was certainly made to realize how deficient both the book and the movie were in their sanitized portrayal of the atrocity of slavery and of the actual attitudes and experiences of African-Americans during that period. However, there are many specific small details about plantation life in North Georgia in the nineteenth century that have proved to be surprisingly accurate. And the novel is not entirely a whitewash. For example, in the opening scene at Tara, the strappingly handsome and athletic Tarleton twins have just been expelled from the University of Georgia, "the fourth university that had thrown them out in two years." Mitchell says, "Stuart and Brent considered their latest expulsion a fine joke, and Scarlett, who had not willingly opened a book since leaving the Fayetteville Female Academy the year before, thought it just as amusing as they did." These are strong, condemning words coming from the invisible author.

Other impressions I gained from favorite movies: the willful, ruthless Southern belles played by Bette Davis in *Jezebel*, for which she won an Oscar in 1938, and as Regina Giddens in Lillian Hellman's *The Little Foxes*, a role premiered by Tallulah Bankhead in the hit Broadway play. Bette Davis was a Yankee born and bred in Massachusetts, but Miriam Hopkins, Davis's antagonist in the classic 1943 comedy *Old Acquaintance*, was a real-life speed-talking Southern belle, born in Savannah, Georgia and raised near the Alabama border. Then there was that British import, Elizabeth Taylor, as a refined Virginia girl experiencing culture shock when she marries a Texas rancher in *Giant*, based on a bestselling Edna Ferber novel. Elizabeth Taylor again as the Mississippi-born Tennessee Williams's smoldering cat on a hot tin roof, set in a plantation house in the Mississippi Delta. Or Taylor yet again as the troubled Catherine of *Suddenly, Last Summer*, who is menaced by a formidable iron magnolia, the imperious New Orleans matriarch Violet Venable, played by Katharine Hepburn and modeled on Williams's own overbearing Southern belle mother. Williams created a tragically more fragile version of the Southern belle in Blanche DuBois in *A Streetcar Named Desire*, where the crudely vital New Orleans street scene is contrasted with the fading pastoral memories of Blanche's decaying family estate in Laurel, Mississippi—Belle Reve, literally "beautiful dream," encompassing the illusions and delusions of the Old South.

However, nothing really prepared me for dealing with a real-life Southern lady of the old school: Ellen Graham, the brilliant senior editor of Yale University Press who discovered my work 30 years ago and made my entire public career possible. It was she who took a chance on a quirky, dissident, 1,500-page manuscript called *Sexual Personae* which had been rejected by seven publishers and five agents. Ellen, who died eight years ago, was born in 1921 right here in Oxford, where she lived for nine years until her father, the noted folklorist Arthur Palmer Hudson, left to teach at the University of North Carolina at Chapel Hill. Both sides of Ellen's family were from Mississippi. Her maternal grandfather, William McNulty Noah, was mayor of Kosciusko and founded and edited the *Herald* newspaper, which is still published as the Kosciusko *Star-Herald*. In the 1920s, Ellen's parents were friends of William Faulkner, whose biographer records how Ellen's mother, Grace, typed at least two of Faulkner's manuscripts and pronounced them "Tripe!" The long tale of my sometimes desperate and anguished give-and-take with Ellen Graham through the years-long process of editorial production of *Sexual Personae* would take a book in itself. Let me just say this: there is no one stronger than a Southern woman!

But it was a superb documentary film released in 1986 that got me seriously thinking about the special assertiveness of Southern women, notably in their relations with men—*Sherman's March*, directed and shot by Ross McElwee, who grew up in Charlotte, North Carolina. This film, which won the Grand Jury Prize for best documentary at the Sundance Film Festival, began as a study of General Sherman's lingering destructive legacy in the South but turned into a pensive autobiographical saga as McElwee's hand-held camera was drawn to the bewitching charm and teasing humor of a series of attractive, confident, and deftly domineering young Southern women. Surely that mesmerizing yet subtly intimidating discourse is a modern adaptation of the verbal style of the Southern belle, about whom the body of scholarship is still relatively limited. McElwee's improvisational documentary made me see how Southern women seize, define, energize, and control the conversational space between men and women—and to a lesser extent between themselves and other women. Even amid merriment, eye contact is intense, somehow combining wary watchfulness with flattering concentration; it's as if, at that moment, no one else exists. Southern women seem to have a knack that Northern women have lost or never had, of interesting and attracting men while keeping them at an approved safe distance.

Now to our three myths. My first model of feisty Southern womanhood is the scrappy old mountain woman, who became a comic stock character as Mammy Yokum in the fictive town of Dogpatch of the *L'il Abner* comic strip, which was created in 1934 by Al Capp and drawn by him for 43 years, at its height reaching a worldwide newspaper audience of 60 million readers. Mammy was tough, blunt, and uncompromising in her archaic pioneer bonnet juxtaposed with the half-masculine motifs of her corncob pipe and clodhopper boots. Capp, the son of Lithuanian Jewish immigrants in New Haven, Connecticut, saw hillbilly culture first-hand when he took a long hitchhiking trip through the Appalachian Mountains to Memphis to see his uncle, an orthodox rabbi. Sleeping in haystacks and mingling with the poor, Capp made on-site sketches that would become the basis of *L'il Abner*. There was an additional impetus when he and his wife saw a hillbilly band performing in downtown New York. It was when hillbilly music, which would soon be called country music, was gaining national attention through a radio program called the *Grand Ole Opry*, broadcast live from the 1920s in Nashville. By 1943, the *Grand Ole Opry* would have its own temple, Ryman Auditorium.

Appalachia as an exotic, self-enclosed culture had been created in the popular mind by literary magazines in the late nineteenth century. This mountainous region, 900 miles long and 200 miles wide, extends all the way from upstate New York to central Alabama. Ethnically, the mountaineers were mostly Scots-Irish who had arrived in the late eighteenth and early nineteenth centuries in Quaker Philadelphia. Finding that area too settled, they traveled west toward Lancaster County, where the Amish still reside, and then turned south to straggle down through the Blue Ridge Mountains. Some have claimed that the notorious Appalachian feuds, one of which lasted 60 years in Clay County and was finally put down by state troopers, had roots in the clan rivalries of the Scottish Highlands. While they were spared in the Appalachian feuds, women according to some testimony were hot-blooded "provocateurs," recording and remembering slights and goading their men on to fight. Appalachia was also Cherokee territory, with frequent inter-marriage occurring between settlers and Native Americans. It may be relevant that Cherokee culture was matrilineal, traced through the female line, with wives having much more power over their children and property than husbands did. Intriguingly, a gender-reversing American institution originated in the L'il Abner strip—Sadie Hawkins Day, where young women pursue eligible men and rope them into marriage. Within two years of Capp introducing the Sadie Hawkins race in a November 1937 strip, nearly 200 colleges, beginning with the University of Tennessee, were staging Sadie Hawkins Day festivities every November.

Capp's Mammy Yokum would be resurrected as Granny Moses, the matriarch of the Clampett family in The Beverly Hillbillies, a hugely popular CBS TV show that ran from 1962 to 1971. The Clampetts strike oil in the Ozarks and promptly decamp to Los Angeles. Granny, played by Irene Ryan in a pioneer gingham dress, appears in every one of the show's 274 episodes. She claims secret skills in folk medicine and keeps goats and pigs in the backyard of their Beverly Hills mansion, where she also cooks up mountain stew in a black kettle. Firing off a shotgun at the slightest provocation, Granny is a dyed-in-the-wool Confederate who excoriates General Sherman and reveres Jefferson Davis—even though the mountain-eers, with their patchwork of poor hilly soil unfit for cotton or rice cultivation, had little to do with slavery. Despite her tiny frame, Granny is fierce, aggressive, and fearless. Her stance of constant, manic combat is a vestige of the trials and priva-tions of the agrarian era, when families who relied on sub-sistence farming could live or die by nature's whims: a bad harvest could well mean starvation over a hard winter. The old mountaineer woman symbolizes persistence, courage, resil-ience, and stoicism, the stubborn will to survive under hostile circumstances.

Mammy Yokum and Granny Moses also offer a powerful persona for aging women, who have few or no models in our youth-obsessed culture. Today, middle-aged women, with their cafeteria menu of plastic surgery, fillers, and Botox, strive to look like 20-year-old girls. Well, I say, forget that! Let young women rule in all their fresh and nubile beauty. Older women of the elite class once had a dowager role to shift into, where they oversaw and dictated the courtship rituals of eligible young men and women. But with our present bias against inherited class privilege, the dowager no longer serves as a useful model. Instead, let's substitute the snappish, irascible, proletarian old mountain woman. She is a crone without being a witch, that supernatural apparition who haunts so many global mythologies. The mountain woman, in contrast, inhabits the here and now. With her irrepressible energy and brusque common sense, she represents active engagement with and mastery of concrete physical reality.

My second canonical Southern persona is the mammy figure, who has been harshly critiqued and almost univer-sally condemned by both white and black academics since the emergence of women's studies and African-American studies in the 1970s. While I respect these objections, partly because of my own indignation about the universal stereotyping slurs against Italian-Americans in movies and TV, I believe the pendulum about Mammy and her descendant Aunt Jemima has swung too far toward the negative, and a partial correction is long overdue. That enslaved African-American women served as caretakers and wet nurses for affluent white children during the antebellum era is well-established. However, some scholars, such as Catherine Clinton, question the age of the women as well as the length and loyalty of their service. There may well have been exaggerations during the postbellum period to support the claim by defeated Southerners of interracial harmony in the antebellum plantation Big House.

The Northern vision of the mammy came first from Harriet Beecher Stowe's epochal *Uncle Tom's Cabin*, the 1852 protest novel that inflamed and expanded the abolitionist movement and helped trigger the Civil War. Stowe's doomed and sickly Little Eva excitedly flings herself into the arms of her black mammy and showers profuse kisses on her, inciting the surprise and revulsion of an otherwise admirable white female cousin, an abolitionist from New England. Mammy and Aunt Jemima became stock characters in the minstrel shows of the late nineteenth century, whose broad comic style can be seen in Al Jolson's blackface performance of "My Mammy" in the first sound film, *The Jazz Singer*, in 1927. That song was so uniquely American that Kurt Weill and Bertolt Brecht parodied it in the Southern clichés of "Alabama Song" from their 1930 Marxist opera, *Rise and Fall of the City of Mahagonny*. During the 1960s, "Alabama Song," as recorded by Weill's wife, Lotte Lenya, would so impress a new Los Angeles band, the Doors, that Jim Morrison hauntingly sang it on their first album in 1967.

Our mental picture of the mammy, however, will forever remain Hattie McDaniel's stupendous performance as

Mammy in *Gone with the Wind*, which garnered her the first Academy Award ever won by an African-American actor. Unfortunately, this tribute is somewhat overshadowed by the facts that have since emerged about the exclusion of the black cast of *Gone with the Wind* from the movie's gala premiere in Atlanta and about their assignment to a back table during the Academy Awards ceremony in Los Angeles, while the white stars, such as Clark Gable and Vivien Leigh, were seated at ringside near the podium. It has justifiably been said that both Margaret Mitchell's novel and the movie show Mammy as so excessively devoted to and identified with her white masters that she has no friends or family of her own. But perhaps this is not the whole story, because Mammy is incontrovertibly portrayed as Scarlett's real mother, in emotional and spiritual terms. Mammy knows, understands, and sharply counsels Scarlett far better than her own mother, who is a classic Victorian-era plantation mistress, pious, conventional, and obliviously preoccupied with her many onerous duties, including ministering to the sick in the servant and slave quarters.

For decades, there has been a flood of commentary on Mammy by women academics calling her things like "desexed," "morbidly obese," even "monstrous." A 2008 book about the mammy theme by an African-American woman scholar acidly portrays Mammy's natural "maternity" as "primitive, instinctual, base." ("Nature" is a dirty word in poststructuralism, which sees only the oppressions of society.) I would argue in contrast that Mammy embodies the physical force, vigor, and power of personality of the country woman and that too much of the recent animus against her seems to be at least partly based on an ambivalence about and even denigration of motherhood in second-wave feminism. Hattie McDaniel's Mammy brusquely speaks and behaves exactly like the bossy Italian-American immigrant women among

whom I spent my early childhood in the factory town of Endicott in upstate New York. Indeed, one of my favorite scenes in
all film is the first moment we see Mammy, leaning out from
a second-story window at Tara and shouting at Scarlett, whom
she boomingly scolds. It always inspires me with a nostalgic
rush of déjà vu, because that is just the way those ferocious
Italian women behaved, including my adored maternal grandmother. Country women, who were raised in the open air,
had big voices and big attitudes. Most of those Italian immigrant women were bulky in build, with powerful shoulders
and arms from doing laundry by hand on washboards. Furthermore, for thousands of years during the agrarian era, fat
was a sign of abundance, health, and stamina. Skinny women
meant famine, disease, and peril in pregnancy and childbirth.
Women academics should not be anachronistically exporting
the current cult of chic thinness backwards to other eras. The
thin ideal is an urban or courtly aristocratic aesthetic that is
a lesser sub-theme in history. And to condemn Mammy for
her weight is to insult the great African-American music tradition of Big Mama blues singers such as Ma Rainey and Bessie
Smith, whose vocal power came from their mass, precisely like
Wagnerian sopranos in opera.

Most sources concur that Aunt Jemima was a development of the antebellum mammy, now in the guise of a domestic servant, one of the few permissible roles for black women
during the Jim Crow era of Reconstruction. In 1893, Nancy
Green, who had been born in slavery, was introduced as the
commercial spokeswoman for a new self-rising pancake mix
at the World's Columbian Exposition in Chicago. Her cooking
demonstration was so wildly popular that guards had to be
assigned to control the crowds. Ironically, an alliance of black
professional women had been strongly pressuring the Exposition's organizing committee to give more exhibition space to

African-Americans, who were virtually invisible. As black men and women rose in the professions after the Harlem Renaissance of the early twentieth century, grinning Aunt Jemima came to seem like a reductive caricature of menial subordination. The Quaker Oats Company, the manufacturer of Aunt Jemima pancake mix and syrup since 1926, has resisted calls to change the brand name, but it did substantially modify its iconic drawing of Aunt Jemima, whose skin has been lightened and whose yellow bandanna and red-checked housedress are gone. The present Aunt Jemima pictured on product packaging is a neatly coiffed career woman with pearl earrings. But surely there are disquieting elements in this transformation, such as class bias as well as an editing of skin color that could be described as reverse racism.

Just last month, a two-billion-dollar lawsuit to recover royalties was filed against Quaker Oats by the family of Anna Short Harrington, who died in 1955 and was one of the last women (among at least seven) to play the role of Aunt Jemima on advertising junkets. Harrington, born in 1897 to a sharecropping family in South Carolina, showed such early talent for cooking that she was employed as a cook by the age of 10. After her husband abandoned her and their five children, she moved with her family to Syracuse, New York, where she worked as a domestic. A representative of Quaker Oats saw her cooking pancakes at the New York State Fair. Starting in 1935, she was hired as a traveling spokeswoman for Aunt Jemima and made a considerable amount of money, allowing her to buy a large house in Syracuse where she took in boarders. However, current information about Anna and the other Aunt Jemimas remains sketchy and contradictory.

One reason I want to protest the routine strafing of Aunt Jemima is that I believe it may have been Anna Short Harrington whom I saw in person when I was a preschool child in the early 1950s. My paternal grandmother, who cared for

me while my parents were at work, took me to see her at the
A&P grocery in my hometown of Endicott, 80 miles south of
Syracuse. Anna, if it was indeed her, was not only the first
African-American I or probably most of the other shoppers
in that immigrant industrial town had ever seen in person,
but she was also the first woman I had ever seen speak in
public. She was electrifying—warm, forceful, and inclusive as
she addressed the crowd from a low platform set up near the
fragrant coffee-grinding machines, where she demonstrated
how to make pancakes and then distributed samples to all. I
thought she was a goddess! Indeed, I conflated her miracu-
lous transformation of poured liquid into white mottled discs
with the priest's handing out white Communion wafers at
our Catholic church up the hill. The now universal attacks on
Aunt Jemima have obscured the real-life professional achievements of those black women who played her role as ambas-
sadors for Southern hospitality. They courageously ventured
into potentially hostile territory and evangelically endorsed
a true artifact of black culture. Because pancakes *are* an art
form, unknown in Europe and very difficult to execute perfectly.

In *Uncle Tom's Cabin*, Stowe's black Aunt Chloe (Uncle
Tom's wife) is a proud head cook in the Big House who is
"much revered in the kitchen" and who is renowned for the
"sublime mystery" of her fried corn cakes, which cannot be
duplicated by her many envious admirers. In his detailed
reports of his tours of the South during the 1850s, Freder-
ick Law Olmsted, the designer of New York's Central Park,
could hardly find words to describe the deliciousness of the
region's butter-drenched fried hot cakes that he saw served
in heaps in home after home, both rich and poor. Surely in
our own time, when there has been a food renaissance via TV
cooking shows often featuring male chefs of folk cuisine like
Emeril Lagasse or Bobby Flay, we can cease looking at Aunt

Jemima as a prisoner of the kitchen. It is dismaying to find African-American women academics assailing Aunt Jemima with elite theoretical jargon explicitly borrowed from Michel Foucault while neglecting to do wider anthropological investigations into the African diaspora. For example, in Salvador da Bahia, the heavily Africanized region of Northeast Brazil, there is a centuries-old tradition possibly originating in Nigeria of black women in white turbans and big skirts frying and selling ground-pea and shrimp cakes called *acarajé* from braziers set up along the streets and roads. The *acarajé* women's folk dress has in fact become symbolic of Brazil itself. They are no servants of a white population; their patrons are fellow Afro-Brazilians. And in Bahia, the religion of Candomblé, a syncretistic fusion of ancient West African Yoruba cults with Portuguese Catholicism, is ruled by old black women reverently called "Mae" (that is, mother or mama, the root of Mammy) or "Tia," meaning "aunt," as in Aunt Jemima. In summary, a major revision and upgrading of Aunt Jemima is drastically needed.

My third and final myth is the Southern belle, who is often identified with Scarlett O'Hara, even though Margaret Mitchell shows her as almost pre-feminist in rebelling against the confining code of the well-bred "lady." Major books by women scholars have documented the often dreary work-filled lives of plantation mistresses, who may sometimes have played a near-managerial role in their husbands' operations, especially during the Civil War, when three out of every four white men were away in the military. The term "belle," meaning "a beauty," is properly applied only to the short period when elite white girls "came out" (or were "turned out," as Southerners put it) and were presented to society as now eligible for marriage. Families on remote plantations might send their daughters to stay for months with friends or family in large cities, even as far north as Philadelphia, in order to meet potential husbands at the constant round of parties, balls, concerts, and riding excursions that constituted privileged social life in the nineteenth century.

The self-advertisement of the Southern belle after her social debut was an exercise in performance art. Indeed, the South was always more open to theater than the moralistic North: it was in Charleston, for example, that Shakespeare was first performed in America. The Southern planter aristocracy believed it was descended from Cavaliers who had fled the Puritan victors in the English Civil Wars—a legend for which no historical substantiation has ever been found. Sir Walter Scott's historical romances of noble knights and fair ladies were avidly read in the antebellum era. The Southern belle was enacting a fantasy of the courtly love tradition, where an alluring but untouchable dominatrix attracted men in droves but broke their hearts. "Courtliness" still lingers in Southern culture, such as in the polite rhetorical flourishes that lengthen the preambles to sentences. One of the central accomplishments in which the belle was coached was called "sociability"—a skill that I believe should be preserved and reconfigured as networking in the modern professional and business world. It is no coincidence that the first college sorority was established in the South—in 1851 at Wesleyan College in Macon, Georgia, which fifteen years earlier had become the first college in the world to grant degrees to women. Sororities would become an important movement for African-American women too, beginning in 1908 at Howard University in Washington, D.C.

The verve of the Southern belle as a virtuoso conversationalist seems to have received little or no scholarly attention. She had to make herself "fascinating" (that was the term used) without breaking any rules of propriety or decorum. Her speech style had an inherent musicality coming from the Southern dialect itself, which was a fusion over several centuries of Anglo-Saxon English with the multiple languages of enslaved Africans, who came from many tribes and regions. The Southern belle, if we may judge from her twentieth-century descendants in classic Hollywood movies, varied a headlong staccato assault of words with graceful glissandos or slides, often taking a lilting upward turn. I conjecture that those slides may have been influenced by the West African melisma, Islamic in origin, that musicologists have identified in the vocal style and slide guitar of African-American blues. The glittering if brief social life of the Southern belle was certainly the product of ethically indefensible exploitation, systemic to chattel slavery. Yet the belle's public activities and performance style deserve study in exactly the way we analyze the evolution of the exquisite French rococo style during the era of Madame de Pompadour and Marie Antoinette, when riots over bread shortages were breaking out all over France and eventually led to revolution.

In conclusion, what lessons can we draw from these three myths—the implacable old mountain woman, the all-embracing mammy, and the flirtatious Southern belle? They represent different modalities of artifice and practicality, of brutal candor and strategic concealment. The postmenopausal mountain woman is a tiny dynamo of sheer will power, harsh and unsparing, standing her ground while peppering her antagonists with buckshot. The mammy, like the ancient earth mother, is tied to the eternal and magnificent rhythms of nature, whose fertility she still commands despite her advanced years. The belle is a shimmering mirage of elegant perfection, occupying a momentary space between careless girlhood and the burdens of adulthood. What ties these three female myths together is assertive speech, which costs nothing and does everything.

31

THE MODERN CAMPUS
CANNOT COMPREHEND EVIL

The disappearance of University of Virginia sophomore Hannah Graham two weeks ago is the latest in a long series of girls-gone-missing cases that often end tragically. A 32-year-old, 270-pound former football player who fled to Texas has been returned to Virginia and charged with "abduction with intent to defile." At this date, Hannah's fate and whereabouts remain unknown.*

Wildly overblown claims about an epidemic of sexual assaults on American campuses are obscuring the true danger to young women, too often distracted by cell phones or iPods in public places: the ancient sex crime of abduction and murder. Despite hysterical propaganda about our "rape culture," the majority of campus incidents being carelessly described as sexual assault are not felonious rape (involving force or drugs) but oafish hookup melodramas, arising from mixed signals and imprudence on both sides.

Colleges should stick to academics and stop their infantilizing supervision of students' dating lives, an authoritar-

[Time.com, September 29, 2014]

* Hannah Graham's body was found on October 18, 2014 in an abandoned house outside Charlottesville, Virginia.

ian intrusion that borders on violation of civil liberties. Real crimes should be reported to the police, not to haphazard and ill-trained campus grievance committees.

Too many young middle-class women, raised far from the urban streets, seem to expect adult life to be an extension of their comfortable, overprotected homes. But the world remains a wilderness. The price of women's modern freedoms is personal responsibility for vigilance and self-defense.

Current educational codes, tracking liberal-left, are perpetuating illusions about sex and gender. The basic leftist premise, descending from Marxism, is that all problems in human life stem from an unjust society and that corrections and fine-tunings of that social mechanism will eventually bring utopia. Progressives have unquestioned faith in the perfectibility of mankind.

The horrors and atrocities of history have been edited out of primary and secondary education except where they can be blamed on racism, sexism, and imperialism—toxins embedded in oppressive outside structures that must be smashed and remade. But the real problem resides in human nature, which religion as well as great art sees as eternally torn by a war between the forces of darkness and light.

Liberalism lacks a profound sense of evil—but so does conservatism these days, when evil is facilely projected onto a foreign host of rising political forces united only in their rejection of Western values. Nothing is more simplistic than the now rote use by politicians and pundits of the cartoonish label "bad guys" for jihadists, as if American foreign policy is a slapdash script for a cowboy movie.

The gender ideology dominating academe denies that sex differences are rooted in biology and sees them instead as malleable fictions that can be revised at will. The assumption is that complaints and protests, enforced by sympathetic campus bureaucrats and government regulators, can and will fundamentally alter all men.

But extreme sex crimes like rape-murder emanate from a primitive level that even practical psychology no longer has a language for. Psychopathology, as in Richard von Krafft-Ebing's grisly *Psychopathia Sexualis* (1886), was a central field in early psychoanalysis. But today's therapy has morphed into happy talk, attitude adjustments, and pharmaceutical shortcuts.

There is a ritualistic symbolism at work in sex crime that most women do not grasp and therefore cannot arm themselves against. It is well-established that the visual faculties play a bigger role in male sexuality, which accounts for the greater male interest in pornography. The sexual stalker, who is often an alienated loser consumed with his own failures, is motivated by an atavistic hunting reflex. He is called a predator precisely because he turns his victims into prey.

Sex crime springs from fantasy, hallucination, delusion, and obsession. A random young woman becomes the scapegoat for a regressive rage against female sexual power: "You made me do this." Academic clichés about the "commodification" of women under capitalism make little sense here: it is women's superior biological status as magical life-creator that is profaned and annihilated by the barbarism of sex crime.

Misled by the naive optimism and "You go, girl!" boosterism of their upbringing, young women do not see the animal eyes glowing at them in the dark. They assume that bared flesh and sexy clothes are just a fashion statement containing no messages that might be misread and twisted by a psychotic. They do not understand the fragility of civilization and the constant nearness of savage nature.

32

WHY I LOVE *THE REAL HOUSEWIVES*

Bravo TV's *Real Housewives* franchise isn't entertainment to me—it's a lifestyle. I watch virtually nothing else on television now, except for occasional documentaries and Turner Classic Movies. I can see the same *Real Housewives* episode multiple times with equal enjoyment. I love the frank display of emotion, the intricate interrelationships, and the sharp-elbows jockeying for power and visibility. I appreciate every snippet—the rapid scene set-ups, dynamic camera work, and crisp editing, with its enchanting glimpses of fine houses and restaurants and its glowing appreciation of beautiful objects, from flowers and tableware to jewelry and couture. And I applaud the *Real Housewives* master theme of the infectious hilarity and truth-telling delirium induced by copious alcohol, that ancient Dionysian elixir! (Get off those boring, flattening anti-depressants, America!)

When Donna Mills left *Knots Landing* in 1989, it was the end of a glorious soap era. I went into deep mourning. Soaps had fallen very far indeed from their sizzling heyday, marked by the dramatic January 1976 *Time* magazine cover showing an anguished, posturing, bosom-baring Susan Seaforth Hayes backed by her pleading real-life husband, Bill Hayes, the

[*The Daily Dish*, bravotv.com, March 7, 2014]

stars of *Days of Our Lives*, with the blazing headline, "SOAP OPERAS: SEX AND SUFFERING IN THE AFTERNOON"!

But over the decades, daytime writers got uppity and began to disdain their own genre. They strained for "importance" and lost their soap soul. In a two-part interview with Michael Logan for *TV Guide* in 1994, I complained about the upsetting decline and accused soaps of abandoning the great female "trash-and-sleaze" style of Old Hollywood. I said that, with her magical ability to produce "one perfect tear," Melody Thomas Scott as Nikki Newman on *The Young and the Restless* was among the last explorers of profound emotion in the grand old mode. My protest evidently struck a chord: I was told that Tony Geary, the famous heart-throb Luke Spencer of *General Hospital*, marched into a network producer's office, slammed that article on the desk, and demanded better scripts.

As TV soaps diluted themselves to the vanishing point, I had to get my soap fix from the vintage movies that started it all: *Stella Dallas, The Women, Dark Victory, Mildred Pierce, All About Eve, Imitation of Life, A Star Is Born, Written on the Wind, Love Is a Many-Splendored Thing, I'll Cry Tomorrow, The Best of Everything, Valley of the Dolls,* and *Mommie Dearest. The Group, Julia, Rich and Famous,* and *Black Widow* also give good soap, with their intense, competitive, woman-on-woman psychodramas. Nearly all those movies had become cult classics among gay men, who were also often connoisseurs of grand opera. Gay men understand the burden of secrets and the ecstasy of the extreme gesture.

Haggard and bereft, I felt like John the Baptist—a voice crying in the wilderness. But then with a thunderclap out of St. Louis came the Soap Messiah—Andy Cohen! (Jesus was Jewish. What's the problem?) In his autobiography, *Most Talkative,* Cohen describes his early passionate devotion to Susan Lucci, who for 41 years as Erica Kane on *All My Children* defined the archetype of the charismatic bitch-goddess for daytime TV. Cohen has always understood the complex emotional core of soaps, a misty, mercurial realm that is beyond words. The torment and tears on *Real Housewives* are real—from Jacqueline Laurita's pained hope for her autistic son in New Jersey to Kandi Burruss's struggle for freedom against her mother in Atlanta.

Cohen has so altered and redeemed the pop culture landscape—which had been suffering for years from snide snark and pseudo-hip cynicism—that he should be acknowledged as a genuine auteur, like maverick film directors. His tastes, instincts, and sensibility now suffuse a staggering number of highly successful TV projects. Not since the radical gay German director Rainer Werner Fassbinder revived and recast Douglas Sirk's "women's pictures" during the 1970s has a single individual so boldly rescued a waning genre and given it such splendid new life. Bravo, Andy!

33

WHAT A WOMAN PRESIDENT SHOULD BE LIKE

Why has the United States, the cradle of modern democracy, never had a woman president?

Incredulous young feminists, watching female heads of state multiply from Brazil and Norway to Namibia and Bangladesh, denounce this glaring omission as blatant sexism. But there are systemic factors, arising from the Constitution, popular tradition, and our electoral process, that have inhibited American women from attaining the highest office in the land.

The U.S. President is not just Chief Executive but Commander-in-Chief of the armed forces, an anomaly that requires manifest personal authority, particularly during periods of global instability. Women politicians, routinely focused on social-welfare needs, must demonstrate greater involvement with international and military affairs.

Second, the President has a ceremonial function, like that of the British royal family, in symbolically representing the history and prestige of the nation. Hence voters subliminally look for gravitas, an ancient term describing the laconic dig-

[Time.com, July 13, 2015]

nity of Roman senators. The President must project steadiness, sober reserve, and deliberative judgment. Many women, who tend to talk faster and smile more than men, have trouble with gravitas as performance art.

Third, the complex, coast-to-coast primary system in the United States forces presidential candidates into well over a year of brutal competition for funding and grassroots support. Their lives are usurped by family-disrupting travel, stroking of rich donors, and tutelage by professional consultants and PR flacks. This exhausting, venal marathon requires enormous physical stamina and perhaps ethical desensitization to survive it.

In contrast, many heads of state elsewhere ascend through their internal party structure. They are automatically elevated to Prime Minister when their party wins a national election. This parliamentary system of government has been far more favorable for the steady rise of women to the top.

The protracted and ruthlessly gladiatorial U.S. electoral process drives talented women politicians away from the fray. What has kept women from winning the White House is not simple sexism but their own reluctance to subject themselves to the harsh scrutiny and ritual abuse of the presidential sweepstakes.

For example, two eminently qualified and experienced Democrats never launched presidential campaigns when they could have over the past 25 years: Senator Dianne Feinstein, with her deep knowledge of defense and intelligence issues, and Congresswoman Nancy Pelosi, the first female Speaker of the House of Representatives and therefore the highest-ranking woman in U.S. history. Yet a marginal Democratic congressman like the boyish Dennis Kucinich had the ambition and moxie to mount two quixotic presidential bids in 2004 and 2008.

Most of the American electorate has probably been ready for a woman president for some time. But that woman must have the right array of qualities and ideally have risen to prominence through her own talents and not (like Hillary Clinton or Argentina's Executive President, Cristina Fernández de Kirchner) through her marriage to a powerful man.

What characteristics would be desirable in a woman president?

She must find a happy middle ground between the trumpet-like triumphalism of Margaret Thatcher, Iron Lady of the Falklands War, and the swooning cult of personality of Evita Perón, dangling boons and bribes before the masses. She should show consistency of ideology, avoiding poll-driven flip-flops. How she manages her campaign signals her executive competence to run the labyrinthine federal bureaucracy.

She must be statesmanlike, pursuing women's progress without playing victim or bashing men. She must deal forthrightly with the news media, a political reality since eighteenth-century Great Britain. In 1984, Geraldine Ferraro, the first female vice-presidential nominee of a major party, held a high-stakes, two-hour, no-holds-barred press conference that was a bravura display of tough, courageous candor. Alaska Governor Sarah Palin's exuberant promise as a national figure was short-circuited by her thin-skinned inability to handle the hostile press. Current GOP candidate Carly Fiorina, though ultimately limited by her lack of government experience, is remarkably nimble in jousting with the media.

Former Cabinet Secretary Elizabeth Dole's bold GOP presidential run in 1999 was torpedoed by her too rote and chirpy Southern-belle delivery, leading to her withdrawal for lack of funding. Dianne Feinstein has a grande-dame gravitas as well as nerves of steel, demonstrated by her heroic composure after the 1978 massacre in San Francisco City Hall.

But today's best model for aspiring women politicians is German Chancellor Angela Merkel, who combines a take-charge persona with engaging spontaneity and zest for life. She is a soccer fan, an opera lover, and a home cook and gardener—a real person, not the prisoner in a gilded cage that our heavily guarded American presidents have become.

34

FEMINIST TROUBLE

CAMILLE PAGLIA ASSESSES THE PARLOUS STATE OF TODAY'S FEMINISM

INTERVIEW WITH ELLA WHELAN, *SPIKED REVIEW*

It's doubtful whether Camille Paglia—cultural critic, academic, and the author of several acclaimed books including, most recently, *Glittering Images: A Journey Through Art from Egypt to Star Wars*—has ever pulled a punch. Since she burst onto the cultural scene in the 1990s, following the publication of *Sexual Personae: Art and Decadence from Nefertiti to Emily Dickinson*—as she put it, the "most X-rated academic book ever written"—Paglia has been a trenchant, principled voice in the Culture Wars, attacking, with one hand, the anti-sex illiberalism of her feminist peers, while, with the other, laying waste to the trendy, pomo relativism infecting the academy.

Above all, Paglia, who some have called the anti-feminist feminist, has remained a staunch defender of individual freedom. She has argued against laws prohibiting pornography, drugs, and abortion. And, when political correctness was cutting a swathe through a host of institutions during the

[*Spiked Review* (U.K.), December 2015]

1990s, she stood firmly on the side of free speech. So, what does she make of the political and cultural state of feminism today? What does she think of the revival of anti-sex sentiment among young feminists, their obsession with policing language, and their wholehearted embrace of victimhood? As *Spiked*'s Ella Whelan discovered, Paglia's convictions burn as brightly as ever . . .

ELLA WHELAN: *On both sides of the Atlantic, feminism, especially on college campuses, appears to be undergoing a resurgence. As a long-term critic of political correctness, do you think today's feminists are too focused on policing thought and speech?*

CAMILLE PAGLIA: After the ferocious Culture Wars of the 1980s to mid-1990s, feminism sank into a long period of relative obscurity. It was kept tangentially alive through scattered websites and blogs until it finally regained media visibility over the past five years, partly through splashy endorsements by pop figures like Beyoncé. The history of feminism has always been cyclic: after the suffrage movement gained the vote for women in Britain (1918 and 1928) and the United States (1920), feminist activism faded away. Forty years passed before second-wave feminism was launched by Betty Friedan, when she co-founded the National Organization for Women in 1966.

The problem with too much current feminism, in my opinion, is that even when it strikes progressive poses, it emanates from an entitled, upper-middle-class point of view. It demands the intrusion and protection of paternalistic authority figures to project a hypothetical utopia that will be magically free from offense and hurt. Its rampant policing of thought and speech is completely reactionary, a gross betrayal of the radical principles of 1960s counterculture, which was inaugurated in the United States by the incendiary Free Speech Movement at the University of California at Berkeley.

I am continually shocked and dismayed by the nearly Victorian notions promulgated by today's feminists about the fragility of women and their naive helplessness in asserting control over their own dating lives. Female undergraduates incapable of negotiating the oafish pleasures and perils of campus fraternity parties are hardly prepared to win leadership positions in business or government in the future.

WHELAN: *You've been critical of the likes of Gloria Steinem and Andrea Dworkin in the past. To what extent do you think the seeds for feminism's current turn towards censorship were sown in the 1960s and 1970s?*

PAGLIA: Steinem, with her media-savvy aviator shades and blonde-streaked locks, pushed the far more pioneering Betty Friedan offstage to take charge of the nascent women's movement in the United States. At the start, Steinem was great—she normalized the image of feminism and made it seem like a rational cause rather than the ravings of frigid sexual freaks. But, by the mid-1970s, Steinem was ruling the roost like the Stalinist politburo. Dissenting voices like mine in feminism were banned from her magazine, *Ms.*, which became the glossy *Pravda* of the movement— anti-male, anti-sex, anti-pop. My wing of pro-sex feminism was driven underground and wouldn't surface again nationally until the early 1990s. Steinem has always been a networking careerist, packaging herself as a saintly, self-sacrificing humanitarian while privately schmoozing with the rich and famous and the media elite. She told the world, "A woman needs a man like a fish needs a bicycle"—even while she was never without a man on the chic Manhattan party scene.

The anti-porn crusader Andrea Dworkin (who died a decade ago) was a rabid fanatic, a self-destructive woman so consumed by her hatred of men that she tottered on the edge of psychosis. Dworkin and her puritanical henchman Catharine MacKinnon (born into wealth and privilege) were extremely powerful in the United States for a long time, culminating in the major media's canonization of MacKinnon in a 1991 *New York Times Magazine* cover story.

When I burst on the scene after the release of my first book in 1990, I attacked Dworkin and MacKinnon with all guns blazing. I am very proud of the role I played in defending free speech and helping the pro-sex wing of feminism to go public and eventually win its great victory over both Dworkin-MacKinnon and the priggish feminist establishment typified by Steinem. Hence the unthinking backward turn of current feminism toward censorship is appalling and tragic. Young feminists seem to have little sense of the crucial battles that were waged and won a quarter century ago.

WHELAN: *Speaking of a backward turn, young feminists today are obsessed with the idea of "rape culture." Do you think that, as the idea of rape culture suggests, sexual violence is normalized?*

PAGLIA: "Rape culture" is a ridiculous term—mere gassy propaganda, too rankly bloated to critique. Anyone who sees sex so simplistically has very little sense of world history, anthropology, or basic psychology. I feel very sorry for women who have been seduced by this hyper-politicized, victim-centered rhetoric, because in clinging to such superficial, inflammatory phrases, they have renounced their own power and agency.

WHELAN: *Are you therefore concerned by the push for affirmative-consent or, as they're otherwise known, "Yes means Yes" laws?*

PAGLIA: As I have repeatedly argued throughout my career, sex is a physical interaction, animated by primitive energies and instincts that cannot be reduced to verbal formulas. Neither party in any sexual encounter is totally operating in the rational realm, which is why the Greek god Dionysus was the patron of ecstasy, a hallucinatory state of pleasure-pain. "Yes means Yes" laws are drearily puritanical and literalistic as well as hopelessly totalitarian. Their increasing popularity simply demonstrates how boring and meaningless sex has become—and why Hollywood movies haven't produced a scintilla of sexiness since Sharon Stone uncrossed her legs in *Basic Instinct*. Sex is always a dangerous gamble—as gay men have known and accepted for thousands of years. Nothing in the world will ever be totally safe, even the plushy pads of an infant's crib, to which feminist ideologues would evidently wish to reduce us all.

WHELAN: *What did you make of Chrissie Hynde's recent assertion that she was at least partially responsible for her sexual assault at the hands of a biker gang when she was 21? Do you think that contemporary feminism is too quick to turn women into blameless victims?*

PAGLIA: I have been a Chrissie Hynde fan since her first albums with the Pretenders, but this scrappy controversy made my admiration for her go stratospheric. I adore her scathing process of self-examination and her bold language of personal responsibility—that is exactly the direction that feminism must take! Hynde (four years younger than me) is demonstrating the tough, no-crap attitude of the rebellious women of my 1960s generation, who were directly inspired by the sexual revolution, created by the brand-new Pill. We took all kinds of risks—I certainly did, with some scary escapes in dark side streets of Paris and Vienna. We wanted the same freedoms as men, and we took charge of our own destinies. We viewed life as a continual experiment, an urgent pressing into the unknown. If we got knocked down, we got up again, nursed our bruises, and learned from our mistakes. Today, in contrast, too many young feminists want their safety, security, and happiness guaranteed in advance by all-seeing, all-enveloping bureaucracies. It's a sad, limited, and childish view of life that I find as claustrophobic as a hospital ward.

WHELAN: *What advice would you give young women today? Or do you think there is an advice overkill and we should be left alone to work things out for ourselves?*

PAGLIA: Each generation must create its own reality and find its own identity. If today's young women want to be passive wards of the state, then that is their self-stultifying choice. One cannot impose a dynamic, expansive, metaphysical vision of existence on timid minds who crave the miniature, like porcelain bibelots of frogs and sparrows. My advice, as in everything, is to read widely and think for yourself. We need more dissent and less dogma.

WHELAN: *What are the main challenges faced by women today, and what* should *feminists be fighting for?*

PAGLIA: Women must find a way to develop their full potential in the professional world without also disrupting and draining their private lives. The corporate business model invented in northern Europe after the industrial revolution is hyper-efficient but also vampiric. Too many people, both men and women, have foolishly conflated their personal identities with their jobs. It's a bourgeois trap and a distortion of the ultimate meaning of life.

The childless Gloria Steinem, who was unmarried until she was 66, has never been sympathetic to the problems faced by women who want both children and a job. Stay-at-home moms have been arrogantly disdained by orthodox feminism. This is a primary reason for the lack of respect that a majority of mainstream citizens has for feminism, which is addicted to juvenile male-bashing and has elevated abortion to sacramental status. While I firmly support unrestricted reproductive rights (on the grounds that nature gives every individual total control over his or her body), I think that the near-hysterical obsession with abortion has damaged feminism by making it seem morally obtuse.

I want universities to create more flexible,

extended-study options for young women who choose to have earlier (and thus safer) pregnancies, and I want more public and private resources devoted to childcare facilities for working parents of every social class. Finally, I call for the investigation and reform of the current systemic exploitation of working-class women (many of them black or Latina immigrants) who have become the invisible new servant class for affluent white women leaving childcare to others as they pursue their feminist professional dreams.

35

ON ABORTION

Like stumbling twin mastodons, both Donald Trump and Hillary Clinton fell into the abortion tar pit this past week. Trump blundered his way through a manic inquisition about abortion by MSNBC's resident woodpecker, Chris Matthews, while Hillary committed an unforced error on NBC's *Meet the Press*, where she referred to the fetus as an "unborn person," scandalizing the vast pro-choice lobby, who treat all attempts to "humanize" the fetus as a diabolical threat to reproductive rights.

While the Hillary flap was merely a blip, given the consistency of her pro-choice views over time, Trump's clumsy performance was a fiasco, exposing in his fiat that women should face "some sort of punishment" for illegal abortions how little he had thought about one of the major issues in American public life over the past 40 years. Following his supercilious mishandling of the controversy over his campaign manager's crude yanking of a woman reporter's arm, Trump's MSNBC flame-out was a big fat gift to Democratic strategists, who love to tub-thump about the Republican "war on women"—a tired cliché that is as substanceless as a druggy mirage but that the inept GOP has never been able to counter.

[Salon.com, April 7, 2016]

Then this week Hillary raised eyebrows when she was asked by conservative co-host Candace Cameron Bure on ABC's *The View* if she believes someone can be both a feminist and against abortion. "Absolutely," Hillary replied, possibly not realizing the implications of what she was saying: "Of course you can be a feminist and be pro-life." Was this an election-year pivot toward conservative women, like Hillary's fantastical praise of Nancy Reagan as an AIDS activist? If it was rooted in genuine conviction, why have we not heard a word about it before? Hillary is usually wedded cheek-by-jowl with the old-guard feminist establishment.

The real issue is that U.S. politics have been entangled and strangled for far too long by the rote histrionics of the abortion wars, which have raged since *Roe v. Wade*, the 1973 Supreme Court decision that defined abortion as a woman's constitutional right under the 14th Amendment. While I am firmly pro-choice and support unrestricted access to abortion, I have been disturbed and repelled for decades by the way reproductive rights have become an ideological tool ruthlessly exploited by my own party, the Democrats, to inflame passions, raise money, and drive voting.

This mercenary process began with the Senate confirmation hearings for three Supreme Court candidates nominated by Republican presidents: Robert Bork in 1987, David Souter in 1990, and Clarence Thomas in 1991. (Bork was rejected, while Souter and Thomas were approved.) Those hearings became freak shows of feminist fanaticism, culminating in the elevation to martyr status of Anita Hill, whose charges of sexual harassment against Thomas still seem to me flimsy and overblown (and effectively neutralized by Hill's following Thomas to another job). Abortion was the not-so-hidden motivation of the Democratic operatives who pushed a reluctant Hill forward and fanned the flames in the then monochromatically liberal mainstream media. It was that flagrant abuse of the Senate confirmation process that sparked the meteoric rise of conservative talk radio, led by Rush Limbaugh, who provided an alternative voice in what was then (pre-Web) a homogenized media universe.

Abortion has been central to the agenda of second-wave feminism since the 1972 issue of *Ms.* magazine which contained a splashy declaration, "We have had abortions," signed by 53 prominent American women. A recurrent rubric of contemporary feminism is Gloria Steinem's snide jibe (which she claims to have heard from an old Irish woman taxi driver in Boston), "If men could get pregnant, abortion would be a sacrament." But Steinem herself can be credited or blamed for having turned abortion into a sacrament, promoted with the same religiosity that she and her colleagues condemn in their devoutly Christian opponents.

First-wave feminism, born in 1848 at the Seneca Falls Convention in upstate New York, was focused on property rights and on winning the vote, achieved by ratification of the 19th Amendment in 1920. Abortion entered the feminist canon with Margaret Sanger's bold campaign for birth control, a violation of the repressive Comstock Act for which she was arrested in 1914. Her organization, the American Birth Control League, founded in 1921, later became Planned Parenthood, which remains a lightning rod for controversy because of its lavish federal funding. Sanger remains a heroine to many feminists, including me, despite her troubling association with eugenics, a program (also adopted by the Nazis) of now discredited techniques like sterilization to purify and strengthen the human gene pool. It was partly because of Sanger's pioneering precedent that I joined Planned Parenthood and contributed to it for many years—until I realized, to my disillusion, how it had become a covert arm of the Democratic Party.

My position on abortion is contained in my manifesto, "No Law in the Arena," from my second essay collection, *Vamps & Tramps* (1994): "Women's modern liberation is inextricably linked to their ability to control reproduction, which has enslaved them from the origin of the species." However, I argue that our real oppressor is not men or society but nature—the biological imperative that second-wave feminism and campus gender studies still refuse to acknowledge. Sex is nature's way—coercive, prankish, and pleasurable—of ensuring survival of the species. But in eras of overpopulation, those pleasures spill into a multitude of directions to slow or halt procreation—which is why I maintain that homosexuality is not a violation of natural law but its fulfillment, when history wills it.

Despite my pro-abortion stance (I call the term pro-choice "a cowardly euphemism"), I profoundly respect the pro-life viewpoint, which I think has the moral high ground. I wrote in "No Law in the Arena": "We career women are arguing from expedience: it is personally and professionally inconvenient or onerous to bear an unwanted child. The pro-life movement, in contrast, is arguing that every conception is sacred and that society has a responsibility to protect the defenseless." The silence from second-wave feminists about the ethical ambiguities in their pro-choice belief system has been deafening. The one exception is Naomi Wolf, with whom I have disagreed about many issues. But Wolf showed admirable courage in questioning abortion in her 1995 essay, "Our Bodies, Our Souls," which was reprinted at the fortieth anniversary of *Roe v. Wade* by the *New Statesman* in London three years ago.

That a pro-life wing of feminism is possible is proved by this thoughtful letter recently sent to me at *Salon* by Katherine Carlson in Calgary, Canada:

Many women like myself (a gay liberal) are deeply upset over the abortion issue. Ultrasound technology has allowed us to see into the womb like never before, and the obvious face of humanity is clear. I totally respected your take on abortion precisely because you never tried to dehumanize the preborn vulnerable. You were clearly pro-choice but made the harsh reality of the decision very clear.

I was thrilled when they took down Gloria Steinem's interview on Lands' End. To me, she is someone who tried to normalize abortion, and I despise her for it. The Democrats have become callous and extreme on the issue, and I feel completely shut out. And obviously, I am no right-winger. I have listened to the testimony of phenomenal women who have survived abortion attempts and were left to die (were saved only because some took their Hippocratic oath seriously).

I am tired of being bullied by women who equate women's equality with abortion on demand. I know some women who use abortion as a method of sex selection and it rattles me to my core.

If you ever decide to write a piece on silenced women like myself, I would be entirely grateful.

I totally agree with Carlson that pro-choice Democrats have become "callous and extreme" about abortion. There is a moral hollowness at the core of Western careerist feminism, a bourgeois secular code that sees children as an obstruction to self-realization or as a management problem to be farmed out to working-class nannies.

Liberals routinely delude themselves with shrill propaganda about the motivation of "anti-woman" pro-life supporters. Hillary deals in those smears as her stock-in-trade: for example, while campaigning last week, she said in the context of Trump's comments on abortion, "Women's health is under assault in America"—as if difficulty in obtaining an abortion is more of an assault than the grisly intervention required for surgical termination of a pregnancy. Who is the real victim here?

Or we have Gail Collins, former editorial page head at *The New York Times*, asserting last week in her column, "Trump, Truth, and Abortion," "In reality, the anti-abortion movement is grounded on the idea that sex outside of marriage is a sin. . . . It's the sex, at bottom, that they oppose." I saw red: where the hell were these middlebrow Steinem feminists of the prestige Manhattan media during the pro-sex insurgency of my rebel wing of feminism during the 1990s? Suddenly, two decades later, the 70-year-old Collins is waving the sex flag? Give me a break!

To project sex phobia onto all pro-lifers is a vulgar libel. Although I am an atheist who worships only great nature, I recognize the superior moral beauty of religious doctrine that defends the sanctity of life. The quality of idea and language in the Catechism of the Catholic Church, for example, exceeds anything in grimly utilitarian feminism. In regard to the Commandment "Thou shalt not kill," the Catechism says: "Human life is sacred because from its beginning it involves the creative action of God. . . . God alone is the Lord of life from its beginning until its end: no one can under any circumstance claim for himself the right directly to destroy an innocent human being" (#2258). Or this: "Human life must be respected and protected absolutely from the moment of conception. From the first moment of his existence, a human being must be recognized as having the rights of a person—among which is the inviolable right of every innocent being to life" (#2270).

Which embodies the more authentic humanism in this

area—the Catholic Catechism or pro-choice feminism? If the latter, then we have much work to do to develop feminism philosophically. In "No Law in the Arena," I argued from the point of view of pre-Christian paganism, when abortion was accepted and widespread: "My code of modern Amazonism says that nature's fascist scheme of menstruation and procreation *should* be defied, as a gross infringement of woman's free will. . . . As a libertarian, I support unrestricted access to abortion because I have reasoned that my absolute right to my body takes precedence over the brute claims of mother nature, who wants to reduce women to their animal function as breeders."

There are abundant contradictions in a liberal feminism that supports abortion yet opposes capital punishment. The violence intrinsic to abortion cannot be wished away by magical thinking. As I wrote: "Abortion pits the stronger against the weaker, and only one survives." My program is more ideologically consistent, because I vigorously support abortion but also call for the death penalty for horrific crimes such as political assassination or serial rape-murder. However, the ultimate issue in the abortion debate is that, in a modern democracy, law and government must remain neutral toward religion, which cannot impose its expectations or values on non-believers.

In an in-depth piece in *The Boston Globe* two years ago, Ruth Graham summarizes one view of the controversial emerging concept of fetal rights in cases where a pregnant woman has been attacked or killed: "It is progressives who have historically pushed to expand civil rights, yet who now find themselves concerned about the expansion of rights to fetuses." Progressives need to do some soul-searching about their reflex rhetoric in demeaning the pro-life cause. A liberal credo that is variously anti-war, anti-fur, vegan, and committed to environmental protection of endangered species like the sage grouse or spotted owl should not be so stridently withholding its imagination and compassion from the unborn.

CAPTION

What's in a picture

IN 1975, ARISTA RECORDS RELEASED *HORSES*, THE FIRST rock album by New York bohemian poet Patti Smith. The stark cover photo, taken by someone named Robert Mapplethorpe, was devastatingly original. It was the most electrifying image I had ever seen of a woman of my generation. Now, two decades later, I think that it ranks in art history among a half-dozen supreme images of modern woman since the French Revolution.

By Camille Paglia

I was then teaching at my first job in Vermont and turning my Yale doctoral dissertation, "Sexual Personae," into a book. The *Horses* album cover immediately went up on my living-room wall, as if it were a holy icon. Mapplethorpe's portrait of Patti Smith symbolized for me not only women's new liberation but the fusion of high art and popular culture that I was searching for in my own work.

From its rebirth in the late 1960s, the organized women's movement had been overwhelmingly hostile to rock music, which it called sexist. Patti Smith's sudden national debut galvanized me with the hope (later proved futile) that hard rock, the revolutionary voice of the counterculture, would also be endorsed by feminism. Smith herself emerged not from the women's movement but from the artistic avant-garde as well as the decadent sexual underground, into which her friend and lover Mapplethorpe would plunge ever more deeply after their breakup.

Unlike many feminists, the bisexual Smith did not base her rebellion on a wholesale rejection of men. As an artist, she paid due homage to major male progenitors; she wasn't interested in neglected foremothers or a second-rate female canon. In Mapplethorpe's half-transvestite picture, she invokes her primary influences, from Charles Baudelaire and Frank Sinatra to Bob Dylan and Keith Richards, the tormented genius of the Rolling Stones who was her idol and mine.

Before Patti Smith, women in rock had presented themselves in conventional formulas of folk singer, blues shouter or motorcycle chick. As this photo shows, Smith's persona was brand-new. She was the first to claim both *vision* and *authority*, in the dangerously Dionysian style of another poet, Jim Morrison, lead singer of the Doors. Furthermore, in the competitive field of album-cover design inaugurated in 1964 with *Meet the Beatles* (the musicians' dramatically shaded faces are recalled here), no female rocker had ever dominated an image in this aggressive, uncompromising way.

The Mapplethorpe photo synthesizes my passions and world-view. Shot in steely high contrast against an icy white wall, it unites austere European art films with the glamorous, ever-maligned high-fashion magazines. Rumpled, tattered, unkempt, hirsute, Smith defies the rules of femininity. Soulful, haggard and emaciated yet raffish, swaggering and seductive, she is mad saint, ephebe, dandy and troubadour, a complex woman alone and outward bound for culture war.

Patti Smith, 1975 © Robert Mapplethorpe Foundation

36

WHAT'S IN A PICTURE: ROBERT MAPPLETHORPE'S PORTRAIT OF PATTI SMITH FOR *HORSES*

In 1975, Arista Records released *Horses,* the first rock album by New York bohemian poet Patti Smith. The stark cover photo, taken by someone named Robert Mapplethorpe, was devastatingly original. It was the most electrifying image I had ever seen of a woman of my generation. Now, two decades later, I think that it ranks in art history among a half-dozen supreme images of modern woman since the French Revolution.

I was then teaching at my first job in Vermont and turning my Yale doctoral dissertation, *Sexual Personae,* into a book. The *Horses* album cover immediately went up on my living-room wall, as if it were a holy icon. Mapplethorpe's portrait of Patti Smith symbolized for me not only women's new liberation but the fusion of high art and popular culture that I was searching for in my own work.

From its rebirth in the late 1960s, the organized women's movement had been overwhelmingly hostile to rock music, which it called sexist. Patti Smith's sudden national debut gal-

[*Civilization: The Magazine of the Library of Congress,*
December 1996/January 1997]

vanized me with the hope (later proved futile) that hard rock, the revolutionary voice of the counterculture, would also be endorsed by feminism. Smith herself emerged not from the women's movement but from the artistic avant-garde as well as the decadent sexual underground, into which her friend and lover Mapplethorpe would plunge ever more deeply after their breakup.

Unlike many feminists, the bisexual Smith did not base her rebellion on a wholesale rejection of men. As an artist, she paid due homage to major male progenitors; she wasn't interested in neglected foremothers or a second-rate female canon. In Mapplethorpe's half-transvestite picture, she invokes her primary influences, from Charles Baudelaire and Frank Sinatra to Bob Dylan and Keith Richards, the tormented genius of the Rolling Stones who was her idol and mine.

Before Patti Smith, women in rock had presented themselves in conventional formulas of folk singer, blues shouter, or motorcycle chick. As this photo shows, Smith's persona was brand-new. She was the first to claim both *vision* and *authority*, in the dangerously Dionysian style of another poet, Jim Morrison, lead singer of the Doors. Furthermore, in the competitive field of album-cover design inaugurated in 1964 with *Meet the Beatles* (the musicians' dramatically shaded faces are recalled here), no female rocker had ever dominated an image in this aggressive, uncompromising way.

The Mapplethorpe photo synthesizes my passions and world-view. Shot in steely high contrast against an icy white wall, it unites austere European art films with the glamorous, ever-maligned high-fashion magazines. Rumpled, tattered, unkempt, hirsute, Smith defies the rules of femininity. Soulful, haggard and emaciated yet raffish, swaggering and seductive, she is mad saint, ephebe, dandy and troubadour, a complex woman alone and outward bound for culture war.

ILLUSTRATIONS

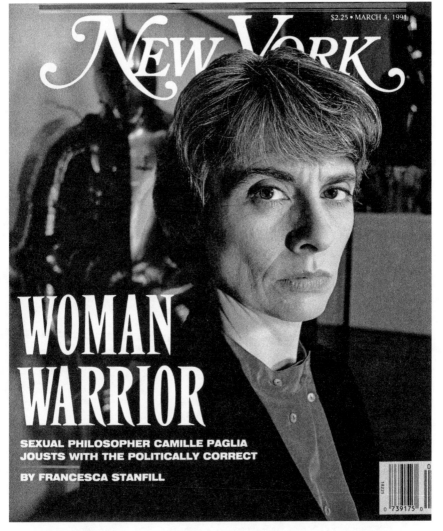

$2.25 • MARCH 4, 1991

NEW YORK

WOMAN WARRIOR

SEXUAL PHILOSOPHER CAMILLE PAGLIA JOUSTS WITH THE POLITICALLY CORRECT

BY FRANCESCA STANFILL

"Woman Warrior: Sexual Philosopher Camille Paglia Jousts with the Politically Correct" by Francesca Stanfill, cover story, *New York* magazine, March 4, 1991. Photograph taken by Harry Benson in the armor room of the Philadelphia Museum of Art. Inspired by early Rolling Stones album covers and Robert Mapplethorpe's portrait of Patti Smith for *Horses*. Violet silk shirt alluded to Oscar Wilde's Mauve Decade.
(**Harry Benson**/New York Media LLC)

"Woman Warrior" by Francesca Stanfill, *New York* magazine,
March 4, 1991. Photograph by Harry Benson of Paglia on guard
with her antique ivory-handled, silver-trimmed Knights Templar
Masonic sword (purchased during adolescence at an upstate
New York country store) on the *Rocky* steps of the Philadelphia
Museum of Art. The persona is defender of the arts.
(Courtesy of **Harry Benson**)

Drawings by John Callahan, published in 1993
in *Willamette Week*, an alternative newspaper in
Portland, Oregon. Gift of the artist.
(© by **John Callahan**. Reprinted by permission.)

"Controversy: Street Fighting Woman. Academic brawler
Camille Paglia takes on the campus establishment," *People*,
April 20, 1992. Asked by *People* for "one shocking picture,"
Paglia struck a *West Side Story* pose with her Italian
switchblade knife in the train tunnel at Swarthmore College.
(**Mario Ruiz**/Getty Images)

A rack of varied clothing was provided for a photo shoot with
Steve Poole for the *Daily Mail* in London in January 1994.
Paglia zeroed right in on a plush purple-velvet Moschino jacket
adorned with gold buttons and cut in a piratical eighteenth-
century style. It took a ship's crew to get her in and out
of those black thigh-high cavalier boots. (© **Steven Poole**)

Another photograph from the shoot with Steve Poole for
the *Daily Mail* in London in January 1994. The clever
crew turned a black shawl into a seaweed-streaming rock.
(© **Steven Poole**)

"America's Most Influential Women: 200 Legends, Leaders, and Trailblazers,"
Vanity Fair, November 1998. *Vanity Fair* invited Betty Friedan, Gloria Steinem,
and Paglia to pose together for Annie Leibovitz. Friedan and Paglia agreed, but
Steinem refused, so the magazine asked the great Robert Risko to do a group
caricature. Headline: "REVOLUTIONARY." Caption: "Friedan, Steinem, and
Paglia are an influential triumvirate—just don't put them in the same room."
(Robert Risko)

SPECIAL REPORT: FASHION'S BRAVE NEW GAY WORLD

THE Advocate

THE NATIONAL GAY & LESBIAN NEWSMAGAZINE | SINCE 1987

OCTOBER 18, 1994

ATTACK OF THE 50-FOOT LESBIAN

Camille Paglia reigns as America's most controversial, intellectual, and intimidating gay woman

ISSUE 666

48220

0 218585 9

$3.95 USA • $4.95 CAN.

"Attack of the 50-Foot Lesbian: Camille Paglia reigns as America's most controversial, intellectual, and intimidating gay woman," cover story, *The Advocate*, October 18, 1994.

"Paglia 101: Confessions of a Campus Radical," cover story, *Girlfriends*, September 2000. Tagline: "Nobody is going to tell me I'm homophobic, okay? I will kick their ass!" Previously published in *Girlfriends* magazine. Reproduced with the permission of Diane Anderson-Minshall and Heather Findlay.

ACKNOWLEDGMENTS

As always, my deepest thanks go to LuAnn Walther, who has been my editor since 1990, when she acquired the paperback rights for my first book, *Sexual Personae,* for Vintage Books. It was her bold idea to separate the most representative of my articles and lectures on sex, gender, and feminism from the mass of my other writings on culture and society. (Material since my last essay collection in 1994 will appear in a future volume.) I am profoundly grateful for her decades of unflagging support, understanding, and advice.

Catherine Tung smoothly coordinated all in-house aspects of the intense preparation of this book. Her admirable precision and tireless help, particularly during the thorny permissions phase, were absolutely indispensable to the timely completion of this project. Altie Karper, Cat Courtade, and Maria Massey oversaw the production process with superb attention to detail. It is a distinct privilege to be a beneficiary of Michael Lionstar's wonderful author photos. For many years now, I have been most fortunate to enjoy the master strategies and witty conversation of two ace publicists at Knopf Doubleday, Josefine Taylor Kals at Pantheon and David Archer at Vintage.

My heartfelt gratitude goes to the visionary editors who commissioned many of the controversial pieces in this book, when it was often risky for them to do so. Leading the list are Herbert Golder and Nicholas Poburko at *Arion*; David Shipley, then at *The New York Times*; Max Boot, then at *The Wall Street Journal*; Alexander Kafka at *The Chronicle of Higher Education*; Ryan Sager, then at *Time*; and David Daley, then at Salon.com.

My agent, Lynn Nesbit, has been a near-oracular source of advice and guidance for a quarter century now. Dorothy Vincent at Janklow & Nesbit Associates remains a paragon of wise counsel. Finally, fervent thanks are due to my friends, allies, and family members (in alphabetical order) who have been so loyal and supportive over the decades: Gunter Axt, Glenn Belverio, Robert Caserio, Lisa Chedekel, Kent Christensen, John DeWitt, Matt Drudge, Kristoffer Jacobson, Ann Jamison, Mitchell Kunkes, Kristen Lippincott, Alison Maddex, Lucien Maddex, Lenora Paglia, Christina Hoff Sommers, and Francesca Stanfill.

INDEX

Page references in *italics* refer to illustrations.

Bellini, Giovanni, 48
Benatar, Pat, 186, 207
Bennington College, xxiii, 96,
    233, 284–85
Berkeley, University of
    California at, xxiv, 128,
    271
Beuys, Joseph, 204
Beverly Hillbillies, The, 249–50
Beyoncé, 185, 270
bibelots, porcelain, 275
Binghamton, State University
    of New York at. *See*
    Harpur College
Black, Cilla, xvii
Blahnik, Manolo, 189
Blake, William, 6, 34, 210
Bloom, Harold, 7, 192
Bogarde, Dirk, 206
Botticelli, Sandro, 154, 155
Bourdieu, Pierre, 204
Bourke-White, Margaret, xii,
    214
Bow, Clara, 55
Bowie, David, xxiv, 203, 204,
    207
Boxer, Barbara, 107
Boyd, Pattie, xvii
Brahms, Johannes, xix
Brecht, Bertolt, 251
Bronte, Charlotte, 98
Bronte, Emily, 98
Brooks, Mel, 88
Brown, Helen Gurley, xviii

Brown, Norman O., 78
Brown, Rita Mae, 215, 233
Brown University, 52, 82, 103
Bruce, Lenny, xxv
Buck, Pearl S., 12
Buñuel, Luis, 205
Burchill, Julie, 235
bureaucracy. *See*
    administrators, campus
Butler, Judith, 112, 195, 203

Campbell, Joseph, 60
Candomblé, 256
capitalism, 74, 80–81, 93, 113,
    145, 169, 195, 196, 209,
    224, 261
Capp, Al, 248–49
Carlisle, Belinda, 186
Carlson, Katherine, 280–81
Carter, Dixie, 242
Cavani, Liliana, 51, 206
Chanel, Coco, 123
Charlie's Angels, xviii
Cher, 55–56
Chisolm, Shirley, 164
Choo, Jimmy, 189
Chopin, Frédéric, xix
Christie, Julie, xvii
Cixous, Hélène, 60, 66,
    115. *See also* post-
    structuralism
Clark, Kenneth, 41, 154
Clinton, Bill, xxi–xxii, 105–06,
    113, 146, 165, 180

PREVIOUS PUBLICATION INFORMATION

"Sex and Violence, or Nature and Art" originally published as part of Chapter One of *Sexual Personae* (Yale University Press, 1990). Copyright © 1990 by Yale University.

"The Venus of Willendorf" and "Nefertiti" originally published as parts of Chapter Two of *Sexual Personae* (Yale University Press, 1990). Copyright © 1990 Yale University.

"Madonna: Animality and Artifice" originally appeared in *The New York Times* as "Madonna—Finally a Real Feminist" on December 14, 1990.

"Rape and Modern Sex War" originally appeared in New York *Newsday* as "Rape: A Bigger Danger than Feminists Know" on January 27, 1991.

"Junk Bonds and Corporate Raiders: Academe in the Hour of the Wolf" originally appeared in *Arion* (Spring 1991).

"The MIT Lecture: Crisis in the American Universities" was originally a lecture delivered on September 19, 1991 at the Massachusetts Institute of Technology, Cambridge, Massachusetts.

"The Strange Case of Clarence Thomas and Anita Hill" originally appeared in *The Philadelphia Inquirer* as "Hill Is Neither Victim Nor a Feminist Hero" on October 21, 1991.

"The Nursery School Campus: The Corrupting of the Humanities in the U.S." originally appeared in *The Times Literary Supplement* on May 22, 1992.

"The Return of Carry Nation: Catharine MacKinnon and Andrea Dworkin" originally appeared in *Playboy* (October 1992).

"A White Liberal Women's Conference" originally appeared in *The New York Times* on September 1, 1995.

"Loose Canons" originally appeared in *The Observer Review* (London) on October 8, 1995.

"Men's Sports Vanishing" originally appeared in *USA Today* on April 9, 1996.

"Coddling Won't Elect Women, Toughening Will" originally appeared in *USA Today* on November 12, 1996.

"Academic Feminists Must Begin to Fulfill Their Noble, Animating Ideal" originally appeared in *The Chronicle of Higher Education* on July 25, 1997.

"Gridiron Feminism" originally appeared in *The Wall Street Journal* on September 12, 1997.

"The Modern Battle of the Sexes" was originally a lecture delivered on December 1, 1997 as part of a series titled "Sounding the Century" at Queen Elizabeth Hall, London, and was subsequently broadcast by BBC Radio 3 on March 7, 1998.

"American Gender Studies Today" originally appeared as "Symposium: American Gender Studies Today" in *Women: A Cul-*

tural Review (U.K.), vol. 10, no. 2, 1999 (http://www.tandfonline .com/).

"The Cruel Mirror: Body Type and Body Image as Reflected in Art" originally appeared in *Art Documentation*, vol. 23, no. 2, Fall 2004. © Art Libraries Society of North America.

"The Pitfalls of Plastic Surgery" originally appeared in *Harper's Bazaar* (May 2005).

"Feminism Past and Present: Ideology, Action, and Reform" was originally a keynote address delivered on April 10, 2008 at a conference "The Legacy and Future of Feminism" at Harvard University, and subsequently published in *Arion* (Spring/Summer 2008).

"No Sex Please, We're Middle Class" originally appeared in *The New York Times* on June 27, 2010.

"The Stiletto Heel" originally appeared as part of the online project "Design and Violence" by The Museum of Modern Art (http://designandviolence.moma.org/) on October 25, 2013, and was subsequently published in *Design and Violence* by The Museum of Modern Art, New York, in 2015.

"Scholars in Bondage" originally appeared in *The Chronicle Review* of *The Chronicle of Higher Education* on May 24, 2013.

"Gender Roles: Nature or Nurture" was originally delivered as the opening statement of a debate on October 8, 2013 at the Political Theory Institute in the School of Public Affairs at American University. Special thanks to Alan Levine and Thomas Merrill.

"Are Men Obsolete?" was originally delivered as the opening statement of "The Munk Debate: Gender in the 21st Century" on November 15, 2013, and subsequently published in *Are Men Obsolete? Rosin and Dowd vs. Moran and Paglia: The Munk Debate on Gender*, edited by Rudyard Griffiths, copyright © 2014 by Aurea Foundation. Reprinted by permission of House of Anansi Press Inc., Toronto (www.houseofanansi.com).

"Put the Sex Back in Sex Ed" originally appeared in *Time* on March 24, 2014.

"It's Time to Let Teenagers Drink Again" originally appeared in *Time* on May 19, 2014.

"Cliquish, Tunnel-Vision Intolerance Afflicts Too Many Feminists" originally appeared in *Feminist Times* on July 14, 2014 (http://www.feministtimes.com/).

"Southern Women: Old Myths and New Frontiers" was originally delivered as the Honors College Convocation Lecture on September 16, 2014 at Sally McDonnell Barksdale Honors College, University of Mississippi.

"The Modern Campus Cannot Comprehend Evil" was originally published in *Time* (Time.com) on September 29, 2014.

"Why I Love *The Real Housewives*" originally appeared on "The Daily Dish" (http://www.bravotv.com/the-daily-dish/news) on March 7, 2014. Special thanks to Bravo Media LLC.

"What a Woman President Should Be Like" originally appeared in *Time* (Time.com) on July 13, 2015.

"Feminist Trouble" originally appeared in *Spiked Review* (U.K.) in December 2015.

"On Abortion" originally appeared in *Salon* (www.Salon.com) on April 7, 2016. An online version remains in the *Salon* archives. Reprinted with permission.

"What's in a Picture" originally appeared in *Civilization: The Magazine of the Library of Congress* (December 1996/January 1997).

ILLUSTRATION CREDITS

A NOTE ABOUT THE AUTHOR

Camille Paglia is University Professor of Humanities
and Media Studies at the University of the Arts in
Philadelphia. She is the author of *Glittering Images:
A Journey Through Art from Egypt to* Star Wars; *Break,
Blow, Burn: Camille Paglia Reads Forty-three of the
World's Best Poems*; *The Birds*; *Vamps & Tramps: New
Essays*; *Sex, Art, and American Culture: Essays*; and
*Sexual Personae: Art and Decadence from Nefertiti to
Emily Dickinson*.

A NOTE ON THE TYPE

This book was set in Scala, a typeface designed by the Dutch designer Martin Majoor (b. 1960) in 1988 and released by the FontFont foundry in 1990. While designed as a fully modern family of fonts containing both a serif and a sans serif alphabet, Scala retains many refinements normally associated with traditional fonts.

Composed by North Market Street Graphics,
Lancaster, Pennsylvania
Printed and bound by Berryville Graphics,
Berryville, Virginia